AF262618

THE

HIDDEN

HAND

Books by Warren Kinsella

Unholy Alliances

Web of Hate

Party Favours (PSEUDONYM JEAN DOE)

Kicking Ass in Canadian Politics

Fury's Hour

The War Room

Fight the Right

Recipe for Hate

New Dark Ages

Age of Unreason

THE HIDDEN HAND

THE INFORMATION WAR AND THE RISE OF ANTISEMITIC PROPAGANDA

WARREN KINSELLA

Signal and colophon are registered trademarks of
Penguin Random House Canada Limited.

The authorized representative in the EU for product safety and compliance is
Penguin Random House Ireland, Morrison Chambers, 32 Nassau Street,
Dublin D02 YH68, Ireland, https://eu-contact.penguin.ie

Library and Archives Canada Cataloguing in Publication

Title: The hidden hand / Warren Kinsella.
Names: Kinsella, Warren, 1960- author
Identifiers: Canadiana (print) 20250118661 | Canadiana (ebook) 2025011867X |
ISBN 9780771021572 (hardcover) | ISBN 9780771021633 (EPUB)
Subjects: LCSH: October 7 Hamas Attack, Israel, 2023. |
LCSH: Israel-Hamas War, 2023-—Propaganda. |
LCSH: Israel-Hamas War, 2023-—Press coverage. |
LCSH: Israel-Hamas War, 2023-—Foreign public opinion, Canadian. |
LCSH: Jews—Canada—Social conditions. | LCSH: Antisemitism.
Classification: LCC DS119.771 .K56 2025 | DDC 956.9405/5—dc23

Book design by Andrew Roberts
Cover art: (hand) ashumskiy / Adobe Stock
Typeset in Garamond 3 LT Pro by Erin Cooper and Six Red Marbles
Printed in Canada

Signal, an imprint of McClelland & Stewart
Penguin Random House Canada
320 Front Street West, Suite 1400
Toronto, Ontario, M5V 3B6, Canada
penguinrandomhouse.ca

2   3   4   5   30   29   28   27   26

Penguin Random House Canada

For Lorna and Douglas

(. . . and for those who fight for the truth)

The propagandist's purpose
is to make one set of people
forget that certain other sets of people
are human.

—ALDOUS HUXLEY

CONTENTS

INTRODUCTION

"You fucking Jew."

That is what the neo-Nazi skinhead said to me. Those were his actual words; I couldn't forget that. It was 1980, in Calgary, and the skinhead and his buddies had been making Nazi salutes. I'd told him to stop. He called me a fucking Jew again, and there was a fistfight.

It happened long ago, that fight. But it was the first time I'd experienced anything like it. The first time antisemitic hatred had jumped out of the pages of my high school social sciences textbooks and into real life.

I'd encountered the skinhead at a musical event where my punk band had been playing. Now, though, I was remembering him mainly because of where I was standing: at the site of another kind of musical event for young people, in Israel's Southern District. Where there had been yet more antisemitic hate—but much, much worse.

I remembered all that as I looked at Rami Davidian, who was talking about what had happened in this sad place.

Davidian is a farmer, with a farmer's big hands. His hair is cut in what seems like a military style, and he's wearing grey jeans and a blue polo shirt. He squints a bit when he looks around him. He is standing in the middle of a crime scene near Kibbutz Be'eri.

A few feet away are hundreds of memorials, most of them just simple poles rising out of the Negev sand. Friends and family have left behind things: a guitar, a T-shirt, some art, Israeli flags, American and Canadian flags, poems, notes expressing love. Atop every pole, however, is a photo of a smiling, happy young person.

If you try to take a photo of the place on your phone, you won't easily fit all the memorials into the frame. There are just too many of them. Each represents a young man or young woman murdered at a music festival, where they went on a beautiful, clear weekend to dance, have fun, and be with friends.

Electronic dance music is big in Israel. So, when the organizers of the Nova EDM festival announced their plan to put on an "event that will take place in a powerful, natural location full of trees, stunning in its beauty and organized for your convenience, about an hour and a quarter south of Tel Aviv," thousands came. Sixteen different DJs from around the world would spin for fifteen straight hours, over October 6 and 7, 2023, a Friday and Saturday. Tickets were about a hundred dollars, and attendees were given the festival's location only a short time before it happened. They were told not to bring weapons or sharp objects.

Nova was roughly four kilometres from the Gaza border, so extra security would be watching over the festivalgoers, who came from across the globe: Americans, South Americans, Canadians, Europeans. It was like Israel's Woodstock, someone had said, but with electronic dance music rather than rock and roll. It was a big event.

It went all night. At around 6:30 a.m. on Saturday, DJ

Artifex was performing, the EDM booming out of a bank of massive speakers. So at first, many did not hear the rockets.

But the sun was coming up, meaning the audience could see the rockets before they heard them. They were arcing across the morning sky, like snakes. People stopped dancing, and then the music stopped, too. Sirens were wailing.

There was confusion, and the crowd started calling out to each other. In Israel, people are used to rocket attacks, and many homes have a *mamad*, a bomb shelter. But there weren't enough shelters at the festival, so people started to rush toward their cars.

Just around 7 a.m. uniformed Hamas terrorists on motorized paragliders began descending from the sky like oversized vultures. Not long after, hundreds more terrorists pulled up, leaning out the windows of Toyota trucks, their modified AK-47s spraying bullets. They began killing everything that moved. They were laughing and joking, something we know because Hamas was live-streaming the murders on Facebook and Telegram.

Later, it was learned that Hamas was surprised by the Nova Music Festival; they hadn't expected it to be there. They invaded Israel to kill Jews in the kibbutzim communities and military bases hugging the border with Gaza, not at a music festival. But they wasted no time, murdering and raping.

That morning, Rami Davidian was at his home in Patish moshav, a ten-minute drive east of the festival site. He was getting ready to have his coffee when the call came. Calmly, Davidian starts telling the story of what happened to him that day.

"It was quarter to seven in the morning," he says. "I got a phone call from a good friend. He wanted me to try to go to [the music festival] to save his son. That was it. That was the start."

He got off the phone and told his wife where he was going, that he'd be back in five minutes. Davidian then jumped in his old car and took off. "I drove out and I find these two beautiful motorbikes on the ground. There are fingers beside the motorbikes. Just the fingers." He looked around, calling out: "Whose bikes are these? Whose bikes are these?" No one responded. He didn't see anyone. He retrieved the fingers but didn't know what to do with them.

He kept driving. He'd lived in the area for a long time, and he saw a pickup truck he didn't recognize. There were some cars on fire, too, so he assumed there'd been an accident. He started to hear gunfire—lots of it. "It's the Sabbath," he told himself. "Why would the Israeli army be out here, practising on the Sabbath? It's our day of rest. It doesn't make sense."

He drove on a bit—not a hundred metres—and made a right. He stopped. "If I'd gone any further," he says, "I wouldn't be here to talk to you today."

He was at the spot where his friend had told him his son would be found. But the young man wasn't there. Instead, about fifteen young people were hiding in the brush, calling out to him, begging him to save them. "There was a whole bunch of young people there—running toward me, yelling, some screaming. Save us, they were saying."

They were weeping. They were terrified. He listened to them. At first, he didn't believe what they were saying. "Their stories couldn't possibly be true here—that there are terrorists that flew in, parachuted into Israel, and they're shooting at everyone." He tried to calm them down. They told him some of their friends had been killed at the Nova Music Festival.

He made a decision. "You're in good hands now," he said. "Don't worry anymore." His car could hold only five people, but all fifteen crammed into it—on the seats, in the trunk, hanging on to the roof—and Davidian raced back to his village with them. He told his son-in-law and other people there that terrorists were in Israel, that the young people at the festival needed to be saved. He got in his car and went back.

He continues: "I was still looking for my friend's son, Ben. I drove back to the place where he was supposed to be and got out of the car. I called out: 'Ben, Ben, it's Rami! Come out!' But there was no one in the area. Then, all of a sudden, I saw a whole bunch of heads pop up. There were more people to rescue. I put all of them into the car and drove them back to my village."

He started to get WhatsApp calls on his phone from frantic parents and festivalgoers who'd heard he was in the area and rescuing people. Unarmed and without a bulletproof vest, he kept driving closer and closer to the site, to where Hamas still were, looking for those who needed to be saved.

"I was about to drive off again when one of the kids said that his girlfriend had been left behind. Please, please, go save her, the boy said. So I went back to where she was."

As he got closer, he saw for the first time Hamas terrorists patrolling the area. He looked at the time on his cellphone. "I was checking to see how long it takes Hamas to patrol around this certain area," he says. "There was a little gap of time. So, every minute and a half, one of the kids would run out and into the car. This happened three times. And they all get into the car, and we drove off."

He went back, even closer this time. Hamas was still there and the Israeli Defense Forces (IDF) were not. He was looking for a girl named Amit. He couldn't see her, but he knew she was nearby. They communicated on their phones. "I played a game of hot and cold, right?" he says. "Like playing Marco Polo. I would honk my horn, and she would text me to say, far or near. And if she could hear honking nearby, she would say, hot, hot. Come out and save me, she said. But when I got to where she was it was already too late. She wasn't alone. There were Hamas terrorists who were kidnapping her."

In Arabic, Davidian called out to the terrorists, saying his name was Abu Rami. "I said, there are IDF soldiers behind us. They're about to get us. Give me the girl and run for your lives, I told them. So, they gave me the girl. I put her in my car, and she was saved." He brought her back to his village, then returned yet again. He was looking for others.

Bomb shelters and dumpsters lined the roads leading to the festival. The young people hid in them when Hamas started shooting, and then they became trapped. Davidian drove to the shelters to look inside because parents had been texting him to check on their kids. "They were sending me messages. My son has a certain colour eyes, my son has these kinds of tattoos. And I would drive around, looking. I went to these bomb shelters, and I found the kids were all dead." He pauses and looks away. "And so I lied to the parents. I actually lied to the parents, because I couldn't bring myself to tell them that that their kids were dead." He pauses again. "It was too much. Too much."

Bodies were everywhere: in the bar, in the festival's medical tent, around the tents in the camping area, in the dancing space, in the parking lots, in the toilets, and even in the garbage containers. There were 375 bodies in all: 357 young people who'd come to the festival to dance and the first responders who'd rushed to the site to save them. Hundreds were wounded, many critically. More than 40 people had been taken hostage. Many of the women, too, had been raped or sexually mutilated in the four-plus hours Hamas had control at the festival site. It was the deadliest concert attack in history—double the Bataclan attack in Paris in 2015 and more than ten times the Manchester Arena bombing in 2017.

Smoke billowing out of dozens of cars that had been set ablaze helped shield Davidian from being spotted by the terrorists. "I went around there," he says, his voice flat. "I saw just the worst things you can imagine. Dead men and women everywhere, naked bodies, body parts, parts of the bodies scattered." Another pause. "Most of the women had been abused. There were very clear marks showing abuse."

A father of four, Davidian said a quick prayer and covered the bodies with whatever he could find. "Then I went to see if I could help anyone else who was alive," he says. Around then, he became aware that it was nighttime, and that the IDF had finally arrived, and that they were taking over. He'd been going for twelve hours.

"It was around 11 p.m.," he says. "So, I said to whoever was there: All right, I'm going to go home now to have my morning coffee." And so he did.

After listening to Rami's story, I go to a *mamad* that has been converted into a shrine of sorts, and light a candle for the hundreds of kids killed at the Nova Music Festival. Standing there, I find myself remembering what the Nazi skinhead had said to me after we'd beat him and his friends in that long-ago fistfight: "We'll be back," he said, and he was pointing at me. "We'll be back."

And, you know? They are.

I have spoken to dozens of people for this book. I sought them out to help make sense of the madness that has gripped the world since

October 7, 2023. Because I cannot recall its ever being this bad. I cannot recall antisemitism ever being like this in my lifetime.

As a citizen, a lawyer, and a political aide, I've been opposing and exposing haters—Holocaust deniers, Islamophobes, incels, gay bashers, and garden-variety bigots—for more than thirty years. Along the way, I've helped to successfully prosecute those who've promoted hate against Jews and Muslims. I've represented and advised several major Muslim and Jewish organizations, and I've learned a lot about those communities, and those who target them. I've seen every variety of hate: spiritual, racial, political, and the kind that targets people because of their gender or sexual orientation. I have seen too much of it.

And even though I'm not Jewish, I've received a lot of Jew-hatred over the years. In 1987, in Caroline, Alberta, an Aryan Nations fanatic, who believed Jews to be the literal descendants of Satan, jammed a rifle in my chest at his group's compound. And in the early 1990s, when I worked for former prime minister Jean Chrétien, the RCMP didn't want me travelling with him: I posed an added security risk because of my published views about racism and antisemitism. Too many neo-Nazis wanted me dead, they said.

Some white supremacist skinheads planned to firebomb my place in Ottawa, resulting in several weeks of on-site protection in 1994. That same year I got a death threat from a skinhead for testifying against a neo-Nazi leader—while still in the courthouse, under police escort. A Ku Klux Klan leader gained access to my place in Vancouver in 1997, necessitating even more security and a rapid exit by my wife and daughter.

In the mid-1990s, as the internet became more ubiquitous, the threats went online with attacks from Holocaust deniers like

Ernst Zundel and David Irving, and many of their fans. Lots of lawsuits by Jew-haters, too. (They lost every single time. Truth is the best defence.) In 2018, a Toronto neo-Nazi publishing a "newspaper" mused in print about me being "bludgeoned to death." His hate sheet included tributes to Hitler and Nazism; it advocated rape; it vilified gays and Muslims; and, more than anything else, it promoted antisemitism. After lots of effort, we got that man sent to jail for a long time. In 2019, there was a bomb threat at my office from a follower of the People's Party of Canada. I lost staff over that one because they were afraid to come into work.

Over the years, I've written five books about racism and bigotry and antisemitism, as well as hundreds of newspaper columns and stories, and in all that time I've formed the opinion that antisemitism is a shape-shifter. It isn't practised by one ideology—it's embraced, at different moments in history, by every ideology, right and left. It is an ideology unto itself, in fact, one that is older than capitalism, communism, and all the other isms. It adapts; it changes with the times. It endures, like a pestilence for which we have no cure.

Where does it come from? To me, the simplest explanation is usually the best one. Antisemitism is rooted in envy and resentment. Those who've worked in politics can tell you that resentment is a very powerful force—one that, when harnessed by a soulless candidate and a glossy ad buy, can topple governments.

Resentment about the extraordinary resilience of the faith of Jews, resentment about their strength as a people, resentment about their obvious love for each other and God. The antisemites— from the Jew-hating skinheads making Nazi salutes at a punk show to the Jew-hating Islamists slaughtering young people at a music festival—seethe with envy and then hate. They are losers and, like all losers, they hate those they perceive to be winners, those who they think have power: Jews.

At the dark centre of all antisemitism—with its conspiracy-theorized manifestations, like "Zionist Occupation Government," and "international bankers," and "globalists"—is just that one, simple thing: envy. Envy about those things that Jews have. And envy about those things they imagine Jews to have, like immense wealth—along with control of media, information, technology, culture, and politics.

If the unspooling of sanity since the events of October 7 has shown anything, it's that Jews have less power, not more. It's almost as if history has played a practical joke on the Jewish people—falsely depicting them as powerful, and then robbing them of it. If Jews were truly as controlling and dominant as antisemites claim, they wouldn't now be getting beaten up, and shot at, and firebombed, and their voices wouldn't be serially disregarded by police, prosecutors, politicians, and the public.

For that's what has happened in the world since the attack on Israel: Schools for Jewish kids being sprayed with bullets. Synagogues and community centres and businesses being vandalized and even firebombed, their charred walls covered in swastikas and tributes to Hamas. Jews being chased and attacked in the streets for simply wearing the symbols of their faith. Imams speaking at rallies in Western cities and calling for Jews to be slaughtered. Jewish neighbourhoods being targeted by mobs screaming abuse and making Nazi salutes. Jews and the Jewish state being vilified by political parties in legislatures from coast to coast. Union leaders and university professors openly and unapologetically promoting Hamas. Campuses being occupied by antisemites who express hatred of Jews while the people in charge do little or nothing about it.

I've led and worked on many political campaigns over the decades, and along the way I've learned the strategies and tactics of another kind of war, the information kind. This book is about the present war of words and images—a propaganda war—that is being waged against Jews, the Jewish state, and more broadly, the West and its values.

Make no mistake: this is a real war. It has been underway for a while now—and it's targeting the hearts and minds of millions, mainly our young.

And we are losing that war.

Israel declared it was in a state of war against Hamas on October 8, 2023. Weeks later, they began moving ground troops into Gaza.

From the very start, there were widespread demands for an immediate ceasefire. From the start, too, there were angry protests against the government of Israeli prime minister Benjamin Netanyahu. There were marches and encampments organized to oppose Netanyahu and the war.

The encampment that has probably lasted the longest—and where the anti-Netanyahu protests have been among the most intense—is in a surprising place: right beside the Tel Aviv Museum of Art and directly across from the headquarters of the Israel Defense Forces on King Saul Street.

In Israel.

Hostages Square, as it's called, began in the same month as the Hamas attack. Some families pitched tents there and commenced demanding that Netanyahu do more to secure the release of their loved ones. In time, Hostages Square would grow to about the size of a city block. It boasted a large stage with a powerful

PA system, a life-size replica of the tunnel network where the hostages were taken, a piano for anyone to play, tables where BRING THEM HOME T-shirts and bracelets are sold, and many displays—among them a long dining table with places set for all the missing hostages, sculptures depicting peace and loss, empty chairs representing the number of those still held captive, and makeshift galleries containing the anti-war art of Israeli children. And, everywhere, posters bearing the photos of the smiling hostages, their age, and the words BRING THEM HOME.

Everywhere, too, there are stickers affixed to any flat surface. Two of the most popular ones showed unflattering images of Benjamin Netanyahu: DESTROYER OF ISRAEL, one says. Another: THE FUNDER OF HAMAS. And every single weekend there was a march: demanding an end to the war, demanding the end of the Netanyahu government, demanding more be done to secure the release of the hostages. Thousands of people participated in those marches, which regularly shut down the centre of Tel Aviv.

I went there to speak with the protestors and members of the hostage families, and then to march with them around the headquarters of the IDF. I spoke with many people there. All of them—without exception—had the same point of view. They intensely opposed the war, they fiercely opposed Netanyahu's government, they wanted the hostages home, and they did not understand why the rest of the world didn't see that. They did not understand why people outside Israel hate them, because they mostly want peace, too.

But even in Hostages Square, unanimity was elusive. Jews and Israelis, like all people everywhere, are not a monolith. Some are Zionists, meaning they support a Jewish homeland in the historical Land of Israel. Others angrily reject Zionism and deplore the tragic loss of life in Palestine. Every Jew I've interviewed, however—in the West and in the Middle East, on the political left and right, religious or not—wanted to see the return of the hostages and the end to the conflict. On that, there was common ground. But no one can speak for all Jews or every Palestinian on these differences. I won't do so in this book.

Near the doors to the museum, I stop one woman, who is from Belarus. She has a child who serves in the IDF, and she is not a Jew. Her boyfriend was one of the ones killed at the Nova Music Festival. I ask her why so many people outside Israel don't see that so many Israelis want peace and a change in government, too. Her eyes are ablaze. "They don't have the knowledge," she says, arms crossed. "They don't know the history. It's very diffi-cult for me to see why they don't understand." She pauses. "It's propaganda. That's why they do it. That's what motivates them."

Sitting on a bench, reading a book and waiting for the protests and the march to start, is an older woman, a clinical psychologist. I ask her what Israelis are feeling—about the war, about their government, about the reaction of the world beyond Israel's borders. "It's been very hard for people to hold it all together," she says. "What is happening to the civilian population in Gaza is horrible." It is.

Not far away, another woman is seated. She is younger, with piercings and tattoos, and she is looking at her device. I ask her what she thinks about the war, about the suffering on both sides. "I am against all war," she says proudly. "I am against all suffer-ing. I am very liberal in my opinions." Outside Israel, I tell her, many people her age seem to hate the Jewish state. The young woman looks wounded. "I feel so alone," she says, and she looks as though she's about to cry. "I feel alone. We are alone." She glances around as more and more people arrive for the anti-Netanyahu, pro-hostage march. "We in Israel don't do a very good job in telling our story."

She uses the Hebrew word *hasbara* to describe this. It's a word I hear many times that night. It has no precise English equivalent, which is ironic, because it roughly means explaining, or seeking to explain, one's actions—whether one is right or wrong. Israel, many people tell me at Hostages Square, is very bad at hasbara.

Some older women stop to talk. "How can the world be silent?" one asks me. She's crying. "We want so much to have peace! I know so, so many Muslims who are such good people . . ." She trails off. "It's not about the Bible or something. We are not all religious. We just have nowhere else to go." She looks in the direction of the IDF buildings. "The majority of the world is against us now."

Two other women, wearing anti-Netanyahu T-shirts and carrying signs that read WOMEN WAGE PEACE, are eager to speak with me. "We are against the war!" one says. "I am so mad at our government!" The other woman nods, pointing at my notebook: "Tell the world we are against the war! Tell them!"

A young man approaches, his father and wife beside him. Their cousin had been a hostage. "We don't choose war," he says. "We choose life."

It's like that with everyone, including those who tell me they've served in the IDF. They're tired of the Netanyahu government; some express hatred toward the man. They want the war to end, and they want the hostages to be released. When the speeches begin, hostage families step up to the microphone. Their voices are heard everywhere in Hostages Square, and echo off the walls of the IDF headquarters across the street. The brother of a slain hostage: "Netanyahu has blood on his hands!" The mother of a young woman killed at Nova: "Netanyahu is a liar and a psychopath!"

I am surprised by the intensity of the opposition, by the anger. An Israeli journalist who I agree not to identify speaks with me. "Seventy per cent of Israelis want the war over," he says. "Seventy per cent of Israelis oppose Netanyahu."

I look around. The crowd of Israelis—perhaps as many as five thousand now—starts to chant in Hebrew: "We will never give up! We will never give up!" Then: "You are not alone! You are not alone!"

We start to march up King Saul Street. Inside the IDF compound some construction workers are looking down at us from an unfinished building. As we go by, they wave and give the thumbs up.

⁂

Bari Weiss, the smart writer and editor who founded The Free Press media company, and was recently made editor-in-chief of CBS News, has been asked about the global propaganda campaign that seeks to demonize Israel and Western democracy.

"Now is the time to step up," she declares. "Now is the time to step up for our values. It's normal to walk through city streets with Hamas and ISIS flags? And that is allowed? How did that happen?"

It's happened in part, Weiss says, because of the simplicity and the effectiveness of the message. "The other side has a very clear story," she says. "Their story has a very clear narrative. And a very clear villain. Us." Jews.

The West needs to wake up, she continues, "and listen to what our enemies are saying. They're shouting it! Have we not learned to take these people seriously when they tell us what they mean?

"If we don't wake up," she warns, "it will be a calamity."

Weiss is right, of course; it *is* a calamity. It has been calamitous for Jews and Palestinians alike. But the important truth is this: within mere hours of the horrors of October 7 happening, a worldwide campaign commenced. One that would deny the rapes and torture and murder and atrocities. One that would turn decency inside out, and get people—millions of them—to shrug about antisemitism, and sometimes to even embrace it.

This book is about that campaign. To make that case, I compare the elements of a typical winning political campaign—the messaging, financing, organization, policies, leadership, and so on—to what the variously anti-Israel, antisemitic, anti-West, pro-Hamas campaign is doing, and how that campaign isn't just similar to a well-organized, well-financed, and professionally run political-style propaganda campaign. It actually *is* a well-organized, well-financed, and professionally run political-style propaganda campaign. That is what it is.

Throughout the book I'll refer to myriad groups and points of view. There are those who are not antisemitic—who regard themselves as anti-Zionist, for example, and are opposed to many of the decisions of the government of Israel. And then there are those who are indeed antisemites: the ones who hate Israelis and Israel—and ordinary Jews—because of their faith. In every case, I try to err on the side of caution in determining whether they are truly antisemitic or not. With over three decades of research and reporting on antisemitism and racism, I've always tried to exercise care in describing the beliefs of those who are now seen in the streets, in the news, and on our computer screens: the protestors, the organizers, the fundraisers, the leadership.

And, in observing many of those protests that have paralyzed cities across Canada, the United States, and much of Europe since October 7, I was struck by one important question that hasn't been asked nearly enough: Is it all just a coincidence, or was it planned? In particular, how could Israel—so obviously the victim of a terrible and monstrous crime on that day—be transformed into a global pariah within a matter of hours, before it had even organized itself enough to strike back at Hamas? And how could so many people outside Israel be unaware of the opposition to the war, and the disdain for Benjamin Netanyahu, within Israel?

I will offer two answers. One—obviously, inarguably—anti-Israel sentiment and antisemitism are far worse, and far more widespread, than any of us have ever considered. Two, antisemitism—targeting Jews and the Jewish state—has been amplified by a cruel but effective propaganda campaign, the likes of which few of us have seen in our lifetimes.

What is happening, what we're seeing on our streets and on our TV and computer screens, isn't always "organic." Not every protest against the Jewish state—and, too often, Jews themselves—is spontaneous. A movement this widespread, effective, and well funded, in such a short time? Every seasoned political strategist will tell you: It needs bodies, like any political campaign. It needs workers, it needs organizers, it needs money.

Ultimately, it needs a hidden hand guiding it.

ONE

A HATEFUL STRATEGY

Eylon Levy eats a slice of watermelon.

Watermelon is green, white, black, and red, same as the colours of the Palestinian flag. Online, a watermelon-slice emoji has become an unofficial symbol of Palestinian defiance and, sometimes, aversion toward the Jewish state. Improbably, it has also become something of a visual representation of the post–October 7 war—what Levy calls "the information war."

After October 7, Levy became one of the best-known spokespeople for Jews and Israel around the world. He was everywhere: CNN, Fox News, Sky News, BBC, CBC, and other mainstream media. And, as he thinks about his answer to the question, he is here, eating some watermelon. Before he can be asked whether it's perhaps a symbolic attempt to recapture an image used to promote extremism or even terror—or simply if he likes watermelon—Levy asks the more pressing question:

"What do they want?"

What do the invisible forces behind an apparently well-funded, well-organized propaganda war against Jews, the Jewish state, and the West want, in the end? What is their strategic goal? What are the policies they hope to impose, when and if they win this war?

Levy's answer is a long one, but it sounds like he knows every word of it to be true.

"There is an attempt by Israel's enemies to weaponize and militarize misinformation against Israel. Because Hamas's goal is not only to kill Israelis and shatter national morale, it's to poison global public opinion against Israel. It's to create tension and friction between Israel and its allies. It's to make good, ordinary, decent people turn against Israel by convincing them that Israel is evil incarnate. That is the meaning of the campaign to charge Israel with genocide, extermination, starvation, and being a white supremacist, colonial, apartheid, fascist state. And to throw every nasty word in the dictionary at it.

"It is a campaign to try to convince people that the descendants of the victims of the Nazis are the new Nazis, and therefore to make people think if the Nazis didn't finish the job, maybe we should. And if someone else will do that, then more power to them.

"They want to change Western public opinion—so that, on the day they are ready to launch an all-out war on Israel, ordinary Western citizens will stand idly by and say, 'The Jews had it coming.' Because they look at Israel not as a democratic nation-state, fighting for its life against barbaric Islamist terrorists, but as the incarnation of people that have no right to exist. Now, in the course of the information war, we see all sorts of made-up allegations against Israel that quickly gain traction on social media, get picked up in the mainstream media, and then the damage has already been done by the time the lies are refuted."

That, he says, is the strategy—and the tactics and the policy—of the hidden hand guiding the explosion of anti-semitism and hate around the world, post–October 7. As Levy says, the strategy is to isolate Israel and its allies. And the tactics at the foundation of this strategy involve pushing conspiracy theories and lies online, in the media, and on the streets. So far, that campaign has been successful, Levy says—far more successful than anyone had ever thought it could be. Which is why he changed the course of his life and commenced fighting in the information war.

Levy was born in London in 1991, to Israeli émigrés working in real estate. He had a facility for language from a young age, joining debate clubs and attending University College School, an acclaimed private school in Northwest London, whose motto is *Paulatim Sed Fermiter*, which is Latin for "Slowly but surely." Yet moving slowly has not always been Levy's favoured approach.

He went to Oxford for philosophy, politics, and economics. While there he attempted to debate George Galloway, the former British member of Parliament who'd pledged to make his riding "Israel free," calling the country an "illegal, barbarous, savage state." When Galloway found out that Levy held Israeli citizenship, he walked out of the debate. Later, Galloway posted on his Facebook page, "I refused this evening at Oxford University to debate with an Israeli, a supporter of the apartheid state of Israel. The reason is simple: no recognition, no normalization. Just boycott, divestment and sanctions, until the apartheid state is defeated. I never debate with Israelis nor speak to their media."

In so doing, Galloway put Eylon Levy on the map. Levy thereafter obtained his master's degree in international relations at Cambridge, writing his thesis on Jewish refugees from the Arab world. "Israel [has] found that neither the regional political situation, nor international opinion were sympathetic to its arguments," Levy wrote. After October 7, that dilemma was to become the defining focus of his public life.

He did a stint in the Israeli military, as is required of almost every citizen, and eventually became the chief news anchor at the English-language Israeli public television station, IBA News, making him even better known. In 2021, Israel's president, Isaac Herzog, hired Levy to serve as a media adviser. He worked for Herzog in that capacity for two years.

And then October 7 happened. On that morning, Levy was thirty-two years old and no longer working for the government. Like everyone else, he watched the coverage of the attack on TV, in shock. He deliberated for a few days, and then made a decision. "I set up a little mini studio at home, propping a laptop on a pile of books and a lamp on top of a big tub of protein powder," he says. He sent out a tweet. "I said I'm a former adviser to the president, and I'm available to do interviews." And that's what he did. Many of them.

Not long afterward, he got a phone call. The office of Israeli prime minister Benjamin Netanyahu wanted him to return to government service and join a team of spokespeople to help deal with international media in the National Public Diplomacy Directorate. Levy quickly agreed. At the Kirya military headquarters in Tel Aviv he started working with Mark Regev, a renowned former diplomat who would lead the Israeli side in the burgeoning information war. Soon enough, Levy was fielding many interview requests. One exchange attracted a lot of attention.

In what's called a double-ender—with Sky News anchor Kay Burley in Britain and Levy in Tel Aviv—Burley noted that a proposed hostage deal would see 150 Palestinian terrorists traded for 50 Israeli hostages. Did that mean, she asked her guest, that Israel valued Palestinian lives less than Israeli lives?

Levy didn't answer right away. Instead, his eyebrows—which are very dark, and hard to miss—shot up. He said nothing for several seconds. Then: "That is an astonishing accusation. If we could release one prisoner for every one hostage, we would obviously do that. We are operating in horrific circumstances. We're not choosing to release these prisoners, who have blood on their hands. We are talking about people who have been convicted of stabbing and shooting attacks. . . . It is outrageous to suggest that the fact that we are willing to release prisoners convicted of terrorism offences—more of them than we are getting our innocent children back—somehow suggests that we don't care about Palestinian lives? Really, that is a disgusting accusation."

Their exchange went viral, making Eylon Levy a star within Israel and in the English-language Jewish diaspora around the world. "Levy—or at least his eyebrow raise—has become a household name in Israel," *The Jerusalem Post* wrote. "[Levy] has raised eyebrows all around," said the London-based *Times*. The clip had garnered sixteen million views online, Fox News noted.

But not everyone was pleased. Sara Netanyahu, the prime minister's wife, was reportedly unhappy about Levy's increasing profile in English-language media—and about accounts that he, along with hundreds of thousands of other Israelis, had participated in the massive protests against her husband's planned judicial reforms. The fact that Levy had done so before October 7, and before he was working for the government, apparently did not placate her. He started to be seen less on TV. When asked where Levy had gone, the Netanyahu government claimed it wanted to present a more "diverse" image to international media. Eylon Levy—an Israeli with Iraqi blood—was effectively out.

In political life, when someone is defeated or dismissed, they often disappear. Levy did the opposite. He redoubled his efforts and recommitted himself to exposing hateful propaganda—this time as a private citizen again, travelling widely, speaking to whichever media outlet would have him. Nor does he plan to give up his mission—the stakes are simply too high. "Israel is an outpost of the West. Israel is on the front lines of the West, against the forces of barbarism," he says.

"I think that the big story of the first half of the twenty-first century is that there are three democratic states that are at risk of extinction at the hands of aggressive neighbours: Israel at the hands of Iran and its proxy armies. Ukraine at the hands of Russia. And Taiwan at the hands of China. The future of the West—the future of the free world—depends on how the West deals with these three countries.

"Do they stand up for them? Do they give them what they need to fight and protect their sovereignty? Or do they let them go under? Because a world in which Israel falls to Iran, Ukraine falls to Russia, and Taiwan falls to China?

"That will be a very dangerous world, indeed."

"Take a leaf from Israel's book," says Eylon Levy. "And realize that freedom and democracy do not sustain themselves. They have to be fought for—they don't exist of their own accord."

Those who are on the other side of the information war—Iran, Qatar, Hamas, Hezbollah, several far-left NGOs and non-profits and charities, and, increasingly, Iran's allies in the Chinese and Russian regimes—are not hiding their ultimate objective, Levy says. While they represent what he regards as an axis of evil, Levy agrees that they're mostly honest about what they want. Years before October 7 they'd been pursuing their anti-Israel, anti-West strategy, more or less openly. After October 7, he says, they started ramping it up dramatically and have achieved a level of success that they themselves did not expect.

That's why it's foolhardy to believe that they'll be persuaded to moderate their beliefs, Levy emphasizes, or that they'll now abandon their strategy. They've been too successful already, he says; why give up now? "Do not underestimate enemies who do not share your values, your openness, and your commitment to freedom and equality. Do not. They see the world very differently. Westerners assume that, ultimately, everyone wants the same thing, and we're all the same deep down. But I think that actually disrespects the diversity of human opinion. Some people think very differently and have very different priorities. Sometimes, when some people say things, you should believe them. You should understand what the implications of that would be, if they had their way—instead of trying to downplay it. Or think that if you ignore it or deny it, it will go away."

It won't, Levy says. Case in point: the Hamas charter. The terrorist group's policy objectives are explicitly laid out in their charter, which is not unlike a Western nation's constitution. Hamas's first charter, revealed in August 1988, is formally called the Covenant of the Islamic Resistance Movement. It acknowledges that Hamas is the Palestinian arm of the Muslim Brotherhood. The Brotherhood, or Society of Muslim Brothers, are Sunni Islamists who founded their organization in Egypt sixty years earlier, in 1928. The Muslim Brotherhood's ultimate objective is the same as that of Hamas: to establish, by force if necessary, a global caliphate ruled by Muslim sharia law. "Islam is the only solution," the Muslim Brotherhood's founders declared, and Hamas embraced that credo with ferocity.

Their 1988 charter reflects it. Written during the first intifada—the Palestinian uprising from 1987 to 1993—the first Hamas charter does not obscure the group's intentions. It is not a subtle document. It makes some half-hearted attempts to bridge the gap between the Palestinian Liberation Organization and the nascent Hamas, but elsewhere it doesn't disguise the main goal: a worldwide Islamic empire, one without Jews or infidels or non-believers, achieved through violence.

Because Hamas held power in Gaza by 2017, their second charter—released that year—is the "softer, kinder" version, the one they wanted the public to see. The newer version gamely attempts to smooth the hard edges in their founding document, but, in reality, Hamas has never renounced the 1988 charter. It remains the terrorist group's supreme statute, their ultimate law. The one above all else.

The 1988 charter best describes what Hamas is—as well as their tactics, strategy, and policies. It defines Hamas as an "Islamic resistance movement," and it calls for a "complete embrace of all Islamic concepts of all aspects of life" and "conversion to Islam" by everyone. The charter goes on to declare Hamas's intention to "rid the land" of people who are "unclean, vile and evil"—namely, Jews, Muslim opponents, and non-Muslims.

The ultimate goal of Hamas and its ilk is Islamic rule "over every inch of Palestine"; according to the charter, "there is no life" for those who do not accept Islam—only "annihilation." The "Zionist invaders" will be killed off, the charter decrees, "no matter how long it will take."

In the charter, Hamas and the Muslim Brotherhood call

ceasefires "so-called peaceful solutions and international conferences [that] are in contradiction to the principles of the Islamic
Resistance Movement." It says they are "all a waste of time." Peace
talks only help "the infidels," says Hamas. All that is permitted is
jihad: that is, what has come to mean holy war.

The charter describes the propaganda war now being waged
against Israel and the West. It is an "ideological invasion" designed
to "upset the thoughts, disfigure the heritage, and violate the
ideals" of the enemy. This ideological invasion is important,
Hamas proclaims, because of Jewish "control of the world media,
news agencies, the press, publishing houses, broadcasting
stations. . . . They were behind the French Revolution, the
Communist revolution and most of the revolutions we heard
and hear about, here and there. With their money they formed
secret societies, such as Freemasons, Rotary Clubs, the Lions,"
as well as instigating world wars, the Balfour Declaration, and
the League of Nations. "There is no war going on anywhere,
without having their finger in it," says Hamas.

The Hamas charter is almost cartoonish in its rhetoric, but
it attaches deadly seriousness to the organization's strategic
objective: the end of Israel and, ultimately, the liberal West. For
anyone with a passing knowledge of Hamas, it should be no
surprise. Violence, as they themselves admit, has long been their
defining characteristic. Both the 1988 and the 2017 charters
emphasize another dimension, too: propaganda.

Hamas's main—some would call its only—strategy has
always favoured the use of propaganda. Such efforts, Hamas states
at the conclusion of their founding charter, "suppl[y] strategic
depth . . . [in] all information spheres, in time and place."
Tactically, Hamas says, a propaganda victory can be achieved

with "explanatory bulletins, favorable articles and booklets [to] enlighten the masses around the Palestinian issue."

"*Jihad*," they conclude, "is not confined to the carrying of arms and the confrontation of the enemy. The effective word, the good article, the useful book, support and solidarity—all of these are elements of the *jihad* for Allah's sake."

Propaganda can accompany bullets, Hamas says. From the very start, Hamas, the Muslim Brotherhood, and their allies were unafraid to use words and images to achieve their strategic goal.

Because "*jihad* is not confined to the carrying of arms."

While Eylon Levy is a soldier in the current information war, Gary Wexler saw the war coming.

Thirty years ago, Wexler—an affable, easygoing author and professor who lives in California, far from the Israel–Hamas battlefront—sounded a warning that, clearly, not many people heard.

After the atrocities of October 7, and after he had some time to think about what he'd witnessed in the media, in the streets, and online, Wexler wrote a piece for the New England–based *Jewish Journal* titled "The Inside Story of How Palestinians Took Over the World." The headline was obviously an overstatement, but his thesis resonated with many: namely, that the communications landscape has witnessed something like a takeover.

Following October 7, it appeared that the anti-Israel, pro-Hamas campaign became more widespread, more extreme, and more violent with each passing day. None of this surprised Wexler.

"I'll tell you the story," he says. "Many years ago, I was hired by the Ford Foundation to create a marketing institute for their grantees in Israel. The grantees were Jewish and Arab, and they were all within the green line—the green line being the official border. When you're interviewing at that level, for marketing, for communication, you have to get in deep."

It was the early 1990s, around the time of the Oslo Accords. People in Israel and the West were starting to believe that peace in the Middle East was finally at hand, and that Shimon Peres would help deliver a better world. Wexler recalls that people were almost giddy with hope in those days.

"With the Arab organizations I was interviewing, as soon as I started getting into the questions, there was an immediate shutdown. [They said] you should meet with Ameer Makhoul when you go up to Haifa, and he will give you the answers. So the first time I heard that, I thought, Okay, that's fine. Second time I heard that, I thought, That's pretty interesting. By the third, fourth, and fifth time, I realized Makhoul was probably monitoring this whole thing I was doing, and people were reporting back to him. And so I realized this guy was obviously very important."

Wexler did what he'd been told. He sought out Ameer Makhoul. Makhoul was the executive director of Itijaa, an Arab civil rights organization. From the start, the encounter didn't go well. "When I got to his office, the first thing Makhoul says is, 'you're not welcome here, Gary Wexler.' Then he says: 'You are the Gary Wexler who's been asking all the questions.' It was intimidation, obviously." Makhoul seemingly knew everything that Wexler had done in life—just about every school, every club, every activity—and made a point of letting him know it.

Then Makhour—skinny, bespectacled, intense—leaned in and described, in detail, what was going to happen in the not-so-distant future.

"Just like you Jews come to organize Zionist events on campus, we will start to have our own people on campuses. We will start organizing our events." Makhour paused, glaring at Wexler. "We will be bringing in our people from across the world. We will be bringing students from across the world to work in our refugee camps, in our villages. We will have our own communication system."

Makhoul told Wexler that the Palestinian side would recruit Palestinian campus activists in America and all over the world. He said they would be bigger and better than anything the "Zionists" had ever done. And just like the Jewish groups, his side would put together global pro-Palestinian organizations. Makhoul also told Wexler that, just as Jews create public relations campaigns and events for Israel, so would the Palestinians. "But we will get more coverage than you ever have," Makhoul said. It was clear to Wexler that the messaging would not only be pro-Palestinian, which is legitimate in and of itself, but deeply hostile to Israel and the Jewish people.

"You wonder how we will make this happen, how we will pay for this?" Makhoul asked, not waiting for an answer. "With money from the European Union, Arab and Muslim governments, wealthy Arab people and their organizations."

"And then he stopped and says to me: 'So, Gary Wexler, how do you feel about what I'm saying?' And I just said to him, I'm here on behalf of the Ford Foundation to collect information. And he kept pressing me and pressing me, until finally I just got up and left."

The years went by and Wexler says he started to notice things that Ameer Makhoul had predicted. "I began to see all these things develop over the years. You know: BDS, Israeli Apartheid

Week." Almost every terrorist attack, almost every confrontation, started to resemble a propaganda victory for the Hamas–Hezbollah–Iran axis. There was the 2010 "Gaza Freedom Flotilla" organized by Turkey and others, where ships ostensibly carrying aid were intercepted by Israeli troops, and nine activists were killed. For the anti-Israel side, the event was a public relations bonanza. "I watched, and I thought, This is brilliant," Wexler recalls. "This is what Makhoul had said. I knew that Israel was going to board the ship, and I knew it was going to become an international incident, and I knew the media were going to be all over it. And I thought, These people are absolutely brilliant."

The tipping point for Wexler, a sign that the propaganda Makhoul had predicted would infiltrate the West was having an effect—perhaps more so than anyone had imagined—was the success in recruiting young Jews.

"They turned these Jewish students—who went to Jewish schools, went to Jewish camps, went on birthright trips—they turned so many of them around to become allies [to the anti-Israel side]. These Jewish students think that they discovered all this on their own. But they don't realize that they've been manipulated through a very sinister process to become aligned with Hamas and the rest."

The anti-Israel campaigners have pursued "a brilliant, brilliant strategy," Wexler says, forging alliances with various Indigenous, minority, and anti-colonial groups. To do so, the forces that Makhoul spoke of have also been very active online, he agrees. "They're using influencers who they have been working with on these campuses. Their online effort isn't just messaging. It's bringing people to events, it's community organizing."

These are the things that Ameer Makhoul foretold, Wexler notes, and they've mostly come true. In the streets, in the corridors of academe, online—virtually wherever young North Americans and Europeans gather these days—hatred for Jews and the Jewish state is too often seen in plain view. Pollsters observe that young people, more than any other demographic, have been captivated by it.

Wexler concludes, remembering that fateful meeting many years ago, "I look around and say: My God, this is what Ameer Makhoul said was going to happen. I now see his hand everywhere."

And what of Ameer Makhoul? In 2010 he was arrested and charged with espionage for Hezbollah, to which he confessed. He provided Hezbollah with reports on weaknesses in Israeli defence, Israel alleged, and on where civilians gathered and were vulnerable. He spent nine years in prison. After his release in 2019 he went back to Itijaa, the organization he was at when he met Wexler. Makhoul did not return repeated calls for comment.

Itijaa's name, Gary Wexler notes, means "the direction."

On October 7, 2023, the campaign started. Surprising things began to happen.

Lowell High School is in San Francisco's Parkside District, where the average household income is nearly $200,000 a year. A top ten public high school in California, it has been named a "distinguished" and "blue ribbon" school multiple times and is routinely ranked in the top one hundred high schools in the country.

It's also racially diverse, with about half its students considered Asian, about 20 per cent Caucasian, and the remainder Hispanic, Latino, Filipino, or Black. The author Naomi Wolf went there. So did Nobel laureates and ambassadors and professional athletes.

Just ten days after October 7, hundreds of Lowell High School students marched out of class. Other Bay-area high schoolers did likewise. It was part of a "national student walkout," they said. Students waved Palestinian flags and held signs declaring FROM THE RIVER TO THE SEA, PALESTINE WILL BE FREE. They didn't call for the hostages to be released, nor did they condemn Hamas and its brutal attack on innocent civilians. One of the fresh-faced student organizers spoke to the media: "We are here together to show unity against the genocide that is occurring in Gaza and to stand against the violation of human rights that have been going on."

Except: genocide? Israel hadn't even begun ground operations in Gaza, some noted, and it hadn't occupied the Strip since 2005—after which an uneasy ceasefire went into effect. Like many of the protests and much of the rhetoric flourishing online up to that point, the student walkout seemed like a thoughtless way to mark the savagery of the October 7 attacks.

The students claimed they had organized the walkout on their own, but that wasn't entirely true. It turned out that members of the local chapter of the Arab Resource and Organizing Center (AROC) had helped the students before, during, and after their walkout. According to the Anti-Defamation League, AROC "consistently engage in strident and extreme anti-Israel activism and traffic in anti-Semitic tropes." (AROC has not responded to repeated requests for comment at the time of writing.) Later it was confirmed that AROC representatives had quietly met with students in the school's quad area before the walkout— "unidentified adults," a San Francisco Unified School District report called them—and were escorted off campus when they were discovered.

AROC had provided students with a "toolkit" in a Google Doc under AROC letterhead, laying out a detailed communications plan for the day. It was a professional-quality blueprint for attracting national media attention. And it worked.

The toolkit gave students a list of the demands they should make; legal advice and resources in case they were detained; lines to use with the media; social media content to share; and even graphics to download for signs and banners. Said AROC in their toolkit: "Leave the halls of your school within 10-15 mins of starting, and mobilize outside! Begin chanting and hold space outside the school! If reporters show up, you can speak with them and use our talking points below."

The document went on: "Chants are a great way to engage your audience and have your message heard. Below are chants that are used widely during demonstrations in support of Palestine. Choose chants that you feel best fit the environment you are facing at your school. Some good practice tips: Practice saying these chants out loud before the day of!" One chant AROC recommended: "Israel Israel you can't hide—We charge you with genocide!" Some of the upper-class high school students even chanted this in Arabic: "With our souls, with our blood, we will bring you back, Gaza."

With the assembled media, the AROC talking points were repeated by the students more or less verbatim: "We refuse to stay silent when entire Palestinian families in our towns are getting massacred and millions are getting forcibly displaced from their homes. Teachers have a responsibility to teach about the occupation and root causes of the current war on Gaza." Then, ensuring the walkout got maximum coverage, AROC held a televised press conference on the steps of San Francisco City Hall. There, they were represented by a Jewish woman who made critical remarks about Israel. It was an approach the opponents of the Jewish state would use frequently in the coming months: inoculate themselves against charges of antisemitism by drawing attention to the minority of Jews within their ranks.

The protest was big news and thus a big success. It looked like the walkout had been entirely conceived by the students, recalling the youthful anti-war protests of the late 1960s and early 1970s. The local NBC affiliate termed the day "very powerful," and actually reported that a single anti-Hamas poster at Lowell High School was a cause for "fear" among Muslim and Arab students. Not one Jewish student or parent was interviewed by NBC.

The walkout made for dramatic television, and was seen across North America—given that it was one of the earliest post–October 7 student protests against Israel, and that its participants were so young and diverse. For many people, it was their first glimpse of what would become a pattern of student protests over several months, across the continent and Europe.

The walkout was devised to look spontaneous and grassroots and youthful, but it mostly wasn't. AROC had played a Wizard of Oz role of sorts, directing the students from behind a curtain: what was said, what was done, where it happened and when.

What happened at Lowell High, then, was not what it appeared to be. But, as propaganda, it worked.

Every action, every plan recalled the 1988 Hamas charter: "*Jihad* is not confined to the carrying of arms."

Case in point: in July 2024 *The New York Times* published a detailed, three-thousand-word investigative report headlined "How Hamas Is Fighting in Gaza: Tunnels, Traps and Ambushes." The story had five bylines and was on the front page of the paper's largest edition, Sunday.

Then, as now, the media's focus was on the military war, not the information war. The story detailed the ways in which Hamas had transformed itself into a ghost army, fighting guerilla-style battles with the Israeli military in Gaza. After luring IDF soldiers into areas of Gaza that Hamas had supposedly vacated, the Islamic terrorist group would ambush the Israelis. Only one sentence alluded to the propaganda strategy of Hamas, but it was important:

"Two [Hamas] fighters are tasked with fixing explosives to the sides of a vehicle or firing anti-tank missiles at it, according to the Hamas officer. A third carries a camera to film propaganda footage. A fourth typically stays at the tunnel entrance, preparing a booby-trap that can be activated as soon as the others return, to kill any Israelis who try to follow them underground."

That single sentence—that Hamas terrorists are charged with "[carrying] a camera to film propaganda footage"—testified to the importance Hamas and their allies attach to their communications strategy, at every level. Even in the dying days of their war, when their leaders and their battalions had been decimated by Israel, Hamas continued to propagandize. It has always been central to their strategy, Eylon Levy and others note. And it has changed public opinion in ways that few expected.

Not long after the atrocities of October 7, a veteran pollster contacted me and another journalist to confidentially share some survey results. Neither his name nor the name of his international polling firm was to be cited.

"We are concerned about the reaction," he said. "We have seen the violence and the attacks, and we frankly don't want to be the cause of more."

A few minutes after he called, he sent the survey results, along with the methodology and a detailed breakdown of who was polled, when, and where.

The poll had been conducted in November and December 2023. Nearly two thousand people had participated, across Canada, from all walks of life and political persuasions. The full range of adult age groups had been surveyed as well, he said. It appeared thorough, its methods sound.

"We asked them if they support the destruction of the state of Israel because it has no right to exist," the pollster said. "The majority were against that, or strongly against that. But more than a third of Generation Z, who we consider to be between the ages of eighteen and twenty-six, said they support—or strongly support—the destruction of Israel. Over 20 per cent of Millennials—between the ages of twenty-seven and forty-two—feel the same way."

He continued: "We were surprised by that, so we asked them a question that should normally only get one answer: no. We asked them if the extreme violence used by Hamas, and its vow to kill innocent Jews and not the IDF, was entirely justified.

"Everyone who was older was against that. Except Gen Z and Millennials, again. Forty-one per cent of Gen Z said they supported Hamas, and they supported the killing of innocent Jewish civilians as well. Thirteen per cent of them strongly supported that proposition. Millennials weren't as bad, but they were bad enough—nearly a third of them supported Hamas and supported killing Jews. Those percentages represent several million people."

It got worse, he said. He and his firm decided to ask about Jews in North America, not just Israeli Jews.

"We asked them if they supported the targeting of Jewish citizens here—Jewish people, Jewish businesses—because of what Israel was doing in Gaza," he said. "And it was the same kind of result. Thirty per cent of Gen Z supported targeting Jews here. Twenty-eight per cent of Millennials did."

There were similar findings. The poll was not what would be referred to as an outlier—an aberration, a result that is outside the norm. "No," the pollster said. "We did this poll because other firms were publishing the same kinds of results, and we didn't believe it could be true. And we got the same thing the others did: while the majority support Israel, and support Israel's right to defend itself, a huge chunk of Gen Z and Millennials don't. In fact, they meet the textbook definition of antisemitism. And there's millions and millions of them, across the West."

Around the same time, other public opinion research firms were indeed starting to come forward with data that validated the pollster's numbers. An early one was released by Harvard University and The Harris Poll. It surveyed more than two thousand registered American voters for their views on politics, immigration, foreign aid, and the Middle East. Seventy per cent said they were following the progress of the Hamas–Israel war closely or very closely. More than that—almost 85 per cent—said that October 7 was a terrorist attack.

Again, the same generational divide was evident: a third of American Gen Z and Millennials refused to call Hamas's genocidal attack genocide. An even larger swath of them—60 per cent of Gen Z and nearly 45 per cent of Millennials—said that Hamas's slaughter of twelve hundred Jews and civilians was "justified."

"Justified." Hamas has been designated as a terrorist organization by the United States, Canada, and European governments, but almost half of Gen Z said they supported it and, ostensibly, their tactics. A third of Millennials said the same thing. Older Americans, meanwhile, overwhelmingly—85 to 95 per cent of them—said they supported Israel.

Harvard and Harris asked other questions, about whether antisemitism is prevalent, about Jew-hatred on university and college campuses, whether Jews are "oppressors." Across the board, the results were similar: Generation Z and Millennials opposed Israel and were dismissive of concerns about antisemitism and anti-Jewish attacks. In fact, almost 70 per cent of Gen Z considered Jews "oppressors," Harvard and Harris found.

European surveys showed similar results. In Britain, the pollster Ipsos found in October 2023 that a quarter of eighteen to thirty-four-year-olds supported Hamas—with only 7 per cent favouring Israel. In the following month, as the war grew more intense, a "More in Common" U.K. survey found that a quarter of young adults there considered Hamas to be "freedom fighters" and not terrorists—and nearly 40 per cent of British Gen Z supported the Palestinians over the Israelis. Months after that, in April 2024, a YouGov survey in Belgium, France, Germany, Italy, and Sweden showed that 40 per cent of Gen Z in those countries believed that Israel was committing genocide in Gaza, and that it practised apartheid.

The Center for the Study of Contemporary European Jewry reported that antisemitism had "skyrocketed" in Europe and around the world after October 7. It was "a fire that was out of control," the Center declared. Antisemitic incidents more than doubled in the United States, it reported—and quadrupled in places like Canada and France. Conspiracy theories, attacks, and denials of the atrocities committed against Jewish civilians on October 7 were widespread, it found.

The origins of this kind of thinking were easy to guess. To Eylon Levy and others, ignorance seemed to be the likeliest cause. Even before October 7, an extensive 2020 poll conducted by the Conference on Jewish Material Claims Against Germany (Claims Conference) in multiple countries found a "shocking and saddening" lack of general knowledge about history and the Holocaust among Gen Z and Millennials. The Claims Conference wrote: "Sixty-three per cent of all [Gen Z and Millennial] survey respondents do not know that six million Jews were murdered and 36 per cent thought that 'two million or fewer Jews' were killed during the Holocaust.

"Additionally, although there were more than 40,000 camps and ghettos in Europe during the Holocaust, 48 per cent of national survey respondents cannot name a single one." In France, 70 per cent of Gen Z and Millennials didn't know that six million Jews were slaughtered in the Nazi Holocaust. In Austria, where some death camps had literally been located, a majority of Gen Z and Millennials also said they didn't know six million were murdered. Said the Claims Conference: "[In Austria], more than half (56 per cent) of those surveyed did not know that six million Jews were killed during the Holocaust. That number rose to 58 per cent among Millennials and Gen Z."

Similarly, a large Anti-Defamation League survey conducted with more than four thousand Americans found that "younger Americans are more likely to endorse anti-Jewish tropes." Said the ADL, "Belief in conspiracy theories continues to be one of the main correlates of antisemitic attitudes," noting that antisemitic attitudes were being embraced by younger Americans "at significantly higher rates." And more than half of Gen Z in the United States expressed some degree of comfort being friends with a Hamas supporter, they wrote.

The antisemitic themes being embraced by younger people went back to the Protocols of the Elders of Zion, a century-old fabricated plan describing a plot for global Jewish control. These themes included "Jews stick together more than others," "Jews in business go out of their way to hire other Jews," "Jews are more loyal to Israel than to America," and "Jews always like to be at the head of things." Wrote the ADL's researchers: "Younger Americans are significantly more likely to see the elimination of the state of Israel as a viable alternative." More of them were willing to believe that "Israeli operatives are secretly manipulating U.S. national policy."

The same depressing trend was being reported across the West: swaths of Gen Z and Millennials were anti-Israel and, in some cases, openly pro-Hamas. Older respondents had the opposite view. But every poll seemed to make clear that Hamas's apparent strategy—to capture the sympathy of Gen Z and Millennials—had been successful.

It got worse: a shocking October 2024 British *Daily Mail* poll with J.L. Partners found that one in five Gen Z voters believed Adolf Hitler had some "good ideas." More than a thousand American voters were surveyed, and nearly 80 per cent characterized the Nazi leader as evil. But 11 per cent of the total said he had some redeeming qualities.

All the pollsters said that young people in the West who had expressed doubt or denial about the Holocaust—or enthusiasm about Adolf Hitler—heavily relied on social media to inform themselves about history and current events. University of Toronto professor Robert Brym, who also conducted some of the surveys, did not simply examine the opinions of Gen Z and Millennials on Israel and Palestine—he looked at where those opinions originated. Said Brym in an interview about his research: "What's certainly true is that university students have much more critical views toward Jews and toward Israel than the general population. It runs contrary to decades of research about the relative tolerance of a university student. And it's pretty worrisome."

The main source of the problem was the type of education young people are receiving, Brym said: "I think they've been primed to accept some of the criticism of Jews in Israel—because they have not been educated, I'm sorry to say—in the university system about the historical justification for the existence of the State of Israel. With them, it's been possible to use the argument that this is a pure case of colonization by imperialistic white people over darker-skinned individuals. But that argument is not historically justified.

"I don't think I need to recite to you the three-thousand-year, continuous history of Jews in the area that's currently Israel, or the fact that there have been—before the existence of modern Israel—Jewish states in that area."

Younger people had been taught to discount the historical reality of Jews and the Jewish state, he says, and their reliance on online conspiracy theories has made the problem dramatically worse. "They don't understand the complexities," Brym added. "So they can get away with calling Jews 'white'—when, in fact, over half the population there was born in the Middle East or North Africa, and that their parents were born in the Middle East and North Africa, and that 850,000 Jews were expelled from Muslim-majority countries in the Middle East and North Africa in the 1950s and 1960s. They know nothing about that experience.

"They have nothing to say in response to it, either. So I think they were poorly educated. And they are accepting false generalizations. And it's because they're much more likely to rely on social media than the rest of the population."

Hamas aims to isolate and eliminate Israel and to destabilize democracy in the West—that much is obvious, Eylon Levy says. Less clear, however, is how Hamas, along with Iran, Hezbollah, antisemitic NGOs, and even China and Russia have achieved so much success in getting young people on their side. Those generations are ostensibly better educated than previous ones— but they've still embraced misinformation and disinformation. And antisemitism.

"[Hamas et al.], and their strategy, benefit as well from years of indoctrination in Western universities." Levy continues. "They've gotten young people to believe the whole oppressor/oppressed narrative. They've twisted reality and turned it upside down."

It's obvious to fair-minded people, Levy says, that Israel is a democratic nation-state—the place where the Jews have reclaimed their independence and reclaimed their ancient homeland. It's also obvious that Jews are fighting for survival, he adds, and for its security and prosperity.

"[Gen Z and Millennials] don't see that. They tell a story of Israel like it's some white settler colonial project, as if refugees coming out of postwar Europe—or even Jews from places like Morocco and Iraq and Algeria and Tunis—were somehow scheming all along to create some white supremacist, colonial project." Levy shakes his head. "It makes no sense. It's completely upside down. There are unfortunately too many young people, however, who are automatically primed to believe the worst about Israel and the Jews. And fighting to change that is an immense challenge.

"I think part of the reason [Hamas et al.] have been successful is because so much of modern discourse—at least within progressive circles—assumes that the victim is always right. So if you can make yourself out to be the weak side, the vulnerable side, the oppressed side? Well, then you win the sympathy Olympics. Israel, you see, used to be weak. We used to be powerless. We used to be oppressed—but we pulled ourselves up by our bootstraps. We have power now, and we use that power to defend ourselves and keep ourselves safe. But within a world that says the victim is always right, a world that absolves the victim of responsibility, that divides the world and oppresses the underclass? In that world they've been able to spin a story that the Palestinians are in fact the vulnerable, indigenous weak minority, the one that's been oppressed by nefarious white colonialist forces.

"Give them credit for their strategy," he says. "For being quite clear about what their objectives are. And I'm sorry that this conflict across the sea, in the Middle East, has infected your domestic politics. But it has, hasn't it?

"The question is: What do you want to do about it?"

TWO

THE BIG LIE

Genocide.

The bearded man in sunglasses stood at McGill University's Roddick Gates, his big sign balanced on a concrete bollard outside the iron fence where McGill College Avenue and Sherbrooke Street meet. The sign was about three by four feet. It was unclear whether he was a student. "Who wants to take a picture?" he asked as surprised-looking people walked by. Some of them did double takes, most likely because of what it said on his sign:

ON OCT. 7 ISRAEL KILLED ITS OWN PEOPLE & COVERED IT UP TO JUSTIFY GENOCIDE.

It was what's called a blood libel—one of a long series of provably false claims that Jews murder their own, or others, to achieve some foul end. Harvesting organs of the innocent, draining the blood of Gentile children for dark rituals: these are blood libels.

On the Telegram channel called Uncensored Truths, the man's message was very popular. On TikTok, YouTube, Reddit, and 4chan, too: Israel killed its own people, anonymous antisemites proclaimed. The massacre on October 7 had been a "false flag" operation—a staged event designed to cast blame on someone else. "So basically the Hamas attack was a false flag for Israel to occupy Gaza and kill Palestinians," said a post on the Reddit forum r/LateStageCapitalism. "Expected behavior from nazi wannabes." Online watchdog organizations found that more than half of the antisemitic messages after October 7 were similar: Israel massacred its own people for profit.

Despite the available evidence, most of it in videos shot and promoted by Hamas itself—in which Hamas and their Gazan partisans killed twelve hundred men, women, children, and babies on that day—the "Israel murdered its own people" lie was widely propagated by haters on the margins. In time, it would become one of the most popular tropes in Hamas's information war.

The word *genocide*, however, was somewhat different. From the very start, the notion that Israel had committed genocide was a specific allegation, and broadly popular. It went viral almost immediately. Genocide became universal, tossed around like so much confetti. It was everywhere.

Lauren Post is the words and images expert with the Anti-Defamation League's Center on Extremism. Asked about the word *genocide*—and the other words that the anti-Israel, pro-Hamas campaign uses, over and over—she says, "It is a sophisticated use of language. And it's coordinated."

Post is one of the leading experts on the words and symbols used by Hamas and their propaganda team. "They have put a great deal of care into how a message or image is presented. They have put some real thought into what messages to use with what constituencies. Because some of these symbols find an emotional core with their supporters. And that's what makes them so powerful."

The words and images pushed out by Hamas's apologists online, on signs, in literature, and on the news since October 7, 2023, communicate defiance, dissent, and (often) detestation. They are the sorts of slogans and symbols—some subtle, some not—that communicate the main messages of a global propaganda campaign.

Genocide is a word that was heard and seen most often at the earliest anti-Israel, anti-West rallies and protests. On the search engine Bing, "genocide and Israel" can now be found nearly fifteen million times. Notably, on Google Trends—which measures how certain words and phrases are being searched—"Israel genocide" spiked dramatically several days before Israel had even launched its ground campaign against Hamas. Since October 7, too, the pairing of *genocide* and *Israel* has been a highly popular English-language search term in Canada, South Africa, Ireland, and various Arab states—having reached 100, or what Google calls "peak popularity." Political campaigns are always striving to infect the public consciousness with a slogan or a concept that uses minimal language. The word *genocide* had achieved that degree of maximum awareness in just a matter of days.

A few paces past the man with the genocide sign, past the Roddick Gates and nearer to the McLennan Library Building, an illegal encampment had been set up several days earlier. Signs had been affixed all along the fencing, the majority in English along with some in French, some in Arabic. But the word repeated most was GENOCIDE, or GÉNOCIDE. That was the message, in both Canadian official languages.

The occupants looked to be students, but McGill University had earlier released a statement saying that they mostly weren't. About eighty tents had been pitched near the library walls, with pallet bridges placed over the patches of mud. Trenches had even been dug for rain runoff. Farther north, a couple dozen students were lined up in a haphazard Muslim congregational prayer. Some protestors could be seen distributing food, coffee, and water.

Others were hammering posts into the mud in order to hold up blue tarps that would protect against the rain and sun. Closer to the pathway, some were gathering on benches or patches of grass, sporting keffiyehs or veils, and talking quietly among themselves. They refused to speak to outsiders. As at other university encampments in the spring and summer of 2024, masked "security" kept away those who got too close—and directed reporters to speak to media representatives, who were also masked and using what sounded like prepared talking points. A generator was running, presumably to provide power to a public address system, but nobody was using it yet. Media were forbidden inside the gates of the occupied space, signs proclaimed.

On the other side of the Roddick Gates, a pair of Montreal police officers sat in a cruiser watching the encampment and looking bored. Another cruiser was parked on the other side of Sherbrooke Street. And, farther east, paddy wagons had been parked around a corner, not easily seen. But there.

Earlier, two Jewish students had brought an application for an injunction in Quebec Superior Court to get the anti-Israel protestors removed. McGill itself took no position, which not a few observers saw as odd, given the fact that from the earliest days of the encampment the university had been loudly and regularly objecting to the occupation of their land. Justice Chantale Massé rejected the students' application, saying they had failed to show that irreparable harm was being caused.

And, from the occupiers' perspective, it was possibly true: "irreparable harm" wasn't much in evidence at McGill during May 2024. The school term was over; most students and professors had gone home for the summer. The occupiers looked tired and dirty, but none of them could be seen assaulting anyone, or yelling at the "Zionists" they'd barred from the area (instead, they had signs that did that). The encampment was relatively calm, if tense. Students were still wheeling by on rented bicycles, going to or from exams.

In the next month, however, things turned violent.

"Protestors"—the CBC called them students, but the university had calculated that 80 per cent of them weren't—stormed into McGill's nearby administration building. They forced out anyone who worked there, barricaded doors, destroyed furniture, and unfurled banners deriding the Holocaust. Hours later, riot police arrived, quickly cleared them out—and, once outside, charged at them with batons and tear gas. The mob dispersed, but not before fifteen were arrested.

In July 2024, McGill shut down its campus and sent in private security and provincial police officers to dismantle the occupation. Three dozen anti-Israel protestors were moved out of the space near the Roddick Gates, and a front-end loader and backhoe were used to remove the pallets, tents, and garbage that had accumulated there. The first layer of soil, and what was left of the grass, was stripped away, having become contaminated by human waste. A fence went up, and that seemed to be that.

The McGill protest had been the first and the longest lasting of any of the Canadian university occupations in the spring and summer of 2024. All were illegal, given that all were trespassing on private property. But the owners of that private property, the universities, had mostly permitted the occupiers to stay and grow in number. Among many Jews, students, faculty, and others, there was much unhappiness about that.

At McGill, about twenty tents had been set up at the start, in April 2024. Within days that number ballooned to more than a hundred. In time, the encampment grew to be as big as forty-three thousand square feet, which is about half the size of an average city block. The few students present were from McGill, with others from Concordia University, the Université du Québec, and the Université de Montréal. The occupiers, student and non-student, would do shifts sleeping there. Some professors did, too.

And everywhere at McGill, that word: *genocide*. It was ubiquitous throughout the encampment, on signs, banners, buttons, and T-shirts. Its presence seemed to charge the air. At McGill—and at campuses across North America, in the spring and summer of 2024—genocide was what Israel and its allies were doing to the people of Gaza, they insisted, over and over. Genocide was being committed by the Jews and non-Jews who supported the Jewish state, they claimed.

As words go, it is relatively new. It was coined by Polish lawyer Raphael Lemkin during the Second World War. It combines Latin and Greek words and means, literally, "race killing." The Nazis were intent on killing the Polish people, Lemkin believed, and he was of course right. In time, *genocide* would also come to mean acts that are intended to destroy a group based on its religion, ethnicity, race, or nationality. Wrote Lemkin at the time: "There has been no serious endeavor hitherto to prevent and punish the murder and destruction of millions . . . there was not even an adequate name for such a phenomenon."

So, Raphael Lemkin, a Jew, coined one: *genocide*.

On October 17, 2023, the Gaza Health Ministry declared that the al-Ahli Arab Hospital in Gaza had been bombed by Israel and that five hundred Palestinians had been killed. It was an act of mass murder, many said, and it made headlines around the world. The bombing was widely cited as evidence of Israel's genocidal war. Doctors Without Borders said it was "horrified" by what it called the "bombardments." The United Nations condemned it, too, and said it was an "atrocity."

Even the likes of *The New York Times* appeared to hold Israel responsible, in a front-page story whose headline spanned several columns of print: "Israeli Strike Kills Hundreds in Hospital, Palestinians Say."

But they were wrong. The allegation that Israel bombed a hospital and killed hundreds was false. The hospital was not destroyed (it still stands), and hundreds were not killed (a fraction were, at most). And, most importantly, Israel did not bomb it; Palestinian Islamic Jihad did, something Israel was quick to point out to those who were willing to listen. Human Rights Watch, which is usually no friend of Israel, later quietly confirmed that a Palestinian "rocket-propelled munition" hit the hospital parking lot, not the hospital itself. Of the Gaza Health Ministry death toll, Human Rights Watch said: "[We are] unable to corroborate the count." To that, they added this: "[The Gaza Health Ministry death toll] is significantly higher than other estimates and displays an unusually high killed-to-injured ratio and appears out of proportion with the damage visible on site." For those who accuse Israel of genocide, it was an important point, but it was generally disregarded in the rush to judgment.

The New York Times, however, eventually admitted its errors: "[Our] coverage—and the prominence it received in a headline, news alert and social media channels—relied too heavily on claims by Hamas and did not make clear that those claims could not immediately be verified. The report left readers with an incorrect impression about what was known and how credible the account was."

"Incorrect" was an understatement. When inaccurately accusing anyone of a serious crime, most media organizations will publish a correction notice. To some critics, the *Times* also needed to pledge to abstain from using the unverified claims of Hamas or its agencies when reporting on what was happening in the war in Gaza, and whether war crimes and genocide were taking place. Instead, in the months that followed, media and governments continued to accept the genocide claims of Hamas and its health ministry.

It happened over and over. Throughout the Israel–Hamas war, few have been willing to dispute Hamas's claims. So, immediately after October 7, when the terrorist group and its allies seized on the "genocide" claim, they would successfully propel it into most of the reporting on the conflict. As propaganda goes, it was very, very successful.

But the mere repetition of a lie is not what makes propaganda successful. It needs to find a receptive audience as well.

———

Lesley Klaff is an editor of the respected *Journal for the Study of Antisemitism* as well as a board member of the Louis D. Center for Human Rights Under Law and of Berlin's International Center for the Study of Antisemitism. She's also a professor at one of Britain's largest and best-ranked universities for research, Sheffield Hallam. Since October 7, Klaff has been extensively studying the rapid rise in antisemitism in Britain and beyond, with a particular focus on its effect on students. And with this youthful demographic, she's found, the anti-Israel, pro-Hamas strategy has been highly effective.

"[The campaign] has been incredibly well organized and incredibly well funded," says Klaff. "Many of the students don't know history, so there is a willingness to accept the allegations being made against Jews and Israel. There is an underlying view, to them, that Jews are evil, and therefore capable of genocide."

Long before the events of October 7, Klaff wrote about how such a campaign seemed to be underway in Western nations. Increasingly, she found, Israel's treatment of Palestinians was being compared to how the Nazis had treated the Jews. The result: wrongdoing on the part of Israel was often exaggerated, she noted—and the crimes and atrocities the Nazis inflicted on Jews were minimized. The anti-Israel campaign was effectively inverting the crime that was the Holocaust, she says. It was, Klaff observed, the new antisemitism.

The United Nations General Assembly—like Human Rights Watch and other NGOs—has accepted that genocide is committing grave harm against a group of people for national, ethnic, racial, or religious reasons. The objective, most agree, has to be to utterly destroy the group. That, says Klaff and others, is the first problem: Israel's war against Hamas was always just that—a war against Hamas, not Palestinian civilians. Throughout the months-long war, Israel repeatedly delayed or halted military operations to facilitate the movement of thousands of Palestinians out of war zones. The Allies did not do that at Hiroshima or Dresden, she says.

As Klaff also notes, Israel was responding to a mass slaughter by Hamas that was itself genocidal. Nor did it break any cease-fire: Hamas itself had done that. By raping, torturing, and murdering thousands of non-combatants—unarmed women, Jewish children, and babies—they were engaged in genocide as defined by international law, she says.

Klaff points out that Israel created humanitarian corridors to allow for the temporary evacuation of civilians throughout the Gaza Strip. It held off on military action to get civilians out of harm's way. It worked to get aid—food, medicines—to Gazan civilians, albeit in a sometimes haphazard fashion. And it had emphasized that it wanted Gazans to be able to return to their homes at the war's end.

As appalling an allegation as genocide was to make against Jews, it wasn't in any way new, however. In her research, Klaff found a multitude of historical attempts to equate Israel's military actions in Gaza with the crimes of the Nazis. As far back as twelfth-century England, she says, the Bishop of Norwich popularized the notion that persecuted Jews had themselves become the persecutors. In that case, one of the first known examples of blood libel, a child was supposedly kidnapped by Jews at Easter, tortured, and then "stabbed with countless thorn points, and made the blood come horribly from the wounds they made . . . some of those present adjudged him to be fixed to a cross in mockery of the Lord's Passion."

In the intervening millennium, Klaff says, the transforming of Zionism into "Jewish Nazism" has ebbed and flowed but never really stopped. It had some notable converts as well. No less than Arnold Toynbee, the acclaimed British historian, wrote in his monumental *A Study of History* that "Jews' immediate reaction to their own experience was to become persecutors in their own turn." Zionists, Toynbee concluded, were "disciples of Nazis"— but worse than Nazis because they had actually chosen to emulate their killers. Now, Klaff says, that hurtful view is widespread in the Muslim world and on the left.

And simple ignorance, and lack of education, has made it all worse. "I think there are just a lot of people, such as students—but also regular people—who don't believe in the truth because they don't know what the truth is. They don't know what genocide is. For them, the term has been stripped of its unique force and special meaning." Klaff's voice is weary. "It's been completely emptied of that."

The result: antisemites have reframed the conflict and reframed the narrative, she says. It's propaganda that doesn't deny antisemitism or the Holocaust, but rather does the reverse: it declares that antisemitism is the justifiable result of a new Holocaust that Jews are creating for Palestinians. To the haters, antisemitism is a consequence of Israel's own actions, making it the most potent form of antisemitism yet. It's "a powerful political tool" in the propaganda campaign against Israel and Jews, says Klaff, because it justifies denying the existence of both.

For Klaff, the media are partly to blame for how widespread it has become, mainly because of a multitude of careless reportage on the Israel–Hamas war. "What's going on in Gaza is absolutely tragic," she says. "But there is virtually no coverage of the conflict from Israel's perspective."

Meanwhile, the themes Hamas and allied terrorist groups have used to cultivate the support of young people—that Israel is a white supremacist, colonial state—have become universal: "There's a big propaganda drive underway to 'decolonize' the curriculum," says Klaff. "Progressive people have adopted this colonization narrative—whereby white people are always the oppressors and black and brown people are always the oppressed.

[Hamas et al.] have particularly pushed this narrative in universities. Students think of Jews as white colonizers who went in and stole the land from the indigenous Arab people."

She shakes her head in dismay. "It is an attempt to absolve Hamas of the crimes of October 7 and erase its victims. So we've seen people tear down posters of the hostages. We've seen denials of the rapes. We've seen people say it was an inside job—all of that kind of thing. But even among people who don't make those false claims, the whole focus is on Israel committing genocide, or doing something that is equivalent to the Holocaust but in Gaza. Which effectively moves the attention of people away from Hamas's wrongdoing. It moves attention away from Israel and Jews as victims—and it provides cover for Hamas, and emboldens them and their allies."

For Klaff, the end goal of the strategy "is the elimination of the two-state solution. The goal is to accuse Israel of genocide, to demonize Israel and delegitimize it. To isolate it in the eyes of the world. The aim of the anti-Zionists is not a two-state solution—it's to replace Israel. I think, very much, that is their calculated aim.

"And it has shocked me, frankly, how even intelligent people have failed to see that."

International law is a set of principles, rarely enforced. But international law still provides Israel with the legal justification to defend itself from attacks by Hamas in Israeli's south and from missiles and rockets fired by Hezbollah in Israel's north (as well as from the Houthis and from Iran's proxies in Iraq and Syria). Article 51 of the UN Charter declares that "nothing shall impair the inherent right of collective or individual self-defence if an armed attack occurs against a member of the United Nations." And with both Hamas and Hezbollah, Israel states, the targets of their armed attacks are almost always Jewish civilians, not the military.

If Hamas is known for anything besides the murder of Jews, it is its willingness to set up military operations in civilian areas and hide behind innocent Palestinians. Hamas has, as NATO noted as long as two decades ago, always used civilians as "human shields." If it has any expertise, military strategists observe, it is that. In the nearly four hundred kilometres of tunnels built by Hamas, they note, not a single bomb shelter for Gazan citizens is to be found. That, too, they say, is a form of genocide—carried out against the Palestinian people by its own government. It is a grim cycle: terrorize, provoke a military response, shelter behind defenceless non-combatants when it comes, then publicize the results.

The numbers used to justify the genocide claim simply do not add up, Klaff and other observers say. Despite that, the death toll in Gaza has been cited by media and politicians, countless times, to demand an immediate ceasefire in the Israel–Hamas war. Repeatedly, there have been claims that many thousands of Gazan civilians have been killed by Israel, most of them women and children.

There is reason to believe that the death toll is flawed, however. Throughout the war and beyond, there has been one cited source for all the numbers used by Israel's critics and haters: the Hamas-run Gaza Health Ministry. Hamas seized control of Gaza in 2007 and took complete control of the ministry, ensuring that their own people would run it. The ministry's director general answers directly to Hamas. It has been established that the ministry has permitted Hamas to store weapons in Gaza hospitals, to operate out of them, and in some, to even keep Israeli hostages prisoner.

Neither side allowed any truly independent body or media organization to enter the war zone, which led to governments and media organizations simply taking the claims of Hamas's health ministry at face value. Some, however, did not. Andrew Fox, a former British army officer and senior lecturer at Royal Military Academy Sandhurst, authored a report for the Henry Jackson Society, a U.K.-based think tank. In it, Fox examined Hamas-issued casualty statistics and found that the terrorist group's health ministry had inflated body counts, particularly those of women and children. He alleged that there were "widespread inaccuracies and distortion in the data collection process" used by the health ministry, including "significant daily increases in the reported deaths of women and children that are mathematically impossible."

Not all agreed with that. Airwars is a respected British not-for-profit that tracks and assesses claims of civilian harm in war and conflict zones. With very high ratings for independence and credibility, it's considered "least biased" by the Media Bias/Fact Check organization. Like Andrew Fox and the Henry Jackson Society, Airwars released a report on Gaza casualties in late 2024 but reached different conclusions. Airwars did not mince words: "By almost every metric, the harm to civilians from the first month of the Israeli campaign in Gaza is incomparable with any 21st century air campaign. It is by far the most intense, destructive, and fatal conflict for civilians that Airwars has ever documented. At least 5,139 civilians were killed in Gaza in 25 days in October 2023. This is nearly four times more civilians reported killed in a single month than in any conflict Airwars has documented since it was established in 2014."

In April 2025, another report was quietly released, this time from the Hamas-controlled health ministry itself: many of those listed as war fatalities in Gaza died of natural causes, the ministry said, or did not die at all. Zaher al-Wahidi, the head of statistics at the ministry, told Sky News that thousands of individual deaths had been reclassified. "We realized a lot of people died a natural death," Wahidi said. "Maybe they were near an explosion and they had a heart attack, or [something] caused them pneumonia or hypothermia. All these cases we don't [attribute to] the war." In all, four thousand names had been removed from the casualty lists.

In May 2025, more amendments were made to official figures. In that month, Tom Fletcher, the United Nations undersecretary for humanitarian affairs, stated the following: "There are 14,000 babies that will die in the next 48 hours unless we can reach them." His words caused an explosion of outrage around the world. On the Bing search engine, his name and the word *babies* produced more than half a million results. *The Guardian* newspaper called it "forced starvation," and the governments of Canada, France, and the United Kingdom called the situation "egregious."

It was, however, completely false. Some forty-eight hours after Fletcher made his statement, the United Nations issued a retraction, as did *The Guardian* and other media. Challenged on his choice of words—perhaps surprisingly—by a BBC reporter, Fletcher was undeterred: "I felt we needed to jolt the international community." He was not asked, apparently, if it was appropriate to "jolt" the international community with statistics that were made up.

The numbers debate, however, rages on. Clearly, too many innocent Palestinians have been killed—Israel acknowledges as much. But the fact that the war was ongoing should have perhaps persuaded the media and others to refrain from making the most serious allegation of all—that an actual genocide was taking place, says Abraham J. Wyner. There are simply too many things that could go wrong. And too many faulty assumptions were being made, he says.

Wyner is a professor of statistics and data science at the University of Pennsylvania. In March 2024 he published an important analysis of the Gaza Health Ministry's death toll numbers in *Tablet* magazine, concluding: "The numbers are not real. That much is obvious to anyone who understands how naturally occurring numbers work. The casualties are not overwhelmingly women and children and the majority may be Hamas fighters."

Wyner looked at the total number of Gazan deaths from the start of the war for a period of five months. On a graph, the death toll number grows by the same amount every single day, showing a perfect line going upward. Wrote Wyner: "This regularity is almost surely not real. One would expect quite a bit of variation day to day . . . the Gaza ministry is releasing fake daily numbers that vary too little." This is made far worse, as he sees it, by the fact that governments and news organizations around the world uncritically rely on those numbers.

Sitting in his sunny University of Pennsylvania office, Wyner explains. "There are three major problems with what Hamas's health authority has claimed."

The first problem is how quickly the health authority was able to churn out numbers. "In terms of reliability," he says, "it takes months before you can genuinely sort out casualty counts. [Hamas's health authority] were producing lists of thousands of deceased people almost in real time. That's just not functionally possible. That's not possible without essentially checking everything—especially when we know they were relying on questionable sources, or patently outright fraudulent information happening."

The second problem, Wyner says, is that the ministry clearly didn't distinguish between combatants and non-combatants. "The total casualty count was extraordinarily regular. It had far less variation than one would expect if the counts were real, coming as they were from actual battles and military interactions. . . . And when you see enough anomalies in data that don't seem to make much sense, and then you couple them with the information that you have externally, you come to pretty straightforward and important conclusions. And so I was able to conclude that their numbers just didn't make any sense. Either they were creating casualties that didn't happen or, more likely, they were reclassifying fighters [into] civilians."

The third problem mainly relates to those on the outside of Gaza looking in: "The Western media should have fundamentally ignored what the health authority was saying." Because, as Wyner points out, it was a Hamas satellite—and what it was claiming was provably wrong.

In mid-May 2024, the United Nations was obliged to concede that point: the numbers upon which the genocide allegation was based were incorrect. In that month, the UN Office for the Coordination of Humanitarian Affairs (OCHA) cut the casualty numbers in Gaza by half. At the start of May 2024, OCHA had claimed that 9,500 women and 14,500 children had been killed by Israel. Two days later, it admitted that the real figures were about 50 per cent lower: 5,000 women and 8,000 children. In early June, even the Associated Press reported on the discrepancy: "The proportion of Palestinian women and children being killed in the Israel-Hamas war appears to have declined sharply, an Associated Press analysis of Gaza Health Ministry data has found, a trend that both coincides with Israel's changing battlefield tactics and contradicts the ministry's own public statements."

Some of the blame also rests with Israel's government, Wyner says. "Israel needed to do a much better job of explaining its side. I recall General Schwarzkopf standing in front of the cameras every night back in the Gulf War, explaining what the army was doing, what they had accomplished, what they didn't accomplish, and taking questions. It was on TV every night. It's not clear that Israel could have done press conferences like that. They could have been ignored, who knows. But Israel was reluctant to put out its side of the story. It's only my opinion—but it's been corroborated and represented by others—and my opinion is that Israel has not done a good job explaining what it does militarily."

All of that, perhaps, helps to explain how Hamas and its health authority were able to disseminate inaccurate casualty counts: only their side of the story was being told, without corroboration. Fair-minded people acknowledge—as Professors Lesley Klaff and Abraham Wyner certainly do—that any loss of civilian life is a terrible tragedy and always to be avoided. But to make the case for genocide, which is the most serious crime of all crimes, the evidence first has to be proven beyond any reasonable doubt. Here, Klaff and Wyner and many others say, it simply has not.

The best refutation of the genocide statistical claim, perhaps, is also statistical, and widely available. It's open source as well. According to the Population Reference Bureau of the Census

Bureau in the United States, "The Palestinian population growth rate is among the highest in the world: 3.4 per cent in the West Bank and 4.0 per cent in Gaza." Life expectancy at birth, too, is very high, says the agency.

And, year over year, Palestinian population growth outstrips Israel's by nearly 35 per cent. If the Israelis are actively pursuing a policy of genocide, some grimly note, it is not a very effective one.

The High Aryan Warrior Priest of Canada stirred.

"Jesus wasn't a Jew," he said, without blinking. "Jews are the spawn of Satan and the real killers."

It was a sunny, warm spring day in 1986. A reporter and a photographer for the *Calgary Herald* were standing in the Caroline, Alberta, kitchen of Terry Long, the just-anointed leader of the neo-Nazi group called the Church of Jesus Christ–Christian, Aryan Nations.

The pair had spent many hours with Long, listening to him assert that Aryans were the true chosen people and that Jews were imposters—and the literal descendants of Satan's pairing with the Biblical Eve. Non-whites, said Long, were "mud people," and Adolf Hitler was "Elijah the Prophet." In modern times, he said, Jews were behind ZOG—the Zionist Occupation Government, which secretly runs the world. ZOG had invented the Holocaust to get undeserved reparations and to obscure their own genocidal campaigns against others. They were the ones engaging in genocide, Long said. Not anyone else.

When the interview was done and Long's words were safely preserved on a tape recorder, the reporter decided to challenge him: "Mr. Long, Jesus was always Jewish and a rabbi. And the

Holocaust is a notorious historical fact in which Jews were the main victims of genocide."

The High Aryan Warrior Priest seemed almost bemused. Rather than reaching for one of his many firearms, he went into his family's cluttered living room and returned with a "bible," one published by the Aryan Nations itself. In it, he patiently explained, Jesus Christ was not ever Jewish, and nor did the Holocaust happen in any way, shape, or form; he had a "scholarly" book that showed that, too. Jews were the real killers of the Aryan chosen people, he declared, and the real genocidal force on earth.

"There's proof," he said, pointing at his bible. It was clear that he was serious. Long and the neo-Nazi Aryan Nations had simply ignored accepted history and conjured up a false new reality, one in which Jews were the murderers, not the murdered. He and the Aryan Nations had written their own books to invert the truth. He would not be the last to do so.

Terry Long and the Aryan Nations and every other neo-Nazi and Holocaust denier the *Herald* reporter interviewed that summer—Richard Butler, Jim Keegstra, Ernst Zundel, and others—similarly denied or dismissed the Holocaust. Like lawyers, they argued in the alternative: there was no genocide, they said, but, if there was, the Jews almost certainly deserved it. Jews were the ones who always victimized others, they proclaimed. Jews had never truly been victims themselves.

Terry Long made these terrible claims decades ago. He and his ilk had inverted the truth of the Holocaust and accused Jews of a new holocaust in order to whitewash the sins of Adolf Hitler and National Socialism. And now, many years later, following the barbarity of October 7, a new crop of haters were making very similar claims, and blaming Jews for committing the same acts of mass murder that had wiped out millions of them in the Holocaust. Why?

Because Holocaust inversion pays double the dividends to the pro-Hamas alliance, academics say. On one level, it throws the Holocaust back in the faces of Jews. It trivializes the original genocide, which was something the Holocaust deniers had always done. On another level, it also weaponizes the Holocaust against Jews, and robs them of their past: it steals the historical truth of the Holocaust. It causes pain by hurling the most serious libel of all against Jews, which is that they have become the new Nazis and are themselves committing genocide against Palestinians. Terry Long and Hamas are separated by years and distance, but in their cruelty and duplicity, they are the same.

When he hears the story about Terry Long, Yossi Klein Halevi sighs. This inversion of historical fact, this inversion of genocide, is the latest manifestation of antisemitism, he agrees, but it has also been around for a long time. Longer than Terry Long.

Having just returned to his home in Jerusalem from a tour of American campuses, where the author and renowned Holocaust expert saw and heard too many comparisons drawn between Jews and Nazis, Klein Halevi says: "Holocaust inversion, which is turning the Holocaust and the memory of the Holocaust against the Jewish people—using the Holocaust as one more stick with which to beat the Jews—is done by invoking Holocaust imagery to criminalize Israel. Israel then becomes Nazi Germany. Palestinians become the victims of these new Nazis. And Gaza becomes a ghetto, echoing the Warsaw Ghetto."

He sighs again. "Israel then becomes the successor state to Nazi Germany, and the heir to its genocidal program."

This transformation is relatively new, he continues, and has become widespread since October 7, 2023. It seems impossible, he adds, given the overwhelming amount of historical evidence to the contrary; and while it also seems monstrous, it is indeed happening, in real life, in real time: "There's been a progression of accusations against Israel. Beginning with colonialism, moving to ethnic cleansing, accelerating to apartheid—and now culminating in genocide. And there's nowhere else to go after genocide," he notes, an accusation that's been an integral part of the antisemitic propaganda campaign that commenced early on the morning of October 7.

"That is their ultimate goal," Klein Halevi says of those who fund and oversee the global anti-Israel, pro-Hamas effort. "Because if Israel is a genocidal state, like Nazi Germany was, then Israel becomes incapable of waging a legitimate war of self-defence. Because a genocidal state has no right to self-defence."

In the Second World War, he continues, Germany was not defending itself. It was the aggressor. That has been a key message throughout the current anti-Israel propaganda campaign, he adds. "A murderous state needs to be defeated. It needs to be destroyed. And so the goal of the anti-Zionists is to delegitimize the state of Israel—as a necessary prelude to justifying its destruction."

If they can pin the Holocaust on its actual victims, Klein Halevi says, then Jews and the Jewish state will quickly lose their moral claim to the sympathies, and the protection, of the Gentiles of the West. "This is a much more effective strategy for them. Don't deny the Holocaust, don't deny the fact of the Holocaust. There were gas chambers. Six million Jews were killed. Don't deny that outrage.

"There is a much more effective way of delegitimizing Israel, or stripping Jews of their own history. Not by clumsy attempts to deny the historicity of the Holocaust—but by simply shifting the burden of genocide onto the Jews. The outrage becomes this: the children and grandchildren of Holocaust survivors are now doing exactly what was done to their families.

Genocide.

Between October 7 and the end of November, 2023, anti-Israel and even pro-Hamas protests exploded across Western democracy.

The slogans being heard across the West were strikingly similar. Jews and their allies were stunned by how many were willing to echo the anti-Israel and (too often) antisemitic refrain. In that seven-week period in the United States alone, almost twenty-three hundred pro-Palestine, anti-Israel protests took place globally. Many of them had rapidly devolved into Jew-loathing, pro-Hamas rallies, marches, caravans, demonstrations, vigils, banner drops, and so-called direct actions. Demonstrations in support of Israel dropped dramatically.

The aptly named Crowd Counting Consortium at Harvard's Kennedy School was keeping track of the protests during this period and in the days that followed. The consortium's Jay Ulfelder noted: "Actions in support of Palestine [had] swelled into a geographically broad and demographically and tactically diverse movement that continues to produce scores of events with thousands of total participants almost every day."

In the United States in those early days, the Harvard consortium found that nearly two thousand anti-Israel protests and rallies took place in nearly five hundred cities and towns in forty-nine states, along with Washington, D.C., Puerto Rico, and Guam. Crowd size exceeded a thousand people for about 60 per cent of the protests—which the consortium "conservatively" estimated to add up to nearly seven hundred thousand people. Week after week, the crowd sizes simply grew.

Pro-Israel events also happened very near the start, Ulfelder confirmed, and were strikingly smaller in size—typically with only three hundred or so in attendance. Most of these events were organized by synagogues or national Jewish groups. Some were initiated by elected representatives. No one knew for sure, meanwhile, who had organized the anti-Israel events. It seemed likely that politicians had played only a minor role: apart from anti-Israel Democrat congresspeople Cori Bush and Rashida Tlaib, Ulfelder says, no elected people attended them.

Immediately following October 7 the protests were angry and noisy, but as at McGill in Montreal, they mainly stayed within the confines of the law. After the first few days, however, that started to change. Whatever the cause—the ineffectiveness of the police response, the indifference of too many politicians and prosecutors, the relative silence of the public—some of the protests went from being mainly pro-Palestine to being openly pro-Hamas and anti-Israel. It was a surprising transformation, one that Harvard noted as well.

"One notable feature of the pro-Palestine movement is the variety of tactics it is employing. While nearly all of the early actions were demonstrations, rallies, marches, or protests on public sidewalks and streets, we've also seen a significant increase since mid-October of acts of civil disobedience and other deliberately disruptive actions. Many of these have targeted the offices of U.S. senators and representatives. . . . Others have targeted the offices or other facilities of companies that design or manufacture weapons for the Israeli military, franchises of companies invested in Israel, or public thoroughfares or transit hubs. Over that same time, we have also seen an increasing but still small number of direct actions involving vandalism or other types of property damage at some of those same commercial targets.

"Taken together, these acts of civil disobedience and direct actions have led to more than 1,600 arrests [in the United States] since October 7, with hundreds of those arrests sometimes occurring at a single event. We have seen reports of property damage at 41 pro-Palestine events, almost all of it graffiti or broken windows, while none of the pro-Israel events we've recorded have involved property damage."

The Harvard report continued: "Another notable feature of the current pro-Palestine mobilization is its demographic diversity. Unsurprisingly, many of the actions throughout this wave have been led by Palestinian community, youth, and student organizations acting in concert with other Arab-American or Muslim ones. From the start of the wave, those organizations have also been supported by the same diverse array of anti-colonialist, anti-imperialist, anti-racist, anti-capitalist, feminist, and queer organizations that have supported calls for Palestinian liberation for decades."

In an influential December 2024 essay on The Free Press website, Canadian writer Terry Glavin noted that the ranks of the antisemites had changed. Wrote Glavin: "Almost none of [the antisemitic] verbal or physical assaults are coming from white supremacists or antisemites of the right-wing variety. They are being carried out by self-described progressives, Arabs, and, often, recent immigrants who are operating inside an ideological framework of 'settler colonialism,' which casts Canada, the United States, Australia, and, most of all, Israel, as irredeemably illegitimate constructs of imperialism, capitalism, genocide, and racism."

Similarly, in a May 2024 report in *Tablet* magazine, senior writer at *The Scroll* Park MacDougald described the protestors' prevailing ideology as a "mix of campus progressivism, hardcore Islamism and Arab nationalism, and revolutionary anarchism and communism"—and observed that the protestors themselves make up a rainbow coalition, of sorts, comprising those who are "far left and anti-Israel. Some are foreigners, or the children of foreigners, who have imported the conspiracies and hatreds of their homelands."

The suggestion that most of the post–October 7 antisemitism was coming from the ideological left was credible, studies showed. The Combat Antisemitism Movement (CAM) is a loose coalition of about seven hundred mostly American organizations that (obviously) oppose antisemitism. It has been critical of anti-Israel politicians on both sides of the ideological spectrum—from Democratic representative Ilhan Omar to Republican congresswoman Marjorie Taylor Greene—and has been attacked by Iranian state media as well.

In their Spring 2025 report, *Echoes of the Past and a Warning for the Present*, CAM studied the unprecedented rise in antisemitism around the world in 2024, summarizing their findings this way: "We are now facing the most severe wave of antisemitism since the end of the Second World War, a phenomenon that demands urgent global attention. Jewish communities worldwide have been subjected to an unrelenting onslaught of violence, harassment, and systemic discrimination, fueled by a fusion of far-left, far-right, and Islamist extremism."

Most of the hate, concluded CAM, is now coming from the left: "Far-left incidents surged by 324.8 per cent [in 2024] compared to 2023, rendering the far-left the dominant ideological camp of antisemitic incidents. Radicalized social movements, media disinformation campaigns, and efforts to target Jewish communities under the guise of anti-Israel activism have primarily fuelled this increase." Conversely, CAM noted, far-right antisemitic incidents dropped by around 55 per cent in the same period.

Meanwhile, there had also been a rise in Islamist antisemitism, they noted: "Islamist-motivated incidents increased by 44.3 per cent from 2023, underscoring the dangerous convergence of far-left antisemitism and militant Islamist propaganda. This rise can be traced to coordinated propaganda networks, extremist religious teachings, and recruitment efforts targeting vulnerable individuals susceptible to radicalization."

Far-left and Islamic antisemites had forged partnerships around the world, CAM noted, and as a result leftist and Islamist extremists have "evolved into a global force, leveraging anti-colonial narratives, certain critical theories, and anti-Zionist propaganda to fuel hostility toward the Jewish state and Jewish communities worldwide." The worst places for the explosion in antisemitic hate, they observed, were the United States and then Europe—unsurprising, perhaps, given their relative populations. But the nation that's had nearly as many antisemitic crimes as the rest of the world's countries was Canada.

Concludes the Combat Antisemitism Movement: "The rise of antisemitism . . . is not a historical aberration—it is a defining moment in modern history. If the world fails to act now, we risk entering a new dark era in which antisemitism is not only tolerated but condoned, allowed to fester and become institutionalized. Such a process creates a downward spiral, as hate begets hate, and calls for the extermination of the Jewish state can quickly transform into actions designed to harm and to kill Jews.

"We must act decisively, forcefully, and without hesitation. The Jewish people have endured persecution for centuries—but they will not stand alone. The time for action is now."

Park MacDougald wrote in the same *Tablet* report that many of the protests included "professional radicals and organizers, black bloc antifa thugs, Marxist-Leninist revolutionaries, and Palestinian and Islamist radicals"—many of whom, he said, had acquired experience during the clashes with police during the Occupy movement, Black Lives Matter, and the Seattle WTO and Toronto G20 protests. Meanwhile, Jewish groups were in attendance, too, such as Jewish Voice for Peace and the IfNotNow Movement. But these groups were usually greatly outnumbered by the others.

While the makeup of the protestors seemed to be varied, their messaging decidedly was not: there was a striking homogeneity to it, everywhere. In the early days, Harvard found in its studies, "Free Palestine" was far and away the message heard and seen most often, at hundreds of events, and usually accompanied by demands for a ceasefire, although usually aimed at Israel—not Hamas, Hezbollah, or the Houthis.

And alongside the claim that Israel was committing "genocide," something else was frequently heard: "From the River to the Sea, Palestine Will Be Free."

It sounds innocuous enough: "From the River to the Sea, Palestine Will Be Free."

Superficially, it doesn't seem to explicitly advocate violence. Nothing is named, apart from Palestine. It lacks the potency of *genocide*.

It is, however, a mistake, Eylon Levy, Lesley Klaff, and others say, to regard "From the River to the Sea" as anything other than the flip side of the "genocide" coin. Genocide is the crime; "From the River to the Sea" is the remedy. The two are inextricably linked and have been used many, many times online since October 7, they note. Early on, on the search engine Bing alone, those words produced more than 136 million results.

"From the River to the Sea" first entered the vernacular in the 1940s, but was rarely used. It became more commonplace in the 1960s and 1970s, when he phrase was seized upon by the Palestine Liberation Organization (PLO)—and, later, formally adopted by Hamas in their revised charter. Article 20 of their governing constitution—which elsewhere calls for the complete extermination of the Jewish state, and vanquishing "infidels . . . in the lands of Islam"—declares that "Hamas rejects any alternative to the full and complete liberation of Palestine, from the river to the sea."

For some pro-Palestine protestors (who may not understand the full connotations of the slogan), and for Hamas and Hezbollah (who fully do), the "river" is the Jordan, to Israel's east; the "sea" is the Mediterranean, to its west. Geographically, that's all of Israel. And so to advocate "From the River to the Sea, Palestine Will Be Free" is clearly to call for the removal of the Jewish state and, one presumes, the Jews who live there. That, certainly, is what terrorists—from al-Qaeda's Osama bin Laden to Hezbollah's Hassan Nasrallah to Iranian president Ebrahim Raisi—consider those words to mean.

The Anti-Defamation League says the slogan is antisemitic. The American Jewish Committee says it means "erasing the State of Israel." Under the guidelines of the International Holocaust

Remembrance Alliance—whose work is supported by dozens of countries, including Canada, France, Germany, the United Kingdom, and the United States—"From the River to the Sea" is seen as denying "the Jewish people their right to self-determination, e.g., by claiming that the existence of a State of Israel is a racist endeavor."

"It's clearly anti-Israel now," says Lauren Post, the Center on Extremism's expert in language and symbols. "We also know that some Jewish extremists would say Israel is from the river to the sea as well. Post–October 7, however, these days, shouting 'From the River to the Sea' has a very clear meaning. It's like when they're shouting 'Globalize the Intifada.' It acquired a clear meaning. It's now obviously anti-Israel and, in a lot of cases, antisemitic."

Since October 7, the use of "From the River to the Sea" in public has caused anguish for many Jews. In the United States, for example, the aforementioned Democratic Party congressperson Rashida Tlaib (who claims Palestinian lineage) was censured by the House of Representatives—including by fellow Democrats—for using the slogan online in November 2023. Tlaib's fellow party members called it a "rallying cry for the destruction of the State of Israel and genocide of the Jewish people." (Tlaib later issued a statement saying she strongly opposed antisemitism.) The Joe Biden White House, for its part, has called the slogan "divisive" and has "categorically rejected" it as antisemitic. In Britain, senior Labour MP Andy McDonald was suspended from the party after saying "between the river and the sea" at a rally. Other Labour Party MPs called his use of those words "deeply offensive." McDonald later claimed his words were a call for peace, not for the removal of Jews and the Jewish state.

However benign the slogan's original meaning, after the October 7 Hamas attack many Jews consider those words to be an unambiguous threat: ethnic cleansing of Jews from Israel. "From the River to the Sea" is arguably more destructive than the "genocide" accusation, they say, simply because it's been embraced so widely. Online, those words are invoked often, including by many—as Levy and Klaff noted—who don't know which river and which sea they're chanting about. Almost predictably, the slogan has now been reduced to a social media hashtag, #FTRTTS, often accompanied by a tiny Palestinian flag and/or watermelon slice.

CyberWell is one of the few organizations in the world that's following, and documenting, the surge in antisemitism online since October 7, 2023. A non-profit started in Tel Aviv in 2022, CyberWell differs from other organizations that monitor online hate. It doesn't keep data to itself, for example: it advocates for transparency in its research, and it posts its findings on a cloud-based platform for all to see and use. To do this, its staff uses advanced technology—including artificial intelligence—to track online expressions of hatred. It pays particular attention to the most popular social media platforms (Facebook, Instagram, X, YouTube, and TikTok), analyzing their hashtags, images, and videos, in both English and Arabic.

When CyberWell finds offensive content, it shares its results directly with the platforms' owners and managers, pushing them to delete or de-platform it. In early 2024, for example, CyberWell identified more than 150,000 examples of antisemitic propaganda and pushed for their removal. They had some success in that, reporting a removal rate of around 32 per cent across all the social platforms, an improvement over its roughly 10 per cent removal rate in 2022. It got somewhat better throughout 2024, it says—but then in early 2025 Meta announced that it would no longer moderate content. As a result, CyberWell and others expect that much more antisemitic propaganda will get through, turbocharged by algorithms that make the content a little bit worse every time someone sees it.

Tal-Or Cohen Montemayor is the articulate lawyer and researcher who founded CyberWell and serves as its executive director. She has lots of data, and many thoughts, to share about the harm caused by "From the River to the Sea." CyberWell compiled the numbers and facts to provide the context lacking from the slogan. In May 2024 it submitted a detailed report to Meta's Oversight Board, an independent body that acts as watchdog for harmful speech on Facebook or Instagram, which have more than five billion users worldwide.

In its report, CyberWell wrote that the slogan "is a call for violence and vandalism against Jewish communities, their institutions, and monuments dedicated to preserving the memory of the Holocaust around the world." "From the River to the Sea" is adjacent to another seemingly innocuous call, QAnon's "Where We Go One, We Go All." That pro–Donald Trump QAnon conspiracy theory's slogan—and its affiliated hashtag #WWG1WGA—surged in popularity in 2019 and 2020 on YouTube, Facebook, Instagram, and X (then Twitter). Meta thereafter categorized it as "militarized content," defined as propaganda coming from groups that "have celebrated violent acts, [and] individual followers with patterns of violent behavior."

CyberWell argued that Facebook and Instagram's Meta parent should do likewise with "From the River to the Sea," proposing that it be subject to more and better moderation. CyberWell also pointed out that the slogan had been used at multiple protests and shutdowns where violence had taken place.

"And," as CyberWell noted, "[the slogan] was used as a rallying cry in multiple illegal college solidarity encampments when physically restricting, harassing, threatening, spitting on, and physically harming Jewish students, press, and members of the public." Despite the evidence, however, in September 2024 Meta's Oversight Board ruled that "[we] cannot conclude . . . that the users in the content in question are using the phrase as a call to violence against a group." The "group," Jews, felt differently. Many were outraged.

Online, CyberWell and other internet watchdogs note that examples of the hateful speech associated with the phrase are ubiquitous. One user posted "from river to sea only Palestine exist [sic]. May God destroy Zionist terrorist Jews." Another wrote that "the only good Jew is a dead Jew," alongside the #FromTheRiverToTheSea hashtag. There are many other such threatening messages coupled with the slogan. They wouldn't have been difficult for Meta to find, critics say, if it had looked.

Examples of how "From the River to the Sea" has become a rallying cry for terror groups are also easy to find. The Popular Front for the Liberation of Palestine (PFLP)—a designated terror group in the United States, the European Union, and elsewhere—states on its website: "Armed resistance is a revolutionary righteous and legitimate response. . . . We take the position that the land has been and will be the heart of the struggle, which has no solution but liberating the land, all of the land, from the river to the sea." And the now-deceased Hassan Nasrallah, leader of the PFLP's terrorist partner Hezbollah, said, "Palestine from the river to the sea is the property of the Palestinian people and they shall return to it."

Meanwhile, in North America, Charlotte Kates, the influential spokesperson for the pro-PFLP designated terrorist affiliate Samidoun, said: "We demand a free Palestine from the River to the Sea. And we stand with the Palestinian resistance and their heroic and brave actions on October 7. As they said, long live October 7th!" Palestinian Islamic Jihad, the Fatah militia in Lebanon, Hamas representatives around the world—all have defined "From the River to the Sea" as eliminating the Jewish state. These groups have not hidden what they consider to be its true meaning.

As much as some try to disguise it, the real meaning and purpose of "From the River to the Sea" has become associated with "real-world harm," according to CyberWell, who, along with organizations like NGO Monitor, have informed Meta, to no effect. The slogan needs to be reduced in ranking in news feeds, they say, get less prominence in online searches, have its related hashtags reviewed—and all fundraisers, ads, and monetization tools using "From the River to the Sea" should be banned completely.

Says Cohen Montemayor: "From the River to the Sea originally was used by the Palestinian Liberation Organization [and] it was also used by other Arab leaders in the region when setting the tone for the vision of what was to be done with Israel. In the beginning, they had no interest in a two-state solution. [The slogan] was stating the vision that the only solution for the Middle Eastern conflict was to drive out Jews from the land of Israel.

"Driving out the Jews from the land of Israel was inextricably linked to Palestinian liberation. So, 'From the River to the Sea' was always about the removal of the Jewish population from the place that they're indigenous to, which is the land of Israel. Of course, after October 7, there has been a weaponization of this term both online and offline in the illegal encampments on university campuses, but also in order to harass and target Jews online—as part of the surge in antisemitism that we saw post–October 7."

That surge inarguably happened in the early hours of October 7. It started almost immediately, suggesting to CyberWell and other watchdogs that it had been in the works for quite some time: launching a global antisemitic propaganda campaign can't be done in a single day, Cohen Montemayor agrees.

"From the River to the Sea," however, was not their only message.

"Free Palestine."

In Washington, D.C., two Israeli embassy staff were gunned down in the street in late May 2025. They were assassinated as they were leaving the Capital Jewish Museum by a man who fired twenty-one bullets into the bodies of the young couple, whose names were Sarah Milgrim and Yaron Lischinsky.

The man waited for the police to arrive. When they did, he pulled out a red keffiyeh and started shouting, "Free, free Palestine!" Some time later, when speaking to investigators, the man said: "I did it for Palestine, I did it for Gaza."

A couple of days later, in reports about the dark origins of the alleged killer's hate, it was revealed that he'd written a manifesto titled "Escalate for Gaza, Bring the War Home." In it, he railed against "atrocities committed by the Israelis against Palestine," called for "armed action," and asserted that violence is "the only sane thing to do."

The alleged killer had many years of involvement with something called the Party for Liberation and Socialism. Among other things, that group had celebrated Hamas's slaughter of twelve hundred Jews in Israel on October 7, 2023, and published a statement on that date declaring: "Resistance to apartheid and fascist-type oppression is not a crime! . . . The actions of the resistance over the course of the last day is a morally and legally legitimate response to occupation."

Eleven days after the killings in Washington, there was another attack on Jews, this time in Boulder, Colorado. As a small group of elderly Jews gathered to call for Hamas to release the remaining Israeli hostages, a man threw firebombs at them, injuring eight. A woman later died. Police said the accused had a "makeshift flamethrower," had been raging about "Zionists," and that, like the shooter in Washington, had been yelling "Free Palestine."

The man, an Egyptian national, had reportedly been in the United States illegally. Less was known about how he'd been radicalized. It was perhaps noteworthy, however, that he and the Washington shooter allegedly used exactly the same words: *Free Palestine.*

Those words—like *genocide, intifada, From the River to the Sea,* and others—have been heard many times since the atrocities of October 7. They are ubiquitous, heard and seen often at Israel-hating university encampments and at antisemitic gang-ups outside synagogues and gatherings of Jews across North America and Europe. And now, murder scenes. At the August 2025 killing of two children in Minneapolis, Minnesota, and the following month in Nashua, New Hampshire, when a man was shot to death, the alleged killers proclaimed, "Free Palestine."

The words are important, experts tell us, because hateful words always, always precede hateful deeds. You cannot have one without the other. You cannot fashion a Jew-hating terrorist out of thin air. You need to radicalize him first, the experts note—using words that denude Jews and their allies of their humanity and that obliterate all truth.

The word *terror* is defined as violence committed to advance some ideological cause. What happened in Washington , Boulder, Minneapolis, and Nashua was inarguably terror: using violence to achieve a political goal. And it wasn't difficult to ascertain what that goal was, Eylon Levy and others observed: the shooter in Washington and the bomber in Boulder used the very same words: "Free Palestine."

Such words are not mere slogans, Levy and others say. They're not harmless, like advertising jingles. They're words that have a very specific meaning and a very specific purpose.

They are words designed to radicalize angry young people, and propel them—like bullets—toward their chosen targets.

Just a few days after the October 7 massacre in Israel, dozens of students and others gathered at Harvard University's Science Center Plaza in Cambridge, Massachusetts, for what they called a "week of action" against the Jewish state.

The event was organized by members of the Boycott, Divestment, and Sanctions caucus of Harvard's graduate student union and the African and African American Resistance

Organization (AFRO). The groups had apparently determined their strategy after Harvard's administration, led by president Claudine Gay, declined to meet their demands: divestment "from illegal settlements" in Israel, dropping disciplinary measures against anti-Israel protestors, and the reinstatement of a graduate student who had allegedly assaulted a Jewish student on camera—and who had, in the course of his studies, seemed to praise a terrorist who plotted to bomb a packed downtown Jerusalem movie theatre. (The student denied the allegation and the trial is ongoing.)

So, the Harvard BDS caucus protested. On a cold, cloudy Monday, students and others rallied at the Science Center Plaza, a short walk across from Harvard's historic Old Yard. Some of them held up Palestinian flags, while others looked uncertain. It was, after all, one of the earliest anti-Israel protests. While reflector-vested organizers watched, AFRO co-founder Kojo Acheampong led the crowd in a chant, making frequent use of an Arabic word: "Long live Palestine! Long live the Intifada! Intifada, Intifada! Globalize the Intifada!" The crowd cheered and applauded, their mitts and gloves making it sound a bit muffled. Acheampong defined what "Globalize the Intifada" means: "It symbolizes revolution," he told *The Harvard Crimson*. "So I'm saying we need a revolution. We need liberation everywhere—that's what the intifada means."

Perhaps because it was still early days for the campaign, another AFRO member, Prince A. Williams, tried to be helpful. "I think people unfortunately can be afraid of Arabic—afraid of phrases that they may not understand the history or the context behind," Williams said, also to the *Crimson*. "But ultimately, as

Kojo was saying, 'intifada' is a word that ultimately symbolizes the Palestinian right to resist."

Not quite. Williams's bit of spin was hopeful, but not entirely accurate. Whatever it once meant, supporters of Israel note, *intifada* no longer means anything as benign as "the right to resist." As with "From the River to the Sea," they say, its meaning has shifted indelibly toward menace. For Israelis, it now has a very specific definition—particularly after the second intifada, between 2000 and 2005. In that bloody period, the intifada resulted in more than a thousand Israelis being slain. Most were civilians.

There were many shootings in that intifada, along with stabbings and cars ramming into unarmed Israelis waiting at bus stops. Suicide bombings were a regular occurrence. If the second intifada is remembered for a single day, however, it was a bloody one in October 2000, when two Israeli reservists mistakenly entered Ramallah in the West Bank. The pair were caught, tortured, and beaten. They were stabbed repeatedly and disembowelled, while one soldier had his body set on fire. An Italian TV crew filmed the worst of it and broadcast it around the world, so there was no denying what really happened.

Captured later by the IDF, Aziz Salha recalled what he and the others did to the two young soldiers held in the el-Bireh police station: "We were in a craze to see blood. I entered the room [and] I saw an Israeli soldier sprawled on the floor in front of the door. I came closer to him and saw a knife lodged in his back, near his right shoulder. I removed the knife and stabbed him in the back two or three times . . . while others in the room continued to kick him. I put my hand over his mouth and the other on his shoulder, in order to strangle him." One of them also called one of the soldier's wives, using the man's cellphone. He told her: "We are slaughtering your husband."

Aziz Salha, by his own admission, actively participated in the torture and murder of the two reservists, Yosef Avrahami and Vadim Norzhich. Years later, Salha would be dispatched by an Israeli missile strike. But then and now, that is what *intifada* means to many Jews: the image of Salha waving his blood-stained hands from the police station window. His bloodied hands—all red, facing outward—would later become an important symbol of their own.

The crowd below erupted. They cheered and clapped as one of the soldiers' bodies was tossed out the window and then stomped on. The bodies were dragged away and mutilated some more in the town square. Palestinian police, meanwhile, busied themselves with trying—unsuccessfully—to confiscate any footage of the killings. That was one bit of propaganda they apparently did not want shared with the world.

It's possible that the dozens of pro-Palestinians in attendance at Harvard's Science Center Plaza, and the dozens of people walking by that day, did not fully understand what "Globalize the Intifada" meant to Jews, or the significance of the red hands, or what happened in a Ramallah police station in October 2000. It's possible—but for many Israelis, it's not. They will tell you: they know what *intifada* means to them. In life, as in law: What the wrongdoer means is immaterial. What matters is how the victim experiences it.

As with "From the River to the Sea," "Intifada"—a nebulous call for a worldwide revolution against Israel—was chanted many times after October 7, and in many places far beyond Harvard University. It would lead to the resignation of Harvard's president. Unhappily for the storied university, the "Intifada" chant was also noticed in Washington, D.C., by members of Congress.

Early in December 2023, Harvard president Claudine Gay was called before the House Committee on Education and the Workforce to testify about antisemitism on college campuses. She was there alongside MIT president Sally A. Kornbluth and University of Pennsylvania president Elizabeth Magill. To say that it didn't go well for the three university presidents would be an understatement. While Gay condemned antisemitism, some of the members of Congress—and one in particular, New York Republican Elise Stefanik—zeroed in on what had been said one cold day in October 2023 at Harvard's Science Center Plaza.

"Does calling for the genocide of Jews violate Harvard's rules of bullying and harassment?" Stefanik asked her.

"It can be," Gay said, deadpan. "Depending on the context."

"Depending on the context"—to many, those words would soon become infamous. Claudine Gay resigned a few weeks later for unrelated reasons, but also because she failed to recognize that "Globalize the Intifada" has a "context" that is not benign at all.

To many Jews, it still means death.

GENOCIDE IS NOT KOSHER.

Another sign, another protest. If not for who was holding it, and if not for where it was being held up, the sign would have been the sort of casual antisemitism that seemingly went global after October 7, 2023.

It was objectionable, but not because it was critical of the government of Israel. After October 7, in fact, it was difficult to find a single Jew in Israel or in the Jewish diaspora—on the political left or right—who wasn't critical of the government, led by Benjamin Netanyahu, for its failure to anticipate, and prevent, the horrors of that dark day.

Most of them, publicly or privately, angrily blamed Netanyahu for permitting Hamas to flourish, and for failing to quickly retrieve the hostages, and for conducting a seemingly endless war without clearly understood objectives. Many in Israel said they looked forward to Netanyahu being gone after the war. For months, polling in the country overwhelmingly showed the same thing.

Criticism of Israeli government policy, then, is always acceptable—Jews themselves are among Israel's strongest critics. But blaming individual Jews for what Israel's government does? That, the International Holocaust Remembrance Alliance states, is inarguably antisemitic.

And the sign—GENOCIDE IS NOT KOSHER—was antisemitic, too, because it explicitly associated genocide (the most serious crime) with an important religious precept (the *kashrut* dietary laws of the Jewish faith). What made the sign worse was that it was being held up by a child, perhaps six or seven years old, a few feet from a cenotaph in tiny Picton, Ontario, on a cold, rainy Saturday in the spring of 2024. The cenotaph had been literally dedicated, years earlier, to those Canadians who gave their lives fighting Nazism. Urged on by organizers wearing safety vests, carrying megaphones, and distributing signs and instructions, the anti-Israel protestors were seemingly there to accuse Jews—the primary victims of Nazism—of being the new Nazis.

Counter-protestors were across the street and asked aloud: Who gives a child a sign like that—knowing full well that the child doesn't really understand what *genocidal* or *kosher* means—and tells them to stand in a sacred place, in a driving cold rain on the Jewish sabbath, to act as a propaganda tool?

As the months-long protests against Israel went on and on, however, Jews and their allies felt there'd been far too much of that: too much careless language and deliberate cruelty, communicated by those who didn't understand but targeting those who usually did. There'd been a lot of signs held up, and a lot of slogans chanted, they observed, by people who weren't perhaps fully aware of what they were saying and who didn't bother to educate themselves.

For example, on the very same weekend as the Picton protest, several actors and celebrities showed up at the Oscars ceremony wearing pins with the bloody red hand, among them Billie Eilish, Jessica Chastain, Richard Gere, Cate Blanchett, and Mahershala Ali. Being stars, with all that goes with stardom, it was not unfair to assume they wanted the pins to be seen by the cameras. (Some claimed it merely represented a call for a ceasefire in Gaza.)

Their critics presumed they knew what the red hand represents: in many cultures, it symbolizes death. In the Israel–Gaza context, the red hand is an explicit reference to that infamous image of the now-deceased Aziz Salha, taken after he helped lynch and dismember two Israeli soldiers during the second intifada. In other words, both Jews and Hamas now recognize the red hand as a commemoration of the murder of Jews.

Some wondered: Was *that* what the celebrities were celebrating? Did they—like the child with the antisemitic sign in faraway Picton—actually know what they were saying? Maybe, maybe not. But to many Jews, the corrosive effect remained the same. To them, the red hand is a way of sending a message, one that wouldn't be understood by everyone, but is very well understood by its intended victims.

So, too, the inverted red triangle—a symbol that since October 7 has become very popular with the pro-Hamas fringe, both online and in real life. To others, its meaning is obscure. Lauren Post, at the Center on Extremism, explains. "I have been working in this field for eight years at this point. I've been around the block a few times. And I had never seen the red triangle, for example, used like this until October 7." Sitting in her bright Los Angeles office, she says, "There's been a claim that, Oh, this is just part of the Palestinian flag. There's a red triangle in the Palestinian flag. But it's also a [Hamas military wing] Qassam Brigades symbol, one that they started [using] after October 7 in their propaganda videos. Their videos are unfortunately very well produced. They're like video games almost. And Hamas started putting the red triangle over their targets. Whether that was Israeli soldiers, whether that was military equipment, or whatever. And that turned the red triangle into a symbol of resistance, or something worse. It's very intentional. You don't just pull a message like that out of nowhere."

She continues: "It was new to me. It's a relatively recent development, like the red hands. It's newer, but it has a very specific context. I haven't seen it deployed anywhere else, really, except in the context of the Palestine solidarity movement." She pauses. "I'm sure that some people don't know where it came from, or what it now means, and are just using it because their friends are using it. But for people who know it came from Hamas, it's an intentional choice to use the red hands and the red triangle."

Online the inverted red triangle is very common now, she says, and almost always signals support for Hamas. "It started with some smaller accounts, and then it really started to get deployed from there." Asked if the red triangle's spread was coordinated out of the Middle East, she says, "It wouldn't surprise me."

As Post notes, the inverted red triangle is likely not the red triangle found on the Palestinian flag. That triangle isn't inverted; it's turned on its side, with the longest side, the hypotenuse, vertical. The inverted red triangle has appeared in many places since October 7, she says, and frequently at violent antisemitic protests.

When red paint isn't readily available, pro-Hamas and antisemitic protestors sometimes replicate the triangle using their hands. Then they will forcefully extend it toward counterprotestors (or even passersby, like this writer, one sunny afternoon at the University of Toronto). On those occasions—and when the inverted red triangle is thrust in someone's direction—this is what the experts say it usually means: we've targeted you. Even this: we want to kill you.

At the months-long occupation at the University of Toronto, red triangles were seen in more than a dozen places, some big and some small. They were affixed to boards and signs and banners across from Convocation Hall, where graduates line up every spring to receive their degrees. The presence of the red triangles left Jewish students feeling unsafe—because, they said, the red triangle is the equivalent of rifle crosshairs being scratched onto a photo of a person's head and slid under their bedroom door at night. Or even a swastika.

The inverted red triangle's real-life use in the Middle East clears up any confusion about its true meaning. Says Post: "Our disinformation analyst had been seeing it, and she said to the rest of us, 'I don't like what I am seeing.' It was innocuous, and then suddenly it wasn't innocuous anymore. The red triangle, then, is a really interesting example of a symbol that seemed so innocuous and then was adopted, and adapted, very quickly. It took just a week or two for it to catch on." Corporate logos usually take much longer, she notes.

What a message communicates now, Post says, isn't what it has always communicated—with so many conflicts in the Middle East the region is turbulent, and what's in the present can very rapidly become part of the past. This is especially true of the keffiyeh, the checkered cotton scarf seen at university occupations and violent rallies across the Western world after October 7. For centuries, the keffiyeh was a traditional headdress worn mostly to protect men's heads against the harsh desert climate. It had no religious meaning. The keffiyeh was created by Bedouins—many of whom, ironically enough, are how Israeli citizens, and make up a significant percentage of Israel's population. Many of them now serve in the IDF, often guarding the fences that separate Israel and Hamas-led Gaza.

In the 1930s, during another Palestinian revolt, rebels were ordered to wear the keffiyeh—and not the other popular head covering, the Ottoman fez—to stand out in the coming fight. A couple of decades later, the black-and-white keffiyeh was adopted by Palestinian militants to distinguish themselves from Jordanians, who favoured the red-and-white version. A couple of decades after that, the black-and-white keffiyeh was famously embraced as the permanent fashion accessory of the PLO's Yasser Arafat. And with that, a simple protective covering created by pro-Israeli Bedouins was transformed into a symbol of Palestinian opposition and, sometimes, fear. The meaning changed.

Most of the keffiyehs now seen on our streets are made in China, not Palestine, and have been sold at upscale places like Urban Outfitters. Madonna has worn them, as has Nelson Mandela, David Beckham (who claims Jewish identity), along with actors on TV shows and in movies. Before October 7 the keffiyeh was often worn as a hipster accessory. But as happens so often in the Middle East, its meaning turned into something slightly more ominous for Jews.

People wearing them in France and Germany have been cautioned or fined or even detained. Newspapers in Germany call the keffiyeh "the problem cloth," and liken it to Nazi uniforms. Others call it "a terrorist scarf." A few days after October 7, in Vermont, three students wearing keffiyehs were shot, leaving one paralyzed.

Ironically, when it still ran things in Gaza, the Palestinian Authority also banned the wearing of the keffiyeh, because it had been worn by Hamas in attacks on Palestinian moderates. Since October 7, however, the keffiyeh has arguably been denuded of whatever benign meaning it once had. To many Jews and their allies, it now represents "hate couture," designed to express opposition to Israel or to intimidate Jews. Or both.

To just as many others, it's just a sartorial distraction. At a time when Jews and their allies are being attacked or killed, debates about the implications of the keffiyeh are a trivial sideshow, a topic for TV debate panels but not much else. So, too, the watermelon, seen so often on pro-Palestine or anti-Israel social media profiles.

After the six-day Yom Kippur War in 1967, Israel chose (bizarrely) to ban the display of the Palestinian flag in Gaza and the West Bank. Some claimed Palestinians were being arrested for displaying it anyway. But whenever far-right Israeli legislators have tried to pass legislation permanently restricting people from waving the Palestinian flag, they have failed dramatically. After the Oslo Accords, Israel officially lifted any bans on showing the flag. After October 7, its display has been restricted once again.

Notwithstanding all that, watermelon emojis are now seen on social media as a harmless way of expressing solidarity with the anti-Israel cause. As noted, the watermelon has the same colours as the Palestinian flag: red, green, black, and white. In May 2024 in Israel, a former IDF soldier was spotted eating watermelon in a Jerusalem market and asked about its propaganda value. The former soldier laughed.

"It's watermelon," he said. "Israelis like it, Palestinians like it. The only meaning it has is that it tastes good on a hot day!"

Genocide. "From the River to the Sea." The keffiyeh. A red triangle. The red hand.

Much of what we're seeing online and in the streets involving the anti-Israel or pro-Hamas movement—the words, the symbols, the chants—is propaganda. Much of it, too, can be ominous and threatening to Jews. Like all propaganda, however, it should not all simply be dismissed as mere falsehood. As Edward Bernays wrote in his seminal 1928 work, *Propaganda*, the term is defined as psychological manipulation that seeks to influence and control people using language that often contains a grain of truth. Its purpose is to make one group forget that another group is human.

Cults, which the Hamas–Hezbollah–Iran cabal recall, have recognized the critical importance of language in exercising control over their flocks. Cults have done so, cult deprogrammers say, by relying upon secret phrasings, buzzwords, euphemisms, hashtags, and even mantras. So, too, do scheming politicians, conspiracy theorists, social media influencers, and evangelical religious leaders. And sometimes, deprogrammers say, manipulative language is a defining characteristic of the anti-Israel movement as well. Those who hate Israel have used deceptive words and symbols to manufacture belief and at times, as one expert notes, extremism and then terrorism. "Without language, there are no beliefs, ideology or religion," University of Edinburgh applied linguistics professor John E. Joseph writes. "These concepts require language as a condition of their existence.

"Hamas certainly has beliefs and ideology. To be an ideology—actually any 'ology'—requires being formulated, expressed, transmitted in language. What the particular ideology is about doesn't alter this." Stressing in an interview that he's not a scholar of Hamas, Joseph observes that the terrorist group's use of social media and propaganda has "of course accelerated the rapid spread of [their] discourse in all spheres."

Joseph adds that he's all too familiar with the power of anti-Israel, pro-Hamas propaganda tactics since October 7. "My office sits above a square in which pro-Palestine rallies are sometimes held, and I am struck by what seems to be the power of the rhetorical devices of rhythm and rhyme. *From the river to the sea, Palestine must be free*, chanted by students, most of whom can't even identify the river or sea in question. The poetic force gives it an emotional charge, and maybe, for them, reinforces its ultimately genocidal 'truth.' They then try to double it up by chanting *From the sea to the river, Palestine will live forever*—oblivious to the lack of rhyme between *river* and *forever*."

Language, if used skilfully by those who don't operate morally, can kill off independent inquiry and the truth, say Joseph and others. Such propaganda can almost create a tribe of belief, cult experts like Amanda Montell say, one that uses words and images to insulate itself against the outside world. And by employing deceptions and distortion, cults—and murderous cults like Hamas, Hezbollah, Iran, along with their allies in Russia and China—don't just use language to depict reality, she says; they use it to create a new reality. Repetition and ambiguity—as was often heard at university encampments and at their rallies—then help to reinforce alternative realities and outright fantasies, Montell has written.

The information war waged by Hamas and their allies has embraced us-versus-them slogans and symbols to push their anti-Israel, anti-West congregations toward hate and then violence, Joseph and linguistic experts say. Propaganda language doesn't always invent hateful emotions—but, as Democratic Party communications guru Tony Schwartz once said to this writer, it often surfaces "a responsive chord." That is, it finds and builds upon a pre-existing prejudice or bias in a way similar to confirmation bias: language that strengthens something that's already there.

For the propagandists, this is always arguably language that helps erase alternative points of view, and ultimately those who hold those views. Religious language—such as the language preferred by Hamas and Hezbollah and Iran—"performs" rather than "informs," as Montell has said. It creates a secure, sealed, self-perpetuating world of its own: a hateful and dangerous world, say Jews and their allies.

Since October 7, the engineers of the global anti-Israel campaign have seemingly used harmful language to exercise influence over those most susceptible to it—mainly anti-Israel or antisemitic activists, plus large swaths of Gen Z and Millennials. Many of these young people are perhaps not even aware that they're regarded as lab rats in a global propaganda experiment, experts and pollsters note. The most effective propaganda campaigns, Bernays wrote, are those that are mostly "unseen" and authored "by men we have never heard of."

Much of the haters' lexicon has been pushed out to communicate a precise message using words and images that are deliberately imprecise, analysts say. It's a time-tested communications strategy favoured by the likes of Madison Avenue ad executives, and whether it's selling running shoes or political candidates, it works because it lets language do our thinking for us.

For decades, the Holocaust deniers, white supremacists, and various other antisemites have watched multimillion-dollar mainstream ad campaigns from the margins, and they've learned, communications experts like Gary Wexler say. Disguising one's true purpose is perhaps better, they discovered: let the truth emerge only later, when it's too late.

On the racist right, David Duke was the pioneer of this strategy. As the Grand Wizard of the Knights of the Ku Klux Klan, Duke transformed the image of the Klan—the biggest, longest-lasting modern hate group—using methods pioneered by ad executives and mainstream political parties. He was the one who shed the Klansmen's robes and hoods, dispensed with the cross burnings and the "Heil Hitler" chants, and presented the public with a telegenic, moderate-sounding Klan.

In his propaganda campaigns for the KKK, Duke would go on to promote a word now on the lips of many pro-Hamas, anti-Israel agitators, from university occupations to angry rallies in Western streets: *Zionist*. Duke changed the impact of that word. As every Jew knows, *Zionist* refers to the nineteenth-century European movement that believes Jews originated in an arid bit of land between the Jordan River and the Mediterranean Sea. They were indisputably indigenous to that place, Zionists said. Zionists, like all Indigenous movements, believe that Jews should be allowed to live in peace in their indigenous homeland.

For them, *Zionist* is a good word, one that communicates something positive and strong. For the likes of David Duke and those who've embraced antisemitism and hate, however, it was a dirty word. It became a useful curse.

Since the attack on October 7, 2023, *Zionist* has probably become the most-heard code word of all, but there is little doubt what it means: most Jews are Zionist, and to be anti-Zionist is —to Jews—to be against them, as people. Dr. Martin Luther King, Jr., one of history's greatest opponents of hate, made clear what *Zionist* meant to him: "When people criticize Zionists, they mean Jews. You're talking antisemitism."

As he marketed his new Klan, Duke was more circumspect. Wearing a suit and tie and projecting a moderate, telegenic face to uncritical media, Duke appeared on talk shows and insisted the Klan wasn't anti-Black—it was "pro-white," he said. Modern Klansmen weren't antisemitic, he claimed, they were merely "pro-Christian." The media ate it up. Whenever a microphone was pointed his way Duke would avoid specifics, and always employed language that seemed inclusive, not divisive. His Klan grew, and chapters again spread across North America, as they had a century before.

Eventually, Duke coined the word *Zio* to mean Zionists. The American Jewish Committee, among others, has stated that "antisemites often use 'Zionist' or 'Zio' as shorthand for 'Jew,' while many antisemites attempt to cloak their hate by claiming to be merely 'anti-Zionists.'" At Stanford and other university encampments in the spring and summer of 2024, *Zio* was used often to disparagingly refer to Jews, as protestors would spit the word out like a curse.

Zio was created as cover, the ADL's Lauren Post and others have noted, a cloak to disguise the true intentions of those who say it. In 2017, long before the atrocities of October 7, the former Grand Wizard of the Knights of the Ku Klux Klan deployed his *Zio* neologism hundreds of times in media interviews and speeches. On his website, *Zio* gets thousands of pages of results. For Duke, and for antisemites and Israel-haters now, *Zio* became a pithy way to refer to Jews without acknowledging they're talking about Jews. On social media, Duke's *Zio* appellation won't get one suspended as quickly as other words and images will. It provides plausible deniability, too. (In the spring of 2024, Meta—following the submissions of CyberWell and others—declared that *Zionist* was indeed antisemitic when used in certain contexts.)

"Since October 7," says Lauren Post, "we have been seeing an increase in the *Zio* shorthand, which David Duke popularized. That is very concerning."

Why does there exist such a willingness of so many— university occupiers, anti-Israel protestors, the authors of online antisemitic attacks—to embrace the messages, and images, previously favoured by long-dead Holocaust deniers, and neo-Nazis, and white supremacists? Perhaps, notes Post, one should look no further than David Duke himself, who took to showing up at anti-Israel rallies after October 7.

When asked by a reporter why he was there, the Klansman said it was "to save us from Jewish supremacism and Jewish genocide because we are being genocided.

"Just like the Palestinians."

THREE

JEWSCONTROLTHEWORLD.COM

There is a thread.

In the past, white supremacists and Holocaust deniers and neo-Nazis lost more battles than they won. They would run for political office and usually come last, or close to it. They would try to promote hate in a classroom and get fired. They would stand on street corners shouting about conspiracies and get laughed at, ignored, and sometimes arrested. In public opinion surveys, they, and their views, would register in fractions of puny percentage points.

In the mid-1990s—as the internet became available to everyone, not just scientists and the military—everything changed. Among the first to adapt to the new digital world were the white supremacists and Holocaust deniers and neo-Nazis and, notably, the Islamic extremists. With the tap of a key, they could send their epistles of hate to every corner of the globe, instantaneously, for free. They could do it anonymously, too, beyond the reach of police and prosecutors. Notwithstanding their comparatively small ranks, notwithstanding the limits of their bank accounts, notwithstanding the unpopularity of their message, they could—for the first time—be heard and seen by potentially billions of people. Meanwhile, traditional mass media started seeing their audiences shrink and their advertisers gravitate toward online platforms.

Around the same time, the haters embraced a strategy known to every experienced political strategist: they learned they didn't need to convert everyone to their side. Just enough to prevail in the new information war. And young people were their target.

It's surprising to many, but it is the truth: the neo-Nazis and al-Qaeda were on the internet long before Twitter or Facebook. They had websites, in the early days, that were more visually appealing than those of national governments. They had a message, a strategy. They, the losers, had finally been handed a formidable weapon with which to attack their shared enemy: the Jew.

Along with a revolutionary new technology, this anti-Israel, anti-West coalition had a simple and simplistic (and false) narrative—namely, that Israel is a colonialist, white supremacist apartheid state, like South Africa was, led by racists who are as bad as the Nazis. And since October 7, pollsters note, they have effectively deployed that message to capture the sympathies of millions. Like Donald Trump and others, the Islamic extremists have made effective use of the internet, spreading their propaganda and shockingly winning an army of youthful converts.

That is the thread that connects Hamas with all the haters and the antisemites who went before them: they'd discovered a new way to defeat the enemy.

They had discovered the power of the online campaign.

Muhammad Taha's X account was called RebelTaHa. His profile picture looked to be AI-generated, depicting a bearded, neatly barbered, unsmiling young man. Another avatar showed him smiling and without the beard.

In the early fall of 2023, he was posting in Arabic or English, often using images and memes. One cartoon showed a Ukrainian soldier advancing on a Russian tank, captioned "self-defence." The next one showed a Palestinian civilian throwing a rock at an Israeli tank, captioned "terrorism." Taha had only eighty-two followers at the time, but starting in the early hours of October 7, 2023, that post would be viewed 170,000 times. It began to trend—meaning it was getting much more visibility on social media than usual—and then it went viral.

RebelTaHa's profile was fake. He wasn't a real person.

Three things were notable about "Muhammad Taha." One, even though much of his content was anti-Israel and, like the "self-defence/terrorism" post, often antisemitic, he would some-times affix pro-Israel hashtags to his posts in order to attract a greater number of eyeballs. It was a sophisticated online strategy, analysts said, one that indicated a deeper understanding of how social media algorithms work.

Two, the volume and speed of Muhammad Taha's posts strongly suggested that he was more than one person. Over a two-day period in early October 2023, for instance, Taha posted new content 616 times. Allowing for sleep, that meant Taha was posting new content about twenty times every hour, or some-thing new every three minutes. By any objective standard, that's a significant amount of online activity.

Three—and this was perhaps the most interesting thing of all—Muhammad Taha's fake account came into being in March 2022. For much of the period between then and October 7, 2023, Taha wouldn't post much, if at all. He'd opine about cricket matches, or a mixed martial arts fight featuring influencer Logan Paul. But nothing controversial.

And then, suddenly, Muhammad Taha and thousands of other accounts sprang to life. A quarter of them, says Israeli bot-monitoring firm Cyabra, were a sham. The firm scanned social media in the days following Hamas's attack, tracking some 162,000 profiles that resembled Taha's. "Twenty-five per cent of the scanned profiles were fake," Cyabra concluded. The fake profiles generated 312,000 posts and comments in forty-eight hours—potentially reaching the eyes of more than 530 million accounts in just two days.

In those first forty-eight hours after October 7, a majority of the posts were in Arabic. But by October 10 or so, similar messages—most antisemitic, anti-Israel, and anti-West—started appearing in English. The fake profiles were disciplined and strategic. Initially, they pushed three main narratives. The first was that a huge number of Israelis had been captured by Hamas, and that a prisoner swap was imminent. Those posts were seen about 230 million times.

The second narrative was clearly designed to boost Hamas's reputation, given that stories were spreading in the international news media about horrific murders and rapes and atrocities. These fake profiles sang the praises of Hamas's humanity. One October 7 post—showing a photo of a terrified Shiri Bibas, clutching her redheaded sons Ariel and Kfir, taken hostage at Kibbutz Nir Oz—read: "Palestinian soldiers: no one harm the Jewish woman protect her. She has kids we are people of humanity we knows the value of human not like apartheid regime of Israel. Muslims are not terrorists we are peaceful, Quran teach us peace not terrorism." It was later learned that the three Bibas family members were strangled to death right around the time that post went up.

The "we are people of humanity" post was significant because it went up at 3:47 p.m., its image of Shiri Bibas and her two sons having been taken just hours after they were seized by terrorists. It swiftly acquired nearly three hundred thousand views. The poster—"Khansolidr"—had been on Twitter, like Muhammad Taha, for about two years, with only a few hundred followers. And also like the others, early on October 7 he began acquiring thousands upon thousands of new followers and views.

The third narrative concerned the Al-Aqsa Mosque, one of the holiest sites in Islam. Those counterfeit accounts falsely declared that Israeli soldiers had attacked Arabs praying there—including a twelve-year-old girl—thereby justifying Hamas's attack on the same day. The concocted Al-Aqsa posts reached nearly eight million pairs of eyes.

The sham accounts were quite alike. They displayed similar actions online, and they engaged with each other just as real people would do. After examining thousands of them, Cyabra concluded: "Typically, fake campaigns employ either similar online behavior or strategic connections between profiles. However, this campaign demonstrated a higher level of sophistication by utilizing both approaches simultaneously." Someone, somewhere, Cyabra noted, had apparently gone to considerable expense and effort to create authentic-sounding online narratives to benefit Hamas.

The signs of inauthenticity were there, however. The counterfeit accounts simultaneously shared identical content. Repeatedly, they used the same keywords and hashtags and even emojis, Cyabra reported. And they boosted their audience by connecting to each other and creating the illusion of "conversations." All of this was sophisticated, but it also made them easier to spot. Meanwhile, common Arabic names like Mohammed were used to promote anti-Israel, antisemitic content without attracting too much scrutiny. The fake users posted within a set timeframe in the afternoon, staggering their posts every few minutes, Cyabra said.

Thirty per cent of the fake profiles suddenly became active at 8 p.m. Israel time on October 7—around the time when some in Europe and North America were going online to learn more about Hamas's attack, which in many places in Israel was still raging. Seventy per cent of the material shared by the fake accounts on October 7 was new. That content would then go on to be shared hundreds of thousands of times.

They used brief, simple messages, not unlike political parties do in their campaigns: "Israel is a terrorist state," "Israel = terror," and so on. The fake posters pushed out dramatic graphics, too, many created by AI, Cyabra concluded. One showed Iran's "supreme leader" Ali Khamenei waving a protective arm over a parade of troops. Many of the graphics used colourful national flags to attract attention as well.

Other internet think tanks started to see what Cyabra had seen. CyberWell took a close look at hundreds of thousands of antisemitic (or very antisemitic) posts for the year prior to October 7 and then in the year that followed. Like Cyabra, CyberWell found a concentrated—and what they believed was a coordinated—flood of online antisemitism on October 7 and the days immediately following Hamas's atrocities. It reported: "Overall, in the 11 months prior to October 7, CyberWell's monitoring technology flagged 135,556 posts as highly likely to be antisemitic. In the 11 months following October 7 this number jumped to 185,229—an increase of 36.6 per cent. The most poignant spike being an 86 per cent increase in online antisemitism in the three weeks following October 7."

Said CyberWell's Tal-Or Cohen Montemayor: "The October 7 attacks were actually the most successful hijacking of social media platforms. Hamas flooded the mainstream social media platforms with antisemitic snuff [video] content, broadcasting it to millions of people."

In the months before October 7, CyberWell found, posts mostly promoted the age-old antisemitic notion that Jews wanted to control the world and were seeking global domination. After the attacks, the message changed: Jews were inherently evil and therefore the enemy—meaning they deserved what they got. Posts justifying the killing of Jews also ballooned after October 7, along with rampant Holocaust denial and distortion, CyberWell found. The main focus of the haters in late 2023 and early 2024 was twofold: there were no rapes of Jewish women and girls, and—if a massacre had happened—then Israel did it to itself, to provide a pretext for the resulting Palestinian "genocide." A smaller percentage asserted that "Israel profits from the October 7 massacre."

The same sort of thing was happening across other social media platforms. According to CyberWell, TikTok, X (formerly Twitter, owned by Elon Musk), YouTube (owned by Google), and Facebook and Instagram (owned by Mark Zuckerberg's Meta) permitted about half of the antisemitic content to remain online, even after the worst of it was formally brought to their attention. After October 7, some were surprised to see TikTok and X belatedly improve on their removal efforts. But on X, the Jew-hating content was still receiving millions of views. On Google's YouTube, too—the historic favourite of al-Qaeda, ISIS, and Hamas—nearly three million antisemitic videos were viewed following Hamas's attack.

Asked about their approach to online antisemitic hate, Google's YouTube spokesperson said: "Upon review of CyberWell's report, we removed videos that violated our community standards and terms of service. We don't allow content that promotes violence or hatred towards the Jewish community." TikTok acknowledged receiving questions about how it handles antisemitism, but did not subsequently provide any answers to this writer about these questions or any other matters discussed in this book. (CyberWell has credited TikTok with improving its moderation efforts.) Twitter/X and Meta likewise did not respond to repeated requests for comment on these matters or any other subjects discussed in this book.

Other firms started digging into the data about online hate. The U.K.-based Institute for Strategic Dialogue (ISD) examined YouTube for approximately the same time period. In just one week after October 7, ISD found, there were more than fifteen thousand instances of antisemitic content on the video platform—representing an unprecedented increase of 4,963 per cent from the days leading up to October 7. Part of the reason, ISD said, was an increase in the number of videos focusing on the Israel–Hamas conflict, but even then the proportion of antisemitic comments tripled after October 7. As the other watchdogs discovered, antisemitic YouTube content also promoted violence against Jews, the idea that Jews were the enemy, and significant amounts of October 7 denial—again, that the atrocities were committed by Israel itself, or that Jews profited from it. Cyabra, CyberWell, and ISD all reported that online antisemitism proliferated after October 7, in what looked like a highly coordinated way. And, when measured by views and engagement, the propaganda—anti-Israel, anti-West, antisemitic, and pro-Hamas—was at a level no one had ever seen before.

That it was coordinated seemed very likely, said Cyabra, CyberWell, ISD, and others. Then, in August 2024, the IDF uncovered proof in a raid in Gaza: secret Hamas documents showing the extent of their online propaganda effort. Hamas's web strategy, the documents revealed, was first to guide and direct "Hamas operatives" in the West Bank, in Arabic. They did that by "controlling the narrative being pushed out about issues in Gaza," the Hamas documents declared. Initially, they were also very focused on influencing and controlling "specific activities in the European arena," the documents read, where there is a higher concentration of migrants of Arab or Muslim descent.

To do this, Hamas describes targeting anti-Hamas activists by "neutralizing them" and "damaging their reputation." Their more moderate political rivals in Fatah, too, were targets: the documents describe reputational attacks online that were "aimed at damaging their public image[s]."

A year later, the IDF discovered yet more documents detailing Hamas's online communications strategy. The documents revealed that Hamas maintained a team of fifteen hundred propagandists in "command centres" across the Gaza Strip. The team was led by Abu Ubaida, the spokesperson for the murderous al-Qassam Brigades, the military wing of Hamas, starting in 2007—until he was eliminated by Israel in August 2025.

Abaida had built up Hamas's propaganda capacity over the past decade. Most of his team were field operatives: every Hamas battalion and brigade had a designated propaganda officer who, under Ubaida, "managed psychological operations efforts." Under those, Hamas propagandists were "operational documenters" who'd been trained in field photography. Using the latest GoPros and digital equipment, these operatives were expected to film guerrilla actions against the IDF and transmit it back to their command centres—in real time. It didn't matter if a unit was wiped out by the IDF—what mattered was the footage. Their motto: "The action is less important than its documentation."

To do all this, all that Hamas's propagandists needed were laptops and an internet connection. Footage they captured would be used in broadcast-quality videos put together by a team of trained Hamas editors. Other editors were assigned to listening to Israeli media in order to determine when and how to deploy the propaganda online.

Abu Obaida, the IDF found, was involved in every single major Hamas operation—including stage-managing the release of hostages for maximum effect. Said one anonymous IDF official about the trove of secret Hamas documents: "Hamas understands its strength lies in asymmetry against us, and how it tells its story. This is one of its most effective weapons, and why it invests so heavily in it. No Hamas operation happens without the propaganda network playing an integral part."

The Hamas online propaganda strategy was meticulous, Israeli intelligence sources said. One Hamas document described some of its tactics in detail: "Management of numerous communication campaigns—both counter-campaigns and offensive campaigns—aimed at sowing confusion and influencing opponents. . . . Targeting hostile activists who incite against the [Hamas] movement, particularly foreign activists, by neutralizing them, damaging their reputation, and exposing their schemes and handlers. This activity has led to the retreat of several activists

[and] the attacks against them have also resulted in some being labeled with derogatory titles that have remained."

The document described "increasing the activity of the electronic team belonging to the organization. This effort greatly contributes to promoting the movement's narrative, attacking opponents, reducing their communication tools, and countering [opponents] on social media.

"The [Hamas] social media messaging team has significantly contributed to combating and limiting the enemy's narrative by deleting hundreds of posts, accounts, and pages of the movement's opponents. The notable results include destroying publications and platforms of the occupation. It is known that on social networks, it is difficult to close occupation platforms or remove publications from them for several reasons. However, by analyzing these platforms and exposing their vulnerabilities, the messaging teams have succeeded in closing many platforms, including those harming the Brotherhood."

Hamas was effectively relying upon strategies pioneered by Western political parties: changing the channel and relentlessly attacking their enemies. When under attack, or when the target of protests, Hamas was diverting attention to other issues, sowing division, or going after the pro-Israel, pro-Western side with disinformation and misinformation. Their critics, the documents showed, would be linked to "the occupation" and would be swarmed by waves of fake online profiles like RebelTaHa.

In all, Hamas had a 160-member Gaza-based "electronic team," as they called it. The team could boast as many as 1.2 million immediate followers on social media, and they regularly posted in groups and forums with an additional 25 million followers. The strategy was to use "advanced technologies [which are] designed to flood social media in a very short time," Hamas declared. The effort would be assisted by limiting "rival" narratives using the techniques Hamas had outlined in the documents retrieved by the IDF.

Hamas's focus on social media and online platforms was a highly effective strategy, the Israeli intelligence sources say. Like Western governments and multinationals, Hamas and its allies still maintained a presence in mainstream media, but—like everyone else—they knew it was less efficient and less powerful than it had once been. Social media is fast, low-cost, and reaches much larger audiences, 24/7. Moreover, Hamas's allies in Russia, China, and Iran had built up a huge online infrastructure to act as an echo chamber for Hamas propaganda, the intelligence sources said. The fake accounts were a key part of the early online strategy of Hamas and the rest.

Oded Vanunu, the chief technology officer at CheckPoint Technologies, said in an interview at his state-of-the-art offices in Tel Aviv that the fake profiles had two main objectives: "distributing fake news, and vandalism online." Most of them were state sponsored, he said, by Iran and other Hamas allies.

"They are building a bot army," Vanunu said, noting that artificial intelligence was making that task easier with each passing day. "They are creating a human-like network. Around October 7, so many bots were unleashed. It was at a level I have never seen before in my life."

Cyabra's conclusion about the Hamas online campaign, which mirrored findings by Vanunu, CyberWell, and others, was that "the fake campaign was well-coordinated, with the fake accounts precisely knowing what to spread, which narratives to promote, and which hashtags to use. Additionally, they exhibited similar behavior, posting simultaneously during the same hours, with many accounts being created between July and October 2023." All of this suggested that the Hamas-backed online campaign had been put together long before October 7, they said—and that it had been created to deny, or justify, the terrible events of that day. It had been planned, not unlike the Hamas military campaign itself.

Concluded Cyabra: "The rapid execution of the fake Hamas campaign enabled the profiles to shape the narratives and significantly influence the ongoing discourse."

And they did all that on October 7, 2023. The very first day—and on every day since.

Online, Hamas didn't really hide what they were planning to do.

For those who'd been paying attention online, it shouldn't have been a surprise. For months, Hamas had been posting videos of its terrorist members openly preparing for a wide-scale attack on Israel. In the many meetings of their senior leadership, they called it "the big project."

One Hamas video, released in late 2022, showed battalions being trained to take hostages and to fly motorized paragliders into Israel. Another video, just a few months later, showed Hamas training to breach the border with Israel and destroying communications towers. Other videos showed training exercises in a full-scale mock Israeli settlement in Gaza, south of Khan Younis. It looked like the real thing, down to the signage and building design. In another video—part of what Hamas called the "Strong Pillar" training exercise—uniformed terrorists stormed a counterfeit Israeli military base; they'd even built a life-sized model of a tank, complete with Israeli flag. The video showed Hamas jogging through cinderblock buildings, capturing people portraying Israeli prisoners. It was filmed near the town of Beit Hanoun, only about a kilometre from the Israeli border.

There was additional evidence of what was to come, not all of it online. *The New York Times* would later report that Israel's military—months before October 7, 2023—even possessed detailed Hamas plans for an attack on Israeli civilians. The forty-page plan described rocket attacks, border vulnerabilities, and how to destroy surveillance cameras on the barriers between Israel and Gaza. It also identified the location of Israeli military forces and communications hubs. Later, it would be learned that Hamas knew who was responsible for security in individual communities, where they lived, and where arms were stored. They even knew who had a dog.

Hamas's "big project"—called Jericho Wall by the IDF—circulated within the Israeli military. It was eventually dismissed as far-fetched. "It is not yet possible to determine whether the plan has been fully accepted and how it will be manifested," one IDF analyst wrote.

Not long after that, a warning was sounded by a veteran analyst within Unit 8200, the IDF's fabled signal intelligence agency. She reported that Hamas was conducting intensive training exercises that were identical to what was described in the forty-page plan. The analyst's concerns were dismissed by a colonel, who said "the scenario is imaginary." The analyst pushed back: "It is a plan designed to start a war. It's not just a raid on a village."

She was ignored. No steps were taken to prevent an attack. No politicians were alledgedly briefed, either.

So, on October 7, 2023, at 6:29 a.m., air raid sirens started wailing in Jerusalem, warning citizens to take cover. It was a

Saturday, the Sabbath. It was also a religious holiday, Simchat Torah. Everyone in Israel will tell you they remember exactly where they were when the sirens began. It would go on to be the bloodiest attack on Israel in its history, and the biggest slaughter of Jews since the Holocaust.

Thousands of Hamas rockets were fired from Gaza—at Tel Aviv, at Jerusalem, and at smaller towns and cities. Simultaneously, Hamas terrorists and some Gazan citizens—on foot, on motorcycles, using trucks and farm and construction equipment—broke through fences bordering Israel in more than sixty places. Others entered Israel by sea and by paragliders, just as they had in the online training videos.

Israel Defense Forces confirmed that more than two thousand Hamas terrorists had crossed into southern Israel from Gaza, invading two dozen kibbutzim farms and even the town of Sderot, which has a population of thirty thousand. Once they accepted that an attack was underway, the IDF and the Israeli government frantically urged its people to hide—but many citizens could not. They didn't take shelter because they didn't hear any warnings, and they didn't know what was happening until it was too late: Hamas had used percision drone attacks to destroy communications hubs, just as they'd outlined in the forty-page Jericho Wall plan. Many Israelis in the kibbutzim didn't know Hamas was attacking until terrorists were physically in their towns and neighbourhoods, going door to door, slaughtering people.

Some Israelis learned about the attacks as they were underway, in real time, by looking at Hamas's online propaganda channels or the social media accounts of family, friends, and neighbours. Hamas was live-streaming its attacks on Telegram, their preferred social media app. Elsewhere, they broadcast their atrocities using the social media accounts of Israeli hostages, on Facebook, WhatsApp, and Instagram. They also used hostages' cellphones to call victims' families and friends and taunt them about what they were doing.

There was footage, hours of it. Most of it came from what Hamas recorded themselves, on GoPros and live-streamed, or was found on their phones after they were captured or killed by the IDF. The GoPro footage was high-definition and very clear. One could see, and hear, most of it.

Months after the attacks, the most senior Hamas official outside Gaza, Khalil al-Hayya, denied that. "Those videos were published by the Israel occupation," he said. "They weren't published by us." Around the world, October 7 denial was widespread.

In November, families of some of the October 7 victims gave their permission to the Israeli government and the IDF to show some of the Hamas videos to journalists and politicians in the West. The objective was to bear witness, they said, to what had been broadcast online by Hamas, or what had been captured by Israeli security or dash cameras. Journalists and politicians were not permitted to film or record any of it, but they probably couldn't forget any of it, either.

In the forty-three minutes of footage, Hamas terrorists—most of them in military gear, top to bottom, no T-shirts or jeans or the like—take selfies with the bodies of the people they've killed. Over and over they yell "Allahu Akbar!"—God Is Greater. There were many Gazan civilians, too, participating in the pogrom.

The videos showed the decapitated heads of babies and children, babies with bullet holes in them, and babies and children who'd been burned until all that one could see was the outline of their little bodies, arms reaching up.

One video shows a girl, perhaps six or seven, wearing Mickey Mouse pyjamas, her tiny frame covered in blood and dirt. An even younger girl, wearing a sundress with blue butterflies on it, has her hands arrayed across her chest like little broken pieces of china.

Another video shows the Hamas terrorists firing automatic weapons at cars carrying Israeli families. The windshields crack and shatter, there are sprays of blood and viscera, and the cars slow to a halt. The terrorists pull the Israelis out and shoot them in their heads, over and over and over. The Hamas terrorists—and, sometimes, Gazan citizens—cheer and dance beside the bodies. In some places, they leave behind ISIS flags.

At the yellow metal gate to Kibbutz Be'eri, a short distance from the site of the Nova Music Festival, a clip shows a resident drive up in his car and wait for the iron gate to open. The terrorists step out from some bushes and shoot the man, many times, and then jog into the kibbutz. Once inside, they can be seen creeping past rows of single-storey white homes. They don't speak, but can be heard breathing on their videos. Once or twice they say, "Where did they go?" They are looking for civilians to kill.

In another video segment, terrorists creep up to the rear of a home in a kibbutz, where a child's swing is seen. Music is playing, and a cellphone is glowing on a table. One terrorist reaches up and slices a window screen with a box-cutter, then shoots a woman who is huddled on the floor, trying to hide.

A lengthy video, likely taken from home security footage, shows a man running out of his house, carrying one son, the other son rushing ahead of them. They are in their underwear. They run into what the Israelis call a *mammad*, a fortified concrete bomb shelter. A few minutes later, one of the terrorists is seen throwing a hand grenade into the spot where the man had taken his boys, killing the man. The boys are shown going back into their house, bloodied, crying out for their father. The younger one says he can't see. He doesn't seem to have his eye anymore. "We're going to die," he says to his brother.

More footage, slightly less clear because the light is dim, shows two terrorists silently enter a kindergarten, passing by little knapsacks hanging neatly on the door. From another camera, a woman is seen hiding inside a room there, under some of the pillows the children use at nap time. There is no sound. She's alive— and then, moments later, she appears to be dead, or close to it. The terrorists carry her out, and she is not seen again. It was later learned that Hamas took corpses that day, also to be held hostage.

Another video shows a woman hiding under a desk in a kitchen. She is crying. The terrorists shoot her three times, and the crying stops. Some footage shot at night shows the bodies of women and girls, naked from the waist down. Smoke is rising from the genitals of one of them. Nails appear to be stuffed into the genitals of another.

In one lengthier video, a foreign worker—dozens were killed or kidnapped on October 7—is seen lying on the ground near a wall. He's bleeding from a gunshot wound to his chest. The man moves his arms a bit. One of the Gazans, not in any uniform, takes a hoe and starts hacking at the man's neck. He is trying to behead the man. "God is great!" the killer screams every time he brings down the blade on the man's neck.

A woman, dead, is seen holding a dead child in her arms. They are in a dimly lit room. Other dead children and adults can be seen as well. The terrorists stand, looking at the bodies. Periodically, they fire more bullets into the adults and children and cheer.

At a bus stop in Sderot, which isn't far from the border, a video shows a jumble of bodies of senior citizens. They had been on a sightseeing tour, and the terrorists killed them all. Their bodies are lying twisted on the ground like broken twigs, left among the canes and the walkers and the dirt.

Some of the footage simply plays audio, captured on intercepted phone calls to and from Hamas terrorists. One is calling his parents in Gaza. "Dad," he says in Arabic, "I'm talking from a Jewish woman's phone. I killed her and her husband. With my bare hands, Dad. Dad, I killed ten, ten with my bare hands." His mother comes on the line. "Mom, your son is a hero! Kill kill kill them!" Another exchange, also caught on tape, captures another man's voice: "Let history be my witness," he says. "That this was the first man I killed. The first one. A Jew. Give me a knife, I swear to you by God I will cut off his head."

In another audio recording, two terrorists can be heard talking about a dead Jew. "Bring him and crucify him," one says. One man laughs. "We've totally slaughtered them."

There are many more videos taken at the Nova Music Festival in Re'im, mostly captured by soldiers and first responders. There, nearly four hundred young people were killed in cold blood. In some earlier footage at Nova, one young man tries to hide at the rear of a car. A terrorist sees him, walks over, and shoots him in the head. There is a lot of footage like that.

At the end of the IDF footage—forty-three minutes of it, but it feels as if it's gone on for forty-three weeks—a first responder finds the bodies of the young people at the music festival. There are dozens of them, bloodied and splayed out in the dirt. "Is anyone alive?" he asks, and there is silence. "Give us a sign of life. Is anyone alive?" But no sound comes.

Some of the video footage came from the IDF. Some came from Israeli home security cameras, or dash cams. Most of the video footage, however, was shot by Hamas terrorists themselves, and later found on their bodies.

And it had been promoted by Hamas on the internet.

High-definition videos showing headless babies, sadistic murders, decapitations, torture, extreme violence: the Hamas footage, unlike the Nazis' clandestine record-keeping during the Holocaust, was designed to be seen and shared. But by whom?

At its height, al-Qaeda—Hamas's terroristic grandparent—developed a training manual that they blandly titled *Al-Qaeda Training Manual*. One of its dominant messages is that communications and violence aren't contradictory, they're complementary. As its authors wrote:

> *by pen and gun*
> *by word and bullet*
> *by tongue and teeth*

Al-Qaeda relied heavily on the written word for their propaganda; ISIS and Hamas also favour images and video clips. But most counter-terrorism analysts agree that al-Qaeda was really the first to make use of the nascent internet to propagandize.

The *Al-Qaeda Training Manual* describes their communications strategy, which would come to be known as a hybrid war. While pedantic among themselves, al-Qaeda's leadership generally had no interest in academic debates with their ultimate victims: "The confrontation we are calling for with the apostate regimes does not know Socratic debates, Platonic ideals, no Aristotelian diplomacy. It knows the dialogue of bullets, the ideals of assassination, bombing and destruction, and the diplomacy of the cannon and machine-gun."

Every act of communication requires an audience. The main audience for al-Qaeda, ISIS, and Hamas and their Islamist allies has always been their own supporters, sympathizers, and soldiers. Outsiders were mostly secondary, Israeli intelligence sources say. Even when bin Laden appeared online before the 2004 U.S. presidential election—standing behind a podium rather than holding an AK-47, as he often did, to proclaim: "People of America, this talk of mine is for you and concerns the ideal way to prevent another Manhattan [9/11]"—even then, his main audience wasn't the West. It was his own people. He went on in the videotaped address to rationalize the atrocities of 9/11, and to crow that the murders of three thousand innocent people had "by all standards, exceeded all expectations."

His first objective with that video, and all his online communications—until he was eliminated by order of Barack Obama—was to buttress support within his own movement, intelligence operatives note. The sympathies of Westerners were not the prime concern of Osama bin Laden and his ilk. Their priority, always, was to awaken the *ummah*, the Islamic Nation, which they believed had fallen asleep. If al-Qaeda, ISIS, and Hamas needed to rely on the technologies of the West to awaken slumbering Muslims, so be it.

Their message was designed to distinguish their group from the outside world. Not to join it.

———

Avi Melamed nods. Melamed is a gruff former Israeli intelligence officer who resides in Jerusalem. He's thought to understand contradictions in Islamic propaganda better than most, and he's willing to speak on the record.

When asked why Hamas—and al-Qaeda, and ISIS before it—continue showing their followers committing atrocities in videos they post online instead of trying to cultivate a better image in the West and acquiring Western converts, Melamed says: "First, we have to understand something.

"In the Gaza Strip, like in other places in the Arab Muslim world, you've got a mindset that has been evolving for many years, one that is very alien to Western minds. I'm talking from an intelligence perspective when I say: the way they evaluate moral standards is quite different from us. I'll give you a disturbing example, something that is very relevant to [the video evidence] we've seen of October 7. Sexual assault. Sexual assault in Muslim society, in the Muslim world, and in the Muslim culture, is something that can result in very severe ramifications. If you are in the Gaza Strip and even harass a woman, in fact, you may find yourself in a life-threatening situation. It is totally unacceptable to them. But assaulting non-Muslims? That is something acceptable to them. Different cultures [have] different perspectives."

So, pro-Palestinian posters and leaflets proclaiming RAPE IS RESISTANCE littered Manhattan streets in April 2024. And online, hashtags and memes approvingly containing that shocking statement circulated for months before that. The United Nations—no historical ally of Israel—concluded in March 2024 that rapes and gang rapes had indeed occurred in multiple locations in Israel on October 7, perpetrated on Israeli women and girls by members of Hamas. In their twenty-four-page report, the UN investigators wrote: "Credible circumstantial information, which may be indicative of some forms of sexual violence, including genital mutilation, sexualized torture, or cruel, inhuman and degrading treatment, was gathered."

Hamas and their supporters in the Middle East have a binary communications strategy, Melamed says. They have one hardcore message, almost always in Arabic, for radicalization purposes, and to rile up their base. And, he says, they have a comparatively kinder, gentler message, too—usually in English or other Western languages—for propaganda purposes, and to burnish their image outside the region. The objective, often, is to bring in potential supporters in the West with the more benign message, adds Melamed. And then, using shrewd propaganda, to radicalize potential supporters, or make them more willing to shrug about terror—as they do, horrifically, with "Rape Is Resistance."

Hamas and its supporters simply don't see things as Westerners do, says Melamed. They don't express themselves in the same way that Westerners do. They would celebrate the atrocities of October 7, yes. But they also knew the effect the Hamas footage could have on Western audiences: they knew the horrific images could alienate potential supporters, donors, and recruits beyond their borders. They particularly knew that the accounts of extreme sexual violence and beheaded babies would spread, rapidly.

So, they had a communications strategy for that, too: denial.

It was an old strategy using a new platform. Decades before, in the wake of the Allies' victory in the Second World War, neo-Nazis had a dilemma. Six million innocent Jews had been slaughtered by Hitler's regime in one of the biggest recorded acts of genocide in human history. So, if they were to be successful in rehabilitating the reputation of National Socialism, the new Nazis needed to minimize or deny the Holocaust.

The Holocaust deniers and doubters created their own think tanks. They held conferences. They wrote papers that sounded academic. They issued news releases and convened press conferences. They raised money. And, when the internet arrived in the mid-1990s, the aspiring Nazis immediately saw its value. Britain's David Irving, Canada's Ernst Zundel, France's Robert Faurisson, American Ku Klux Klansmen Don Black and David Duke—all were among the nascent internet's earliest adopters. Their main message was denial. The Holocaust, they said, was a "holohoax," a lie perpetrated by a worldwide Jewish conspiracy. And Israel wasn't a country but rather another concoction of that conspiracy.

Zundel, who was prosecuted and then deported from Canada for his views, told the Supreme Court that "the Holocaust is a myth fabricated by an immensely powerful Jewish-Zionist conspiracy to win lucrative war reparations from the Germans, to make them feel ashamed and a pariah in the eyes of other nations, and to win political and economic support for the State of Israel." On his own website he was even more direct: "Over the years, the numbers of [Jews killed in the Holocaust] have changed drastically. Hardly anyone can keep the lie straight any more. . . . Pick your favorite number—facts don't matter, truth does not matter, death certificates don't matter to the Holocaust-promoters and liars!"

Denying acts of violence against Jews is as old as Judaism itself. For centuries before the birth of Christ, serial horrors have been endured by Jews. Those atrocities, in turn, have been denied by those committing them, minimized, or dismissed even by those watching it all unfold. In the past, antisemitic denialism took the form of grubby leaflets passed out at secret night rallies or in the ravings of the likes of Zundel, speaking to their puny flocks, illuminated by nighttime cross burnings. Now, however, the new deniers merely need to tap a keyboard and their hateful dispatches will be seen instantaneously, globally, by millions. That was the strategy Hamas embraced, too.

October 7 was another Shoah, another catastrophe for the Jewish people. It had been well documented by Hamas itself: in many ways better documented, Lesley Klaff and Yossi Klein Halevi say, than the Holocaust had been. As a result, the anti-Israel alliance would embrace an audacious strategy. They would deny the very crimes they themselves had documented—but would turbocharge their denial by adding algorithms and hashtags and bot farms.

Because of that, Hamas were much more effective than Zundel had been—and, notably, their denials of October 7, 2023, were circulating before any of its victims were even in the ground. Denial, agrees CyberWell's Tal-Or Cohen Montemayor, was the principal objective from the start.

October 7 and the days that followed, she says, were the beginning of a massive and coordinated online propaganda campaign. The messages: deny October 7, or—where that wasn't feasible—justify it.

It's impossible to develop and deploy such a coordinated global online propaganda campaign in a single day, Cohen Montemayor points out. But the Hamas propagandists had been quietly laying the groundwork online for years, and knew that some demographics in the West would be receptive to their messages, she says. Hamas's propagandists had other assets, too: access to millions to finance the campaign and bot farms in Egypt, Britain, and America to push out their propaganda. Their biggest asset, she says, was that they knew October 7 was going to happen before it did, and they were ready to swiftly reach millions of people in multiple languages.

"We found evidence of October 7 denials—and support and celebration of it—as early as October 8, 10, and 11," says Cohen Montemayor. "And we have evidence of accounts on X's platform with only three thousand followers tweeting out October 7 denial and misinformation—and then getting three million views. That's highly, highly suspicious." For the first few days after October 7, Hamas's main online strategy was to deny the sexual violence committed against Israeli women and girls as well as the utter brutality of it all—the burnings, the beheadings, the torture, the cold-blooded murders.

"With October 7 denial, unlike Holocaust denial—which was kind of limited to these fringe groups—we were seeing antisemitism in the mainstream, but it was amplified by algorithms so it would be viewed by millions and millions of people."

CyberWell produced a voluminous report on October 7 denial, released in January 2024. It found that Hamas, Hezbollah, Iran, and their cohorts in Russia and China had been disseminating a barrage of antisemitic propaganda around the globe: "There were no acts of rape; the State of Israel orchestrated the violent events; and Israel and the Jews are profiting from the massacre." All of it was a violation of the social media platforms' own policies. CyberWell looked at just 313 specific examples of online Jew-hatred on Facebook, Instagram, TikTok, X, and YouTube. What they found "had a far-reaching impact, collectively garnering over 25 million views, [but] after being reported to the platforms, only six per cent was removed." The worst early offender was X. Even after CyberWell brought examples of antisemitic tweets/posts to the attention of the platform owned by far-right billionaire Elon Musk, only two per cent of it was removed. Said CyberWell in the weeks after October 7: "X is the leading platform hosting October 7 denial content."

CyberWell was not alone in identifying X/Twitter as a major platform for online Jew-hatred. The experts at the Combat Antisemitism Movement and the Network Contagion Research Institute (NCRI) reported a dramatic rise in extremist, anti-semitic users rejoining Twitter after Elon Musk assumed control of the company, and an immediate 136 per cent rise in anti-semitic threats and attacks on the platform. To some, it was pre-dictable: Musk is a right-wing free speech absolutist who makes fascist salutes and unfunny jokes about the Holocaust. Neo-Nazis, white supremacists, and Islamic extremists followed Musk's lead, flooding his platform with hateful messages. Said NCRI: "They [registered] with the expectation that Musk would provide a more hospitable platform for their brand of extremist content, joining Twitter at a rapid rate."

The antisemitic surge that followed Musk's acquisition of the platform marked a dramatic increase from the pre-Musk era. Neo-Nazis, white supremacists, and Israel-hating jihadists like Hamas had a shared enemy. Says Joel Finkelstein, NCRI's chief science officer and director, "There is almost a horseshoe effect mobilizing against the Jewish people, with white supremacists, Black Hebrew Israelites, Islamists and others working together on the only cause that unites them—a hatred of Jews."

After Musk acquired Twitter, it became "a safe space for hate," he said, but also a pathogen for its spread. It swiftly became an online platform where it was acceptable, some critics said, to sow seeds of hate. Initially, the lie promoted most often on Twitter/X by Hamas and its adherents was "There was no rape."

As on the placard at the gates to McGill University, "Israel did it" was also promoted, along with the claims that Israel "profits from the October 7 massacre"—again, an identical strategy to the one pioneered by Holocaust deniers many decades before: outright denial of the murders and rapes or, if forced to accept that some crimes happened, shifting the blame for them to Israel.

For about half of it, the October 7 denial took place on X. A quarter of it was on Facebook. TikTok was next, with around 20 per cent of the denial. YouTube and Instagram made up the remainder. As CyberWell put it in their report: "The central role that social media played during the Hamas massacre of Israeli citizens is historic and unique. First, Hamas terrorists harnessed social media as a vehicle of psychological torture, live-streaming their brutal attack. Second, Hamas terrorists and their sympathizers exploited social media as a mass misinformation and disinformation machine, amplifying claims that deny the reality of the atrocities [or] asserting that the victims, survivors and first responders are lying or exaggerating their experiences."

One English-language tweet from a verified X account, @HadiNasrallah, read: "The US and Israel are lying about Gaza. No babies were beheaded and no women were raped. They want to justify the genocide happening now in Gaza." That post was put up five days after October 7. It was viewed almost three million times. Another post took the form of a meme—a favoured approach of Western neo-Nazis and white supremacists, given that memes are harder for automated moderation software to detect. It depicted two women facing each other, talking. One says, "Killing babies and rape is not resistance!" The other woman, wearing a keffiyeh, says, "Those things did not happen. That is proven disinformation and you're racist and Islamophobic for believing it. Mainstream media has now retracted any reports of those things happening because there was no evidence." That post, offered up less than a month after October 7, was "liked" tens of thousands of times.

American political commentator Jackson Hinkle, who has three million followers on X and a history of posting anti-Zionist rhetoric—and has been kicked off YouTube, Twitch, and Instagram for what YouTube stated were "repeated violations" of their policy that prohibits denying events like October 7—jumped into the orgy of denial. Hinkle posted that "ISRAEL ADMITS they fired on their OWN CIVILIANS with APACHE ATTACK HELICOPTERS!" His post was swiftly recirculated by hundreds of Arab-speaking accounts. Two of his posts that denied the killing of babies acquired 3.5 million views. Another post Hinkle favoured came from a Hezbollah-affiliated account.

The denial was seen across platforms. A TikTok video showing a young woman included this statement: "First of all, we find out there were no beheaded babies . . . there were none. No dead babies, okay? . . . There are no rapes. No one was raped." Other posts would reluctantly accept that atrocities had taken place but claim that Hamas wasn't responsible. One video proclaimed that "it's the Zionist soldiers and settlers who unalived [sic] Israelis and raped them." Some even sought to revisit the truth of the Holocaust, declaring in Arabic above the now-infamous 1941 photograph of Adolf Hitler meeting with the Grand Mufti of Jerusalem, Haj Amin al-Husseini: "Hitler was on the right path . . . if the Jews were honest, they would not have tried to distort the Palestinian resistance in the Al-Aqsa Flood operation. They lied that the resistance slaughtered children and raped women. Likewise, what they told us about Hitler [was] a lie and slander."

One of the first social media posts that denied Hamas did anything wrong, and which blamed Israelis, came just hours after the massacre on October 7. A user ostensibly in Lebanon had only six thousand followers—but his denial posts rapidly acquired nearly 400,000 views. The online "newspaper" *Electronic Intifada* played an early and important role in October 7 denial, its posts seen by some five hundred thousand followers on X. In that case, one correspondent posted that Hamas couldn't have committed the atrocities at the Nova Music Festival because it didn't have the organizational capacity to murder on that scale. Hours later, however, he changed course and posted that there was "no evidence" of any atrocities. Those posts also garnered tens of thousands of views.

The deniers received a helping hand early on from Qatar's Al Jazeera, which picked up on the false posts about infanticide. Its reporting was then amplified around the planet by bot farms and fake accounts in Iran, China, Russia, and throughout the West, Cyabra and others noted. Al Jazeera's popular website, AJ+, played a unique role in the dissemination of fake profiles, disinformation, and antisemitic propaganda, some charged. A comprehensive December 2024 report by the Combat Antisemitism Movement (CAM) described the Al Jazeera social media outlet as a key tool driving online "anti-Western . . . anti-Israel" content. Cyabra assisted CAM by probing thousands of accounts interacting with AJ+ content in late 2024. It found that a third were fake, with "a strong emphasis on anti-Israel propaganda." Wrote CAM: "Fake profiles were instrumental in redirecting traffic from X to AJ+'s TikTok account, often sharing identical messages and links to orchestrate cross-platform engagement. This deliberate manipulation focused on promoting specific AJ+

TikTok videos tied to highly contentious anti-U.S. and anti-Israel narratives, amplifying their visibility and shaping key public discussions." (Al Jazeera had not responded to requests for comment at the time of writing.)

The fake accounts would boost false claims of Israeli atrocities, Cyabra said, such as that almost "every school [was] bombed or destroyed," or that people were "martyred in the bombing of the Baptist Hospital." Israelis are "born with an infinite hatred, a hatred unlike any other," the fake accounts posted.

On Al Jazeera's main news site, allegations of babies being beheaded—a fact the extremists wanted denied then and now—was "baseless," it claimed. Those reports were then fed back into the social media machine and relied upon as yet more October 7 denial. Frequently, these well-known Arab-speaking social media accounts would also claim their information came from "confidential sources," thereby avoiding the need to provide proof. Meanwhile, writes CyberWell, "While journalists and reporters led denial discourse on X, TV stars and celebrities led denial discourse on TikTok and Instagram." It was an online denial loop: Al Jazeera was amplified by the likes of the extremist Hinkle, who was boosted by lesser-known Arab-speaking social media voices—who would then feed back yet more disinformation. And that denial loop, CyberWell and other internet watchdogs observed, was continually growing ever larger and ever more effective.

All of this—denying the violence, mocking the victims of violence—is prohibited by the rules of every major online platform, from Meta to TikTok to X to YouTube. In some cases, and in some countries like Canada and Germany, it's even against the law. But the platforms weren't doing nearly enough to stop it in the months after October 7. Says Cohen Montemayor: "These guys already have rules on the books. And I know they are more capable of removing antisemitic content online than they are presently doing."

So, the new denials of October 7 spread like wildfire—aided and abetted by a new technology, and age-old antisemitism.

Like political parties in the West, like multinational companies, Hamas's objective has been to control the narrative.

Some of their videos are slick and professional-looking, and present a moderate and accessible public image. One video posted on a Hamas Telegram channel, for example, shows terrorists in camouflage and carrying automatic weapons, carefully guiding a crying infant in a stroller past an Israeli home that has been destroyed. "Hamas fighters showing compassion for children," proclaimed the video, which had been viewed online hundreds of thousands of times.

Another Hamas propaganda video, shot at Kibbutz Holit on October 7, shows a terrorist patting the back of a wailing baby—and on the same shoulder where he's carrying a Kalashnikov. In another video, a terrorist makes a show of bandaging the foot of an Israeli toddler, then holds the boy on his lap. In yet another, a terrorist off-camera instructs a Jewish boy on how to say *bismillah* in Arabic—"in the name of God"—and the frightened boy does so in a Hebrew accent. And in yet another, a terrorist holds up two Israeli children and says, "Look at the mercy in our hearts. These kids—we didn't kill them like you do." (Nineteen Israeli children were murdered by Hamas and Gazans on October 7.)

Experts agreed that the videos were ham-fisted attempts to attract support, sympathy, and new recruits in the West. Many people outside the Middle East, of course, were repelled by them. But Hamas mainly produces such videos for extremists in the Arab and Muslim world, analysts say. And, however amateurish they may be, the videos generally work with their target audience. The *bismillah* video, for example, was seen 1.4 million times, and 75,000 "liked" it. Many left behind glowing comments, such as the one praising "the morals of the fighters of the Islamic resistance."

There are those videos produced by Hamas, however, that are clearly intended to terrify people in the West. So, on its Telegram channel on October 7, standing beside charred homes inside Israel, one Hamas terrorist aims his camera at the body of a dead Israeli, blood running down a sidewalk, and says in Arabic, "Time for photographs." A Hamas terrorist standing nearby fires rounds in the air as if in celebration of the slaughter. A video released immediately after October 7 shows Israeli hostages, covered in blood, with this caption in Hebrew: "This is what awaits you when you enter Gaza." Another one promises to live-stream executions of Israeli hostages.

Their binary approach to propaganda is foreign to the West. But it's an online strategy aimed at two very different audiences, Avi Melamed says: Muslims and non-Muslims. It has been highly effective, too, with young people in the Middle East and in the West, he adds, who have grown up playing single-player shooter games and have seen plenty of bloody violence online. "There is a logic to what they are doing, unfortunately. Hamas and the others were accurately reading the evolving mindset in the West, where some were romanticizing slogans like 'Resistance.' Hamas was seeing how some of those concepts were being romanticized in the West."

There was an additional benefit to this quixotic online revolution. For al-Qaeda, ISIS, and Hamas, Melamed says, online platforms have always provided valuable insights into Western thinking—particularly the thinking of Gen Z and Millennials—and how to manipulate them. Peering at their devices, often oblivious to history and fact, what these young people see being generated online by Hamas and its allies gives them "a very distorted perspective," according to Melamed. The consequences have been disastrous for Israel and the West, he says, and—over time—have greatly benefited the three major Islamic terrorist organizations.

Al-Qaeda was founded in 1988, the same year in which the National Science Foundation Network (NSFNET) was created. NSFNET was the earliest internet, created by linking five supercomputers in the United States. Al-Qaeda, for its part, was the creation of four veterans of the Soviet–Afghan war, Osama bin Laden and Ayman al-Zawahiri among them. At the outset, al-Qaeda and the internet were both loosely structured, bearing little relation to what they would become. Both were essentially a decentralized network of networks, really, with no formal organization, no hierarchy, and no single location. A military analyst at West Point would later marvel at that, writing that al-Qaeda was "strikingly similar to the Internet with its unstructured network [and] reliance on a decentralized web of nodes."

From the start, al-Qaeda recognized the boundless opportunities the fledgling internet presented for recruitment, propaganda, and the spread of terror. At its peak, al-Qaeda would operate nearly six thousand internet platforms, and by the mid-2000s was adding about nine hundred new ones every year, taking the form of websites, chatrooms, blogs—and, later, social media accounts. Al-Qaeda was one of the earliest converts to the internet, and was in fact active online years before most social media platforms even existed.

Its first web presence was launched in February 2000, the same year in which internet use exploded globally with the spread of broadband access. The site was hosted in Pakistan and, notably, in China. Initially, al-Qaeda used it to share lengthy (and, to many, boring) theological treatises by bin Laden and al-Zawahiri, but it wasn't a stable platform and crashed too often. A new site, called "The Call," replaced it a year later, in 2001. Other al-Qaeda web properties then started to proliferate.

In June 2001, al-Qaeda debuted visual content that would become the model for what Islamist terrorist groups did online thereafter: a slick two-hour video called *Destroying the American Destroyer Cole*, recounting al-Qaeda's attack on the U.S. Navy vessel the year before. The video related how a small boat pulled up alongside the *Cole* during a scheduled fuel stop in Yemen. The two men aboard, both al-Qaeda operatives, made friendly waves at the American ship, and then they detonated a massive amount of explosives. In the resulting explosion, seventeen U.S. sailors were killed and the *Cole* was left with a forty-by-sixty-foot hole midship.

Al-Qaeda's in-house digital production team put the video together. In the years to come, the terrorist group would use *Destroying the American Destroyer Cole* for recruitment and to terrorize. Following their lead, ISIS and then Hamas would also produce slick video content to spread their message, to spread fear—and to radicalize.

At the start of the millennium al-Qaeda dominated the internet, much more than any other Islamic terrorist group. ISIS, however, would ultimately become more effective—because ISIS was virtually an internet entity in and of itself. It revolutionized the way in which terrorists used online platforms to radicalize and recruit, moving online terrorism far beyond what al-Qaeda had done. In so doing, it essentially changed the formula for terror. Al-Qaeda was preoccupied with expunging non-believers and infidels, but ISIS had a different approach: converts to their cause were welcome, wherever they resided. And their cause—just as with the white supremacists and neo-Nazis who seek a whites-only ethnostate—was to use force to set up their own Islamic country. A caliphate, an Islamic state, just like the Umayyad and Ottoman Caliphates of the past.

To achieve that, ISIS was prepared to spill more blood online than al-Qaeda had done. And unlike al-Qaeda, ISIS didn't need a ruling from a cleric like Osama bin Laden to carry out an attack. It simply encouraged its supporters to go and kill someone, anyone, at any time. "Smash [your enemy's] head with a rock, or slaughter him with a knife, or run him over with your car," ISIS spokesman Abu Mohammad al-Adnani declared in October 2014. So, for example, Canadian ISIS supporter Martin Couture-Rouleau did precisely that, running down two Canadian Forces soldiers in Saint-Jean-sur-Richelieu in Quebec. He killed one, Warrant Officer Patrice Vincent. After a high-speed chase, Couture-Rouleau was shot to death by police. Just two days later, another online ISIS convert, Michael Zehaf-Bibeau, shot Corporal Nathan Cirillo in the back at the National War Memorial in Ottawa, killing him. Minutes later, Zehaf-Bibeau was killed in a shootout with security on Parliament Hill. Both terrorist attacks happened in the same month that al-Adnani had issued his directive online.

From its captured territories in Syria, Iraq, and Libya, ISIS directed, or was linked to, fatal terror attacks in Paris, London, Berlin, Brussels, Manchester, Amsterdam, and many other places around the world. Between 1999 and 2016, it's estimated that the group killed thirty-three thousand civilians. In their territories, too, they enslaved enemies and forced marriages with captured women and girls. They kidnapped thousands, they recruited child soldiers, they killed journalists, they engaged in mass rape, they robbed and extorted, and they destroyed historical sites. Most notoriously, they tortured and massacred thousands of dissidents—with beheadings, burnings, beatings, and even crucifixions. In the West, starting in and around 2014, they attracted the attention of millions with their online decapitations.

ISIS beheaded captured Syrian soldiers. They beheaded American freelance journalist James Foley, Lebanese and Kurdish soldiers, and Afghan police officers. They beheaded Steven Sotloff, an American journalist with *Time* magazine; British aid workers David Haines and Alan Denning; and American medical aid worker Peter Kassig. They beheaded, among others, a French mountaineering guide, deserters, two Japanese businessmen, Christian Coptic Egyptian construction workers, and a Croatian topographer. They carried out so many beheadings, in fact, that the subject has its own lengthy Wikipedia page: "Islamic State Beheadings."

We know how these people were killed because ISIS often murdered them in front of their high-definition cameras, just as Hamas would do on October 7. In many of the ISIS snuff films—like the ones featuring Foley, Sotloff, and Henning—there is some reference to a recent news event to establish its date. The location is somewhere in the desert. The victims, kneeling and sometimes wearing orange Guantanamo-style coveralls, read a statement given to them by ISIS. Masked ISIS terrorists are usually standing behind the men. One of the terrorists typically makes some statement, too, railing against Israel and America and the West. Then the terrorists grab the victim and hold him down while another terrorist beheads him using a long-bladed knife. All on camera.

The beheading videos were aimed at two different audiences with two very different messages. As terrorism expert Rita Katz put it in her book *Saints and Soldiers*, "the execution was more than simply punishment of an enemy; it was theatre. It was a message of intimidation to the public . . . and an invitation to jihadists around the globe: Don't wait to act." Most of all, Katz says, ISIS was saying to its radicalized recruits, "it doesn't matter how many people you killed in an attack, or whether you won a battle; what mattered was how you leveraged it via propaganda."

To leverage its propaganda, around the time of its beginnings in 1999, ISIS (then called the Islamic State of Iraq and the Levant, later called simply IS or ISIS, or its Arabic name, Daesh) was a dedicated Twitter user. Twitter was faster than the other platforms, it was global, it was free—and, importantly, it was also terrible at moderation. At the worst of it, Twitter was littered with at least seventy thousand ISIS accounts in multiple languages. There were ISIS bots, sock puppets, and operatives. There were recruitment accounts, fundraising accounts, media accounts, and accounts on how to travel to the ISIS caliphate— and, of course, easy-to-understand accounts about how to make bombs or carry out attacks with whatever was available: guns, knives, motor vehicles.

Eventually as many as fifty different ISIS online media hubs in different countries were aimed at different audiences. ISIS would ultimately become "the first terrorist group to hold both physical and digital territory," said Jared Cohen, director of the Google Ideas think tank. By the mid-2010s ISIS had become the unrivalled leader in online propaganda jihad. Their internet-based messages were "projectiles," ISIS crowed; the objective online, always, was to "shatter the morale of the enemy." With Twitter and other online platforms, ISIS had managed to make terrorism sexy, as Rita Katz and others noted.

When its executives finally became aware of the extent of their ISIS problem, Twitter didn't know how to deal with it. Hundreds of ISIS accounts were removed by the social media platform, only to quickly spring up again, like weeds. When their main Twitter account—@IslamicState—was resuscitated after being unsuccessfully banned for the hundredth time, ISIS taunted Twitter with an image of a birthday cake. Eventually, however, Twitter succeeded in eliminating many, but by no means all, of the ISIS accounts.

That would turn out to be the least of ISIS's problems. By 2014, a global military coalition was moving against it—cutting off its funding, cutting off its supply of new recruits, and killing ISIS fighters by the thousands with as many as 170,000 bombing sorties. The anti-ISIS coalition was led by the United States and made up of a number of countries, among them Canada, the United Kingdom, France, Jordan, Australia, Saudi Arabia, Turkey, and the United Arab Emirates. The final outpost in ISIS's caliphate, Baghouz Fawqani in Syria, fell in March 2019. That effectively meant the end of ISIS as a physical force. Online, however, they continue to exist, and maintain thousands of online accounts to this day. They also continue to recruit Muslim teenagers from Central Asia for the affiliate ISIS-K (meaning Khorasan province in Iran). One of their most active voices online uses the pseudo-nym Sulaiman Dawood al-Kanadie and emanates from the West—more specifically from somewhere between Montreal and Toronto. His presence has been seen on Facebook, Twitter, and Telegram. In September 2025, Global News reporter Stewart Bell revealed, the ISIS propagandist was arrested and ordered into an Edmonton de-radicalization program.

For al-Qaeda, ISIS, and Hamas, their chosen platforms move around. When one platform becomes too restrictive or too effective at stamping out extremism, they simply jump to another. What remains constant, however, is the twofold objective of whatever they put online: first, to terrorize.

And, second, to recruit and radicalize.

Don't ever believe that the majority in the Muslim world are enthusiastic about their young men getting radicalized, former Israeli intelligence officer Avi Melamed says. They are shocked and alarmed by it. "There are many voices in the Arab and Muslim world who are very critical of this increasing Islamic radicalization," he notes. And the vast majority of Muslims oppose terror, he adds.

"In the West, some will say radicalization is just a counter-reaction to Islamophobia. That's totally, totally missing the big picture. There is a very vibrant discussion happening in the Muslim world that condemns radicalization. Many, many voices in the Arab and Muslim world condemn it. And some of them accept that they bear some responsibility for it. They will say, 'We have to find ways to stop this, because in some circles in the West there are those who are receptive to radicalization, whatever the reasons.' Many times, of course, it has to do with an individual's psychology or personality. But there are other reasons for it—like romanticizing that distorted picture [of the Middle East] on social media."

A few Islamist terrorists may have been fated at birth to become mass murderers, but certainly not all. Online radicalization, the likes of Melamed say, is how al-Qaeda, ISIS, and Hamas—and others, from jihadi to neo-Nazi—have transformed the terrorism landscape in the new millennium. All are movements that now flourish because of, and on, the internet. And they're not just the terrorists of old: similar to what ISIS became, they mostly exist as internet platforms, Melamed and others note. And the online world permits them to radicalize recruits more effectively than ever before.

Intelligence and counter-terrorism police agencies agree with that. The head of the European police agency, Europol, states that "the online environment plays a key role . . . it facilitates self-radicalization and the spread of terrorist propaganda." The European Commission's Counter-Terrorism Agenda adds that "the spread of radical ideologies and terrorist material accelerates through the use of online propaganda, with the use of social media becoming an integral part of the attack itself." And the National Security Branch of the Federal Bureau of Investigation says, "No matter the format, the message of radicalization spreads faster than we imagined just a few years ago. Like never before, social media allows for overseas terrorists to reach into our local communities to target our citizens as well as to radicalize and recruit."

Terror radicalization works in much the same way that cults groom converts. The language cults and terrorists use actually defines who they are, cult deprogrammers note. This is particularly true when they use repetition—"linguistic rituals" like chants, prayers, turns of phrase—that can draw people further away from reality. For cultists, extremists, and terrorists who are already predisposed to believe something, specialized and repetitive language reshapes the inside and outside world. And it gives them the licence to embrace an ideology they were already sympathetic to.

Which is the case with the aspiring jihadists being radicalized online: most of the time they're eager to find radicalizing content, and they quickly find a lot of it on the internet. The statistics tell part of the story. In the United States alone, the National Consortium for the Study of Terrorism and Responses to Terrorism (START) has published data showing that social media played an outsized role in radicalizing and mobilizing 90 per cent of terrorist lone actors, a significant jump from the mid-2000s. Fortunately, START says, online radicalization doesn't always lead to successful terrorist attacks: those who are radicalized on social media and take steps to act on their hate tend to be less successful than those who also receive face-to-face terrorist training, simply because open social media platforms make it much easier for police to catch them (and much harder to train them). That said, the trend line remains worrying, according to START, because a radicalization process that used to take as many as eighteen months is now down to about a year, and is rapidly getting much more efficient. As START found, "Social media usage in extremist movements accelerates consensus on radical viewpoints and increases commitment."

START continues: "In the last several years, social media has become a nearly ubiquitous method for consuming and sharing extremist content and communicating with extremists from around the world." Three-quarters of them use social media to "consume content, participate in extremist dialogues, spread extremist propaganda, or communicate with other extremists. Islamist extremists displayed the highest rates of social media usage. They were, by large margin, the group most likely to engage with social media as a primary means of consuming extremist content or communicating with other extremists." Half of them were radicalized by social media more than any other factor. Nearly 90 per cent of "lone wolf" terrorists were propelled into violent action by online propaganda, START found.

The 2025 New Year's Day terrorist attack in New Orleans, for example, was carried out by such a "lone wolf." In the early hours of January 1, Shamsud-Din Jabbar mowed down fourteen revellers, killing all. Jabbar was transformed by online content, his brother Abdur Jabbar later said: "[What he did] does not represent Islam. This is radicalization, not religion." His majority-Muslim neighbours angrily denounced his attack. Shamsud-Din Jabbar had largely confined himself to his home leading up to the terrorist attack, obsessively consuming ISIS propaganda online. And Jabbar's radicalization did not happen abroad—it happened in the middle of the United States.

In the al-Qaeda/ISIS era from 2005 to 2016, about two-thirds of known extremists and terrorists used Facebook. YouTube came second, with about 30 per cent. Twitter came third, with about a quarter. Whatever the platform, however, Islamist terrorists used social media differently than neo-Nazis or the far-left extremists of the past. More than any other extremist group, the Islamists "were far more likely to use social media to facilitate travel to a foreign conflict zone," START says. And more of them participated in actual terrorist attacks.

The platforms can't fairly be accused of directly supporting terror. But being recklessly indifferent to its spread? That is a fair criticism. The reason, perhaps, is that when it comes to radicalization of recruits, terrorist groups and social media platforms have a distinctly symbiotic relationship. They both effectively want the same thing, for different reasons: the social media platforms want people to stay online longer (for profit), and so do the likes of Hamas (for radicalization).

YouTube, owned by Google, has always been one of the preferred jihadist radicalization sites, going back to its creation. For example, Berlin-based digital researchers with Democracy Reporting International (DRI) examined YouTube videos about neo-Nazi riots in Eastern Germany in 2018. They suspected that the reason for the neo-Nazis' radicalization was YouTube. After observing the pro-Nazi footage, the researchers then took note of the videos YouTube recommended that they watch next. Soon enough, the researchers were heading down a rabbit hole of ever-worsening hate. Their computer screens were quickly filled with misinformation, Nazism, and terror, all of it more violent than what had preceded it.

YouTube's algorithm—essentially, the recipe that a computer is programmed to follow—had been tweaked, DRI said, to show ever more extreme examples of what the analysts had watched, they said. (YouTube says it has recently made changes to its recommendation algorithm that reportedly reduces the prominence of harmful content.) It was highly efficient as well: when asked how many clicks it took for a YouTube user to be nudged toward online hate, one DRI researcher later said: "Only two. By the second, you're quite knee-deep in the alt-right."

The platform's algorithm worked in the same way with jihadist radicalization videos, terrorist how-to manuals, and many, many beheadings: the longer you stay, the worse it gets. As the DRI researcher put it: "I stay engaged, the ads play."

YouTube has long been one of the worst offenders, DRI and others note. In its early years, the platform hosted a digitized library of speeches and fundraising campaigns by Osama bin Laden. Beneath those videos, comments were always open, mostly to provide al-Qaeda with links to potential new recruits. When a video was posted on YouTube, supporters of Islamic extremism and terrorism—from influencers to link creators—would busy themselves with getting it in front of as many eyes as possible. For recruitment and radicalization, it was a highly effective model.

YouTube has made legitimate efforts to suppress and ban the pro-terrorism content. But the videos still get through. When a person uploads a video to YouTube, they're asked to choose the category it belongs to. The terrorists will often label the videos as "unlisted," which makes it more difficult for YouTube's automated moderation system to detect them. Direct links to the unlisted videos then get swiftly shared with supporters and sympathizers over Telegram and other encrypted platforms. Similarly, some YouTube videos are simply pathways to pro-terrorism content—audio will play over a still image, urging viewers to click on a pro-terrorism link, in the video's description section.

YouTube isn't the only social media platform where terrorist groups find an effective way to spread their propaganda. All the online platforms have the same simple imperative: eyeballs equal success, engagement equals profit. The longer someone stays on a platform, the greater its monetary value. In one of his more candid moments, Facebook creator Mark Zuckerberg admitted as much: "We design a lot of algorithms so we can produce interesting content for you. It actually computes what's going to be the most interesting piece of information." Online, the content that is most "interesting" is frequently the content that is the most violent and hateful.

Social media algorithms generally don't distinguish between kitten videos and beheading videos. As long as the content is attracting views and engagement, it's considered helpful by both the platforms and the terrorists. Regrettably, in September 2011, YouTube's leadership team confirmed this when they circulated an email among themselves with this simple subject line: "Watch time, and only watch time."

As things turned out, that was how al-Qaeda, ISIS, and Hamas measured value, too.

⸻

Just two weeks after October 7, thousands of students at more than a hundred universities across the United States and Canada protested "fascists and Zionists," according to the World Socialist Web Site. In Montreal, police were called in to escort Jewish students at McGill University past a well-attended anti-Israel protest. Simultaneously, security had been enhanced to protect Jewish students at three British Columbia universities: UBC, Simon Fraser, and the University of Victoria.

In Toronto, three York University students' associations published seemingly pro-Hamas statements, and refused to retract them even after it was again pointed out that Hamas had raped, tortured, and murdered more than a thousand Jews, and kidnapped hundreds more. Shortly thereafter, hundreds of high school students walked out of classes at schools across the Toronto District School Board to wave Palestinian flags and chant against the Jewish state. Meanwhile, police and Jewish organizations reported that there'd been multiple death threats and assaults happening on campuses in North America, overwhelmingly motivated by Jew-hatred. It was like that across much of North America and Europe. In most cases, the protests and demonstrations had been organized online.

Wherever the protests and shutdowns happened, the common element was young people, pollsters noted: Generation Z and Millennials, those roughly found between the ages of eighteen and thirty-nine. And, they added, Gen Z was the demographic segment with the greatest affinity for antisemitic messages.

Gen Z has been labelled the polarization generation by some, and the designation is apt. Across the West, Gen Z is mostly disinterested in politics, distrustful of democratic institutions, and angrier than other segments. Gen Z, unlike other demographics, is a group that has grown up at a time of massive social, economic, and political upheaval. Unlike previous generations, Gen Z has been forced to lower its expectations about jobs, housing, peace, the environment, and democracy itself, experts note. The arrival of the pandemic simply made this bad situation worse: Covid-19 impeded the career aspirations of many in the Gen Z cohort. It forced them indoors and, most pollsters agree, damaged their prospects and their hopes for the future.

Gen Z, and to a lesser extent Millennials, now express fatalism about that future, telling polling firms about their cynicism and feelings of despair. They express disbelief in "official stories" about history and are more willing to accept conspiracy theories and to support political candidates who espouse them. As a result,

Gen Z has become susceptible to propaganda churned out by any number of bad actors, including Islamic jihadists like Hamas.

Similarly, young men are increasingly embracing "bro culture" and far-right populist politicians and parties across North America and Europe. Meanwhile, young women have been seen heading in the opposite direction, embracing hyper-progressive causes and leaders. Where the Gen Z genders converge, however, is on the Middle East. They increasingly reject the Jewish state, say pollsters. More worrisome, the polls show, this anti-Zionism often transforms into unvarnished antisemitism.

Bad parenting was to blame, some supporters of Israel say, along with radicalized professors and teachers expressing intolerant views. But the main reason, CyberWell and Cyabra and many others have concluded, was that Generation Z had been targeted by a sophisticated propaganda campaign, pre– and post–October 7. And, for this generation, their favoured platform was and is TikTok.

TikTok went from effectively nothing in early 2016 to more than 1.5 billion global users in early 2022. It now has an estimated worth of more than US$50 billion. According to Pew Research Center, 70 per cent of American teenagers use it regularly—and one in six of them use it "almost constantly." Pew says the number of Americans who rely on TikTok for news quadrupled between 2020 and 2023, to more than 50 million people.

Long before October 7, 2023, many in the West raised concerns that TikTok is headquartered in the People's Republic of China, a long-time ally and ardent supporter of Hamas. TikTok has been banned by India, the world's most populous democracy. It has also been forbidden in Muslim-dominated countries like Pakistan, Malaysia, and Indonesia. Most significantly, perhaps, access to TikTok has never been permitted in China, by decree of China's regime. Everywhere, however, antisemitic content is easy to find on TikTok. As the ADL noted in one study: "TikTok claims that its algorithm amplifies content that users are interested in and minimizes other content. However, there is evidence that even users who don't espouse hate are exposed to hateful content, such as antisemitic memes—either because TikTok's algorithm surfaces it, or because they seek it out to critique it."

In the West, dozens of U.S. states have prohibited TikTok use by government agencies, employees, and contractors on government-issued devices. America's federal government, meanwhile, declared that TikTok would be entirely banned if it didn't change its ownership structure by the end of 2024. In early 2025, the U.S. Supreme Court unanimously ruled that it should be banned—but newly returned U.S. president Donald Trump halted the ban after TikTok donated to him and its CEO attended his inauguration. In late 2025, Tik Tok was sold to a group of investors politically aligned with Trump.

Some of the TikTok bans have to do with morality, since TikTok has been linked to child pornography by American attorneys general. (TikTok disputed those allegations—but has stepped up their moderation of such content.) The principal reason democratic nations are weighing bans of TikTok, however, is that TikTok is a platform where users can spread anti-Western propaganda—and because it is seen by many as a willing apparatus of China's ruling Communist Party. The platform is considered no friend of democratic states, and has been shown to be actively involved in the aggressive harvesting of users' personal data, critics charge. Unsurprisingly, TikTok has insisted that the app is independent and has denied supplying user data to China's government.

When a Chinese entrepreneur cooked up the idea for TikTok a decade or so ago, the app was much more benign. It was designed to target teenagers with short videos and accompanying music clips. Around the same time, however, Xi Jinping commenced reforming China and slammed shut the doors the country had opened to Western-style capitalism. Under Xi, the Chinese dictatorship forced TikTok to accept internal Communist Party cells in its workforce. It also clapped chains on TikTok and the rest of the country's burgeoning tech sector—and then passed the twin Cybersecurity Law and National Intelligence Law in 2017.

Those statutes make clear why TikTok has become a social media application unlike the others. The 2017 Chinese laws declare that "any organization or citizen shall support, assist and cooperate with state intelligence work." Given the fact that China does not consider Hamas a terrorist organization—and given the fact that China has supplied Hamas and Hezbollah with assault rifles, grenade launchers, high-end communications equipment, cruise missiles, ballistic missiles, and other sophisticated explosives—TikTok would soon become one of the world's main platforms for anti-Israel and antisemitic propaganda.

The U.S. State Department offered proof in October 2024. Josh Rogin, who monitors online antisemitism for the State Department, wrote in a report: "There's [been] a parallel rise on China's internet of pro-Hamas and anti-Israel content. The Chinese tech companies, which operate under strict instructions from Chinese government censors, have played a big role. Chinese internet search giants [even] went so far as to actually erase the country of Israel from their maps." So, the State Department noted, within days of October 7, Chinese state TV media started broadcasting claims that America was controlled by a cabal of money-hungry Jews. TikTok provided an online amplifier, giving antisemitism a measurable boost in the West.

Now, less than a decade after it launched, TikTok has become a social media behemoth. It usually ranks behind Facebook and YouTube for regular use, but ahead of Instagram, Snapchat, X, and many other social media platforms. For Gen Z, it is their preferred news source.

The problem with TikTok's algorithm revealed itself almost immediately after October 7. When one U.S. researcher, Jeff Morris Jr., engaged with just one TikTok post on the Israel–Hamas war, his feed was swiftly overwhelmed with anti-Israel messages. Morris looked at the resulting data and alleged that "TikTok is being controlled by anti-Israel bot farms—much of which is paid for by Hamas-supporting organizations." Shortly after October 7, one Jewish writer posted a video of herself on TikTok, saying, "For those asking if the Jewish people are okay, how can we ever be okay? How can we ever be okay watching a thousand of our people being ruthlessly murdered, raped, burned and beheaded? Jewish people are NOT okay." TikTok's response was to slap a warning label on the video, reading "Caution: video flagged for unverified content."

On another occasion, shortly after October 7, an American Holocaust educator received what amounted to a Holocaust-denial manifesto via her account, and reported it to TikTok. TikTok said that it did not violate their "community guidelines."

"'Israel' isn't a country," one much seen TikTok infographic read, making use of scare quotes around the word *Israel*. "They are a settler colony." If users of the platform were concerned that TikTok was permitting far more antisemitic and anti-Israel content, they had reason. In March 2024, *The Jerusalem Post* reported that 98.6 per cent of the videos on TikTok relating to Israel and Hamas carried a pro-Palestine or anti-Israel hashtag.

TikTok has rejected ads from families of Israeli hostages as being "too political," but has accepted many from pro-Palestinian groups. Those who attempt to provide content on TikTok about the historical reality of the Holocaust are often flooded with antisemitic comments: "Holding camps are NOT death camps. Even the chimney was built after the war for effect." And: "If it happened—it didn't—they deserve it." On TikTok, hashtags such as #StandWithIsrael got two million views. Meanwhile, #StandWithPalestine got an extraordinary 37.7 million views—almost twenty times as many. #FreePalestine hash-tagged TikTok videos were watched more than fifty times more than pro-Israel videos.

Inside TikTok, anonymous Jewish employees posted that the company had set up support groups for Palestinian employees. Requests for similar help for Jewish employees were denied for again being "too political." TikTok told Fox Business that the claims made "do not reflect the experience of the majority of our employees" and touted TikTok's "strong policies against discrimination and harassment in the workplace." Screenshots released by a senior employee at the company's Israel-based office showed some within the company aggressively promoting Boycott, Divestment, and Sanctions causes, as well as advocating the ban of businesses that operate in Israel, such as McDonald's, Burger King, Pizza Hut, and Domino's Pizza. And, on the company's Lark internal chat system, some TikTok managers and employees allegedly celebrated attacks on Jews by Hamas and other Iranian-backed terrorist groups. A TikTok spokesperson called the allegations "false."

In June 2024, a TikTok moderator was discovered posting antisemitic content on social media, calling for "death to Zionists" and urging that October 7 be made a holiday. "I do not condemn Oct 7 and think it should be made into an international holiday," she wrote on Instagram. Six weeks after the atrocities of October 7, more pro-Palestinian or anti-Israel videos were being viewed on TikTok than the total number of visits to the top American news sites. Younger TikTok users were nearly 20 per cent more likely to hold anti-Israel or antisemitic views after spending just thirty minutes a day on TikTok, said American data scientist Anthony Goldbloom a few weeks after October 7.

As with YouTube and the other social media platforms, TikTok's so-called engagement flywheel—which online platforms use to increase momentum and profit—pushes ever more extreme content toward its users to increase engagement. It seemingly amplifies antisemitic content as a result of its efforts to attract eyeballs. In the ADL study cited earlier, the human rights organization reported that "bad actors appear to be side-stepping TikTok's moderation policies to spread antisemitic content through slideshows (Photo Mode) and hashtags." The ADL noted that the platform was "difficult to study due to the lack of data it shares."

Asked about all these allegations and facts, a TikTok spokesman acknowledged receipt of the questions but did not subsequently provide any answers.

"Young people," Avi Melamed says, "very, very easily fall for sensationalized, romanticized images and rhetoric and symbols. It's very easy to capture their hearts and minds and manipulate them. When you don't have knowledge, when you don't have basic educational skills like critical thinking and media literacy, you are not going to be looking for context and nuance. And it can lead to disaster."

Melamed adds: "As long as you've got a combination of fast-food information and young people who lack the basics in education, groups like Hamas will continue to excel on these social media platforms."

The statistics—in Canada, United States, and Europe—all reflect the same depressing dynamic: many within the younger generations vehemently oppose and even hate the Jewish state, often expressing anger toward anyone who doesn't agree with them. Poll after poll show a pattern: large segments of Generation Z (from eighteen to twenty-seven) and Millennials (from twenty-eight to late thirties or so) have created their own political and historical construct, one where anti-Zionism and anti-Western ideology dominate.

The main "driver" for all this, as pollsters call it, is perceptions of Jews. Many young people regard Israelis and Jews as wealthy and powerful, and therefore see Israel's response to Hamas as unjust. To them, the Jewish state has become the embodiment of the white oppressor, an apartheid state that is aligned with the United States and it is subjugating a weak, racialized minority. And their disdain for Israel and Jews dovetails with the hatred that many Gen Z and Millennials now express toward Western society in general, pollsters note.

This antisemitic (and historic) falsehood that Jews are immensely wealthy and all-powerful is but one reason for the animosity of younger generations, the ADL says. So, too, the racial dimension. Even though more than 60 per cent of Israel's population is considered non-white, polls consistently show many North American and European Gen Z and Millennials believe it is a white supremacist, colonial state. An investigation by PBS, for example, saw youthful anti-Israel protestors repeatedly citing race as a driver of their disdain for Israel. In recent years, they participated in Black Lives Matter protests, the Occupy movement, and Greta Thunberg–style environmental advocacy. Now they're protesting for Gaza and against the Jewish state.

To them, it is all connected.

On October 7, 2023, Israel was unprepared for Hamas's attack. Online, too, Israel was caught off-guard by the pro-Hamas, anti-Israel online propaganda campaign.

From the outset, Israel's messaging was often confused and contradictory, their talking points completely ineffective. The pro-Hamas side generated far more content online, and it looked far more professional than what was coming out of Israel. Even strong supporters of Israel agreed that the other side was winning.

It wasn't entirely Israel's fault, Israeli politicians and intelligence operatives have told this writer. Hamas and their allies had been preparing its campaign for at least two years, they say. They had a small army of spin doctors, and ample resources or support from Iran, Qatar, Russia, and China. They were ready for October 7, and they flipped a switch in the early hours of that day—and unleashed an avalanche of misinformation and disinformation that was difficult, if not impossible, to compete with. As Jerusalem deputy mayor Fleur Hassan Nahoum observed, "Israel is fighting on many fronts, but the [Hamas] social media front is particularly aggressive. And we are painfully outnumbered."

Author and veteran journalist Shraga Simmons, like other Israelis I interviewed, suggests that his country had been losing the media war long before October 7. As he noted at the conclusion of his 2012 study of anti-Israel media bias, *David and Goliath*, "A few years ago when this propaganda war first got underway, there was no government, organization or individual that stood as the prime propagator. Though there were pockets of intense activity—college campuses, European capitals—there was no global coordination. But now [there is] a calculated, centralized strategy for manipulating public opinion in order to defeat Israel. And the glue binding it all together is the mass media."

Videos and photos originating from within Gaza have been greatly boosted by pro-Hamas accounts as well as troll farms that are found in Iran, China, and Russia, Israeli intelligence sources observe. In Putin's regime, for example, the St. Petersburg–based Internet Research Agency (IRA) worked to ensure that Hamas's propaganda would be seen by millions. The agency came to the attention of the West in 2018, when U.S. special counsel Robert Mueller indicted thirteen of its members for pro-Trump election interference. In the 2016 U.S. presidential campaign, Mueller found, the IRA had spent millions through shell companies to boost more than ten million tweets across nearly 4,000 accounts, 1,100 YouTube videos, and 116,000 Instagram posts across 133 accounts—along with 61,500 unique Facebook posts. Wrote Mueller: "Russia's specialists were directed to create 'political intensity through supporting radical groups, users dissatisfied with the social and economic situation and oppositional social movements." Russia even created a Hamas-like group, called United Muslims of America, to promote division and suppress voter turnout for Hillary Clinton. It had more than three hundred thousand followers in 2016.

With the assistance of Russia, China, and Iran, Hamas and its Islamic terrorist axis have become much more skilful than Israel in getting their messaging seen by bigger audiences, intelligence sources say. Members of the Hamas media team have often received training in the West, and their budgets are considerable. As Tel Aviv University propaganda expert Guy Aviad puts it, "Their output is technically of very high quality."

This was particularly true online, where many in the West now go for what passes for news. As the Center for Strategic and International Studies observed in a post–October 7 analysis, "pro-Palestinian content is more concentrated on social media platforms. . . . Gazan journalists have had significant success in reaching audiences on [social media] platforms." Within Gaza, cellphone usage is at almost 100 per cent, one of the highest levels in the world. On X, Instagram, Facebook, and other platforms, Gazans posted innumerable raw, selfie- and diary-style "reports" that weren't being scrutinized by professional editors for accuracy or bias. They soon acquired huge audiences, particularly among women, who favoured Instagram and TikTok.

For instance, one youthful Palestinian Instagram user received little attention before October 7. After the war began, she somehow quickly acquired five million followers, posting photos and clips along with claims that Palestine has endured "75 years of occupation" and "Israeli genocide." Another twenty-something Palestinian with an Instagram account was most preoccupied with photos of her cats before October 7. After that date, in a video diary in which she accused Israel of destroying hospitals, bringing "massacres," "genocide," and "death," her following also somehow ballooned to nearly five million people.

October 7 denial and other anti-Zionist and antisemitic messaging wasn't scattershot. It was fired into the internet ether with a sniper's precision, the likes of Cyabra say, because Hamas and its axis had been tracking their desired target for years. They knew what demographic to target and what messages to use with that audience. Political campaigns and big corporations call this "segmentation marketing": separate, personalized marketing campaigns, which are much more effective and cost-efficient. It's narrowcasting instead of broadcasting.

For big corporations and mainstream political parties, segmentation reduces the risk of wasting time and money on disinterested or hostile consumers and voters. So, Hamas segmented their messaging. On Facebook, CyberWell discovered that the online message was "Jews control the world—or are dominating the world order." On Instagram, it was different: "The Rothschild conspiracy theory"—named after the well-to-do French Jewish family that has long been targeted by antisemites. On TikTok and X: "Jews are the enemy." And on Google's YouTube: "Jews are the synagogue of Satan."

In political and marketing campaigns, micro-targeting pushes out messages that are carefully aimed at specific demographics, based on age, gender, geography, and education. To work, a micro-targeting strategy requires significant resources to accurately identify a specific audience with the right messages on their preferred platforms. Propaganda is no longer leaflets being dropped out of a plane (which, tellingly, is how Israel often communicates with Gazans). Sophisticated propagandists tailor their messaging to snare a receptive audience. Micro-targeted online advertising isn't just used for selling running shoes, CyberWell and other watchdogs say; it can also be used to market hate. From publicly available research and polling results, Hamas and others knew that the anti-Israel—and antisemitic—propaganda effort would work with youthful demographics better than any other. Captivating swaths of those two demographic segments, Gen Z and Millennials, would be easier to do, and the research also shows why.

It is a truism, of course, that people embrace hate because of ignorance. Before and after October 7, such ignorance was was everywhere. One poll, conducted by YouGov for *The Economist* a few weeks after October 7, found that younger respondents were what the magazine said was "remarkably ignorant" about the Holocaust. A fifth of Gen Z considered it a hoax, and a third said they "didn't know" if it was. Meanwhile, the same poll revealed that a third of Gen Z and Millennials believed that "Jews wield too much power." Some commentators insisted that poor educational standards were solely to blame for the results, but this was not the case: YouGov and *The Economist* determined that education didn't really play much of a factor. The number of young people who believed that the Holocaust is a myth was "similar across all levels of education" in the United States.

Lane Kendall, an American researcher who has closely followed the online efforts of Iran, Hamas, and their allies to capture the support of young Westerners, says it's a mistake to dismiss their influence on Gen Z and Millennials. "I think the organizational power of students is underestimated, especially in the West. If you look at countries like Taiwan, or if you look at Korea, those countries didn't become democracies without student pressure."

Hamas and its allies know this, Kendall says. "It's not even about voting. The cultural influence that students have—especially over left-leaning parties in the West—is significant. Centre-left political parties depend very heavily on young voters. And if they have to cater to young voters—and all of a sudden young voters have the same policy objectives that terrorist organizations have—well, now you have terrorist organizations getting the ability to directly influence policymaking decisions at the highest levels."

To illustrate his point, Kendall cites the sums that Qatar, Hamas's main banker, has pumped into Western universities and colleges. From 2001 to 2021, Qatar supplied U.S. universities with up to $4.7 billion. None of the institutions initially revealed the source of the money, even though U.S. law requires it. For example, Qatar supplied Carnegie Mellon in Pennsylvania with nearly $700 million between 2010 and 2022—precisely the period, Kendall and others have noted, when antisemitism had risen dramatically at that university.

The online propaganda, and the propaganda they're getting in university classrooms, have an impact on students' opinions, Kendall says. The money is key. "Finding out where the money's going or who's spending it: there's definitely a correlation," he concludes. "And it's a proven correlation that, where more [Qatari] money is coming to a campus, the more likely [antisemitic and anti-Israel groups] are going to be active on that campus. You can't look at all this and say that there's no relationship. Because you would be lying to yourself."

Education, or the lack of it, was of course a factor, he says. Antisemitism has gone viral among young people, some argue, because they've been persuaded to think that way by professors and curriculums that promote the notion that Zionism is settler colonialism, and inherently racist. Not coincidentally, antisemitism ballooned on university and college campuses in 2023 and

2024, Kendall says, with many accounts of Jewish students being defamed, threatened, and assaulted. So, as three-quarters of North American students reported having witnessed antisemitic incidents during their school year. Antisemitism was rampant, and was reportedly being reinforced online and in the classroom, Kendall adds.

What is most striking about all of these numbers, pollsters say, is that young people haven't always been antisemitic. In fact, historically, they've always opposed it. For more than sixty years, for example, the Anti-Defamation League has conducted regular surveys about antisemitism. And over all those years they found that younger people rejected antisemitic attitudes much more frequently than older people. But just prior to the pandemic years that started to shift, and during the pandemic itself, the period when Gen Z and Millennials were feeling isolated, angry, and confined to an online world, that phenomenon began to accelerate. In and around 2020, conspiracy theories were every-where—about vaccines, but also about Jews.

Tel Aviv University researchers found that antisemitic content went viral just as the coronavirus did, starting in February 2020. Conspiracy theories began to circulate online that Jews and Israelis had created and spread the virus so they could profit from selling vaccines. Those who opposed lockdowns also compared their plight to that of Jews in the Holocaust, thereby minimizing it. Wrote the report's authors, who noted that online antisemitic hatred never stays online: "Right at the outset of the pandemic in 2020, conspiracy theories began to sprout around the world, blaming the Jews and Israel for spreading the virus. The lockdowns, which glued people to their screens at home, contributed significantly to popularizing toxic antisemitic discourse on social networks. In 2021, when the lockdowns were gradually eased, anti-Semites returned to the streets." And the demographics most susceptible to the pandemic-era Jew hatred were Gen Z and Millennials—"populations with no well-defined political or ideological identities," the report said.

The pandemic was like gasoline tossed on the smouldering fire of online antisemitism. By 2024, the ADL reported, Millennials and Gen Z "led the way" in this regard. They had become the first generation in American history to sympathize more with Palestinians than Jews. Those cohorts expressed strong opposition to racism. Jews, to them, became fascistic, apartheid-supporting white supremecists.

Following October 7, then, antisemitism became all the rage.

Marc Ginsburg shakes his head.

"These kids wouldn't know the difference between Gaza and a bagel," the former ambassador says.

Ginsburg, a diplomatic appointee during the Bill Clinton administration, is asked whether those kids—the university- and college-level ones who've accused Israel and the West of "genocide" from Toronto to Los Angeles—could all be coming together spontaneously. Organically.

"No," says Ginsburg, now the head of a Washington-based online watchdog called the Coalition for a Safer Web (CSW). "Not all of them. No way. There's no doubt that what Hamas had in the can was prepared weeks, weeks in advance [of October 7]. They lined up a whole bunch of influencers in Europe, United States, and Canada to push this Hamas content onto mainstream social media platforms."

Ginsburg has considerable experience tracking online hate and antisemitism. Just hours before sitting down for an interview in his Washington office—the walls are adorned with photos of him with Clinton and his friend Al Gore—he met again with a U.S. congressional committee to offer testimony about Iran's efforts to destabilize democracies like America's, often by making use of social media and Hamas-adjacent "influencers." Much more needed to be done to counter the propaganda barrage coming out of Iran and its proxies, Ginsburg said. The long-time Democrat even applauded the tough action the Trump administration has taken against antisemitic campus agitators, often acting at the behest of Iran, Qatar, and Hamas.

With his CSW group, the former ambassador to Morocco has devoted years to tracking and exposing antisemitism and the incitement of violence against Jews. Hamas, he says without hesitation, now runs a sophisticated social media propaganda effort throughout Western democracy. And it's a campaign that particularly relies on popular influencers scattered throughout the West, he says.

He has no doubt that those influencers—and myriad organizers and protestors—are being paid to show up and spew Jew-hatred, Ginsburg says. Money flows in through non-profits, NGOs, and charities in Canada, the U.S., and Europe, he adds, ultimately from Iran, Qatar, and even Russia and China. Says he: "I applaud the Trump's administration's decision to threaten the withholding of federal grants until these universities clean up their act. . . . [The campus anti-Israel activists] are full time and very capable. These paid disruptors are being funded. Who has chartered the buses and then provided them with the transportation to go out and disrupt an airport runway or an airport roadway, to stop people from getting to an airport? This doesn't happen because a kid who's a freshman or sophomore says, 'Guess what? We're going to go out to Kennedy, to Kennedy Airport. We're going to stop every flight, every passenger trying to make a flight.'"

The agitators, who are getting bolder, have training, resources, and the backing of powerful interests, Ginsburg says. A combination of Marxist-Leninists, anarchist groups, and Jew-haters has come together since October 7 to promote violence and enmity toward Jews, he notes.

Ginsburg and his group have evidence, he says. In a report prepared in the wake of Hamas's 2023 attack on Israeli civilians, the CSW revealed that Hamas, Iran, and Qatar "had a sophisticated social media plan ready to spring" on October 7; that, on X, Instagram, and TikTok, the anti-Israel forces worked to "generate support for Hamas [and] leverage foreign social media influencers" in their propaganda campaign; that, while protests on university campuses and in Western streets may have "appeared organic," they were in fact "professionally staffed and funded" by others; and that, after October 7, those extremist groups—drawn heavily from what he says are leftist, Muslim, and anarchistic circles—formed a new "axis of antisemitism."

Ginsburg points to the example of one Canadian group that in 2024 was designated as a terrorist entity by the governments of Justin Trudeau and Joe Biden. Grimacing, Ginsberg says he and his colleagues at CSW spent years trying to convince the Trudeau and Biden administrations to act against Vancouver's Samidoun, which is now considered a front for the terrorist Popular Front for the Liberation of Palestine. "With the Biden administration, you could've hit them over the head with a 2 x 4, but they were always dragging their feet . . . and the Canadian government was dragging its feet a lot longer," says Ginsburg, adding: "Canada has sadly become a petri dish for antisemitism."

The funding, the influencers, the online antisemitism: Ginsburg is asked whether the threat is being exaggerated. He looks out the window of his office, just blocks from the White House.

"Not only is it getting worse," he says, "there's been no real effort by any government to shut it down. We seem to be going at this the wrong way. We're going from the bottom up rather than the top down. We're looking at these grassroots organizations—but, in the end, where are they getting the support from?"

Khaled Hassan grew up Muslim in Egypt. He now lives in England and is a Jew.

His youth was steeped in antisemitism, online and off. To him and everyone around him, it was as natural as breathing. When Hassan was younger, Jews were fundamentally evil, he believed.

Hassan liked to travel, however. He saw different places and experienced different ways of thinking. Radicalization isn't always bad, he says now. In his case, it worked in reverse: he started learning about other points of view and various cultures. He started questioning the beliefs that had been part of his growing up in Egypt. Eventually, slowly, he made the decision to convert to Judaism, he says.

These days he works as an intelligence analyst and runs a counter-terrorism organization. And since October 7 he's been very busy. "Everywhere you look [online], people and groups are willing to accept the Hamas narrative." That's mainly happening online, he says. And it's a type of warfare, as he calls it, that is "completely new."

"Social media is not used to necessarily change the opinions [of young people]," says Hassan. "It's being used to reinforce pre-existing prejudices. Things that were already there. And it is just staggering how they are willing to accept what they are being told."

The understandable desire of young people to oppose authority, he says, is a big part of the effectiveness of the anti-Israel, anti-West propaganda campaign. That is why Hamas and its allies call themselves "the resistance" online and in the real world.

"Resistance," Hassan says. "Resistance. To young people, it's all a form of resistance. And it's particularly successful now because the conflict has been going on much longer, and it is much more devastating on all sides. That has given Hamas and its allies more time to actually promote their narratives. Among young people, interest in that has grown. They did all that before, yes. But Hamas was smarter this time. They knew what to do online, they knew what to say. They knew how to get young people on their side.

"Unfortunately, they have managed to convince people that this is about justice. They managed to convince people that the land of Israel belongs to the Muslims, not the Jews. It's a narrative they've spun very effectively online."

Hassan says that no one should be under any illusion: for Hamas, the war—online and otherwise—is about faith, and establishing a global caliphate. "It's 100 per cent about religion for them," he says. In the early days of this religious war, the preferred weapons were always the Kalashnikovs ISIS used to kill civilians in Paris in November 2015, or the AK-47s Hamas used to slaughter hundreds in October 2023, or the many weapons al-Qaeda used in their serial wars against the West. Their main weapon of choice now, he says, is a smartphone. A smartphone provides valuable insights into the way the West lives, and how to capture their support. If someone is in the anger business, the internet is the best recruitment and radicalization tool in the history of the world.

With their rage about Western excesses—Western indolence, Western indifference, Western modernity—Hamas and their murderous axis intend to conquer the world, says Hassan. And they are dominating in that war, he says, whether those of us in the West care to admit it or not.

Online, and off.

FOUR

NO JEWS, NO NEWS

"Not seventy-five years later, but just months later, and people are already forgetting, they're already forgetting that Hamas unleashed this terror, that it was Hamas that brutalized Israelis, that it was Hamas that took and continues to hold hostages.

"I have not forgotten, nor have you. And we will not forget.

"As Jews around the world still cope with the atrocity and trauma of that day and its aftermath, we've seen a ferocious surge of antisemitism in America and around the world. 'Never again' simply translated for me means: Never forget. Never forgetting means we must keep telling the story, we must keep teaching the truth. The truth is we're at risk of people not knowing the truth. It's absolutely despicable and it must stop. Silence and denial can hide much but it can erase nothing . . . it cannot be buried no matter how hard people try.

"We're at risk of people not knowing the truth."

The speaker was then U.S. president Joe Biden, in a May 2024 speech at the annual commemoration of the Holocaust Memorial Museum in Washington, D.C. He was addressing American Holocaust survivors and American Jews, but likely everyone else, too. "Knowing the truth [and] teaching the truth," as Biden put it, were essential if society is to prevent another Shoah.

Left unsaid in Biden's address was what the president thought about the way the news media had been communicating certain truths about October 7. An earlier press briefing conducted by Biden's press secretary, Karine Jean-Pierre, also conveyed what the White House believed reporters needed to be doing during the Israel–Hamas war. Said Jean-Pierre: "We've been pretty consistent about protecting [journalists] and making sure that journalists are able to . . . gather the facts, report the facts."

Facts matter. But in every war, per the cliché, truth is usually the first casualty. Facts can end up littering the battlefield like fallen soldiers, and lies start to dominate. Since October 7, 2023 (and despite Article 22 in Hamas's charter referring to Jewish control of the media as "ferocious"), that poverty of truth has favoured Israel's enemies. In its media campaign, and in its social media campaign, Hamas and its ilk have utterly dominated the discourse, with the Israeli side—as Israelis say themselves—having had a minimal to nonexistent voice. Over and over in the information war, Hamas and its allies have somehow overwhelmed the Israeli/Western perspective—to the point where the president of the United States felt compelled to issue a warning that truth was losing the battle.

"A lot of people," Biden said during his October 2023 trip to Israel, "are not sure" what are the facts and what is the truth. That big challenge, Biden told Israeli leaders, "we've got to overcome."

It wasn't going to be easy. In fact, from its very first moments, Biden's historic trip was overshadowed by a significant propaganda victory for Hamas. As Air Force One was touching down in Israel, much of the mainstream media was reporting on what had arguably become the biggest news story in the world: namely, that Israel had allegedly bombed Gaza City's al-Ahli

Arab Hospital, deliberately (or recklessly) reducing it to rubble, killing scores of innocent Gazans. Everywhere, this was reported as fact: *The New York Times*, the BBC, CNN, CBS, ABC, the *Evening Standard*, *The Times*, Yahoo News, *The Wall Street Journal*, Reuters, the Associated Press, and many other news organizations. The shocking news had the potential to completely derail Biden's first visit to Israel since October 7.

Except, the hospital was still standing. Five hundred people were not dead (the actual tally was two or three dozen casualties at most). And, while the al-Ahli hospital parking lot had indeed been bombed, Israel hadn't done it. Palestinian Islamic Jihad had, with an allegedly misfired rocket. "Based on what I have seen," Biden eventually told Israel's relieved politicians, "it appears as though it was done by the other team, not you."

In Palestine, the al-Ahli hospital is the only cancer-treating hospital in the Gaza Strip. It was previously known as the Gaza Baptist Hospital, having been run by the foreign mission board of the Southern Baptist Convention (and later the Anglicans). The al-Ahli hospital came to represent something else, however: a glaring example of how experienced and respected media organizations can get things dramatically wrong when reporting on Israel. It has become a problem since October 7, some say.

"When it comes to Western media, most, not all, are completely unfair to Israel," journalist Brian Lilley says. "There are exceptions, like Douglas Murray in the U.K. There are media outlets such as the *Toronto Sun* and *National Post* in Canada, the *New York Post* and *Wall Street Journal* in America. By and large, though, Western media take a singular narrative—that Israel is the oppressor and the Palestinian people are the oppressed. They run every story through that lens."

Lilley is one of the exceptions. He started in Montreal as a radio reporter, then went to Ottawa to cover news—and later was the parliamentary bureau chief for Standard Broadcasting for half a decade. From there, he was hired to help launch Sun News Network. Lilley was anchor for the most popular show on the network, and wrote a book of media criticism about Canada's public broadcaster.

Today he's the most read columnist with Postmedia, Canada's biggest newspaper chain. He freely admits to a conservative, pro-Israel editorial stance. Which is precisely the problem with much of the media coverage of Israel, Lilley says: too many media organizations and publishers claim to be neutral on the subject when they decidedly are not. "If they were fair, they would write and report that, yes, the Palestinian people are oppressed. But the oppressors are Hamas, Palestinian Islamic Jihad, and Fatah." But most media organizations regard Israel only as a fascist, oppressive white supremacist apartheid state, he adds.

Their selection of facts reflects that unfairness, he says. The examples are multiple, going back years, and range from rookie factual errors to egregious instances of bias.

"Terrorist" is a case in point. The Federal Bureau of Investigation defines terrorism as "violent, criminal acts committed by individuals and/or groups to further ideological goals." That is the generally accepted definition, with minor variations, elsewhere. But Western media have had an uneven approach to the use of that word in the ongoing Israel–Palestine conflict, Lilley says.

Writers at different media organizations describe terrorists in different ways. One at the BBC has called terrorists "activists." At the Associated Press: "assailants" and "underground." At *The*

Washington Post: "assassins." With CNN: "attackers." *Los Angeles Times*: "captors." *Orlando Sentinel*: "combatants." *The Philadelphia Inquirer*: "commandos." *The Orange County Register*: "dissidents." One at *The New York Times*: "fighters." *The Guardian*: "freedom fighters." The *Sunday Times*: "fugitives." *The Christian Science Monitor*: "guerillas." *Newsweek*: "insurgents" and "radicals." *USA Today*: "martyrs." *Time*: "militants." *Chicago Tribune*: "nationalists." *Pittsburgh Post-Gazette*: "perpetrators." Fox News: "protesters." *The Seattle Times*: "rebels." *The San Diego Union-Tribune*: "resistance fighters." *Publishers Weekly*: "revolutionaries." *Newsday*: "vigilantes." *The New Yorker*: "warriors."

The substitutions are inventive, but not very descriptive, Lilley says. Reading them, he adds, it becomes apparent why so many Israelis and Jews are upset about how the Western media reports on attacks in which they are the victims. To Lilley, several of those trade-offs—"freedom fighters," "martyrs," "resistance fighters"—are, by traditional journalistic standards, neither accurate nor fair. To some people, they are morally neutral to the point where they no longer serve the reader, listener, or viewer. To Brian Lilley, and those who feels similarly, they are simply wrong.

The most notorious example of that, Lilley says, is the use of the Gaza Ministry of Health as a source by Western journalists seeking casualty numbers (see Chapter 2). Readers, viewers, and listeners are not being well served as a result, he says—and Israel and Israel's allies aren't benefiting either. "The Gaza Health Ministry," he says, "is Hamas."

Lilley points to a related example: while too many in the media apparently believe terrorism never takes place in Israel, he says those same media don't hesitate to use loaded words and phrases to describe the Jewish state: at various times it's been called "colonial," "white supremacist," "apartheid," and "illegitimate." Simultaneously, these news organizations refer to Gaza and the West Bank as "occupied territories," without otherwise applying those words to occupied territories found elsewhere in the world. And this kind of editorializing in straight news reports about Israel is commonplace, Lilley notes, particularly at times of conflict between Israel and Palestine.

Says Lilley: "I've worked in newsrooms across Canada, [and] I've cooperated with newsrooms across the United States and Britain. Most journalists in those countries lean left. In the United States, most vote Democrat. In Canada, reporters have tended to be on the Liberal Party's side—and when I was in the Parliamentary Press Gallery, it was easier to find socialists than people who'd supported and voted for the Conservative government. As those parties and the movements that drive them have lurched further to the left, they've taken up the position that Israel is always wrong and the Palestinian people are always right. . . . So the journalists have taken up the same position."

Unless attributed to a source, however, the use of adjectives in straight news reports is always frowned upon, or strictly prohibited, by news organizations in their style guides. The standard is always to strive for objectivity, balance, and fairness. Despite that, Lilley notes, when the subject matter is Israel, value judgments seem to occur often. A writer at *The Independent* wrote about "the monstrous war crime" and "extraordinary, sinister events" when describing Israel's 2002 incursion into a terrorist base in Jenin in the West Bank. One at *The Guardian* called Israel's attempt to eliminate terrorist cells in Jenin "a crime," and reported that there was "the stench of decaying flesh, of dead bodies left to rot." An *Evening Standard* writer struck a similar tone, reporting that Israel was to blame for a "massacre" and "genocide" in Jenin—where, it should be noted, the Israeli side lost twenty-three fighters and the Palestinian side lost twenty-seven.

Accusing Jews of acting like fascists and Nazis is now routine, Lilley says. It's seen in many post–October 7 news reports, but was also present long before the barbarism of that day. A CBS 60 *Minutes* report accused Israel of "ethnic cleansing" in December 2003, while a January 2009 CNN headline quoted a British lawmaker saying, "Israeli Forces Acting Like Nazis." A reporter at Agence France-Presse declared, "Saudi Likens Gaza Assault to Nazi War Crimes," while a writer at *The Irish Times* wrote that Israel's actions in Jenin "looked uncannily like the attack on the Warsaw Jewish ghetto in 1944."

Lilley shakes his head when reviewing a summary of such examples. A lot of that bad journalism is happening, he says, because of the training journalists are receiving. "We've put a couple of generations [of students] through journalism school in the era of the oppressed versus the oppressor narrative. If you take that narrative and juxtapose it on the ethos I just described—and add in some radical identity politics—you suddenly see why Israel is always at fault. Which is what we see in much of our news coverage."

The worst of it, to Brian Lilley and others, is Holocaust inversion. Holocaust inversion minimizes the immensity of the real Holocaust, Lilley says, and casts the victims of Nazism as the practitioners of Nazism. In editorials it's offensive; in news reporting, he says, it has no justification whatsoever. But it's seen often across large swaths of Western journalism now. The U.K.'s *Observer*, in an op-ed: "Israelis are the Zionist SS." *The New Zealand Herald*: "Israelis are getting the same results the

Nazis got." *Toronto Sun* columnist Eric Margolis, for his part, actually wrote that Israel was pursuing a "final solution" against Palestinians.

Even in an interview with President Barack Obama, NBC's Tom Brokaw made an inappropriate comparison between Nazi death camps and Israel's conflict with Hamas. But Obama was having none of it. "There's no equivalency there," he snapped at Brokaw, clearly unimpressed.

Apartheid, Lilley observes, is a word that frequently gets tossed around as well. A *New Zealand Herald* headline: "Palestinians' Fight Is a Struggle Against Apartheid." *The Atlanta Journal-Constitution*: "Israelis Adopt What South Africa Dropped." The *Hartford Courant*: "An End to U.S. Aid to the Israeli Apartheid System." *The Washington Post,* asking of Israel: "Worse Than Apartheid?" (The column's writer, Robert D. Novak, answered yes.) The phrase "Israeli apartheid" shows up 1.5 million times on the search engine Bing. In comparative terms, studies show, no other Middle Eastern nation comes close to achieving that distinction.

Media characterizations of Israel's enemy receive a very different treatment, Lilley says. Even the weapons Hamas uses to kill Israelis, he adds, are dismissed as not much of a threat. A writer at *The Economist* has called the rockets fired into Israel "rudimentary" and far more harmful to Gazans than Israelis; one at *The Washington Post* wrote that the "amateur rockets" merely "nagged" residents of Israel's south; another at the *Seattle Post-Intelligencer* said the rockets were "falling harmlessly." A BBC writer called the rockets "symbolic" while one at the Associated Press insisted in 2003 that "Palestinians have been firing primitive, homemade Qassam rockets. . . . Most of them miss their target, and those that land cause little damage with their small explosive warheads."

Regarding Hamas itself, a BBC correspondent said their leaders "espouse a more moderate brand of Islamist politics." A *New York Times* writer echoed that account, writing that Hamas was a "militant Palestinian group" seemingly regarded as a terrorist group only by Israel. One, at CNN, published a story in 2002—by which time Hamas's use of extreme violence was notorious—that the terrorist group was known among Palestinians merely "for actions such as building schools, hospitals and helping the community in social and religious ways." Years earlier, in October 1994, a writer at NPR called Hamas "terrific community organizers" who sponsor "business projects like honey, cheese-making and home-based clothing manufacturing."

Even when it's acknowledged that Hamas attacks first, Israel gets blamed, Lilley says. In January 2009, a *New York Times* writer led a story with critics' claim that Israel has had "a wildly disproportionate response to the rockets of Hamas, causing untold human suffering and bombing an already isolated and impoverished population into the Stone Age." When Hamas "won" the election in 2006, an author at *The Guardian* called the result "the best news from the Middle East in a long time." An editorial in the pages of that newspaper, meanwhile, said Hamas would bring "new opportunities to the immense task of building peace."

Patrick Martin, a writer at Canada's newspaper of record, *The Globe and Mail*, has written that Hamas is simply a "Palestinian resistance movement"—and not, as it was when Martin wrote those words, a designated terrorist entity in Canada. *Newsweek's* reporter said that Hamas was "admired for its ethos . . . and their network of social services." A writer at *The New York Times* declared that Hamas was notable for its "philanthropy." Another writer at the *Times* said that Hamas was "fully committed" to a two-state solution, which was categorically false. (Even Hamas says so.)

As recently as September 2024, when Hezbollah supreme leader Hassan Nasrallah was eliminated in an Israeli airstrike, these sorts of mischaracterizations of known terrorists continued. "Hezbollah has a moral compass," said *The Washington Post*, while *The New York Times* opined that Hezbollah wanted "equality for Muslims, Jews and Christians," which would perhaps be news to the several hundred Muslim, Jewish, and Christian civilians it has killed over three decades. The *Times* also stated that "Mr. Nasrallah" was "a powerful orator . . . beloved among many Shiite Muslims" and that he "came across as less dour than most Shiite clerics, partly because of his roly-poly figure, a slight lisp and a propensity to crack jokes. He never pushed hard-line Islamic rules, like veils for women in the neighborhoods that Hezbollah controls." A reporter at *Le Monde* called him "heroic" and one at the Associated Press also heaped praise on him: "Charismatic and shrewd . . . an astute strategist . . . considered a pragmatist . . . idolized by his Lebanese Shiite followers . . . respected by millions across the Arab and Islamic world." *The Guardian*'s correspondent, meanwhile, called Nasrallah "a qualified Islamic scholar, effective public speaker and competent organizer."

In stories about known terrorists, Western media can often sound like unabashed fans as well, Lilley says. The way terrorist Zakaria Zubeidi was depicted, for example, recalled an overwritten restaurant review penned by a newspaper summer student: Zubeidi had eyes "the color of rich toffee," wrote one reporter at *The Washington Post*, who went on to describe another terrorist as having skin "the color of roasted pecans." Meanwhile, a journalist at *The Guardian*, reporting on terrorist Leila Khaled, was similarly glowing: "The gun held in fragile hands, the shiny hair wrapped in a keffiyeh, the delicate Audrey Hepburn face refusing to meet your eye. But it's the ring, resting delicately on her third finger. To fuse an object of feminine adornment, of frivolity, with a bullet: that is Khaled's story, the reason behind her image's enduring power." (It should be remembered that Khaled blew up a TWA plane, Israelis say, while Zubeidi was a bomb-maker and a leader of Hamas's al-Aqsa Martyrs' Brigades.)

Examples of this sort of purple prose abound, Lilley and others note. Abdel Aziz al-Rantisi—who as a Hamas co-founder oversaw the killings of IDF soldiers and the bombing of the Hebrew University cafeteria, murdering seven people—was called a "pediatrician and poet" by a writer at the Associated Press, who then quoted some of his poems about birds. NBC's Martin Fletcher visited Ahmed Sanakreh—another al-Aqsa Martyrs' Brigades bomb-maker—and called him "baby-faced, with black hair sticking up in gelled spikes." PLO leader Yasser Arafat had ordered Raouf Barbakh arrested for refusing to heed a ceasefire and because Barbakh preferred more bloodshed—but *The New York Times* correspondent called him "polite" and "a kind youth counsellor" who dreamed about "planting a garden among the weeds." Someone at McClatchy newspapers said that a terrorist who'd murdered a four-year-old girl with the butt of his rifle and then killed her father was to his people "a hero," "humble," "patriotic," and "a symbol of ascendant power."

Ismail Abu Shanab, a now-dead founder of Hamas, infamously stated that "all Israeli targets are legitimate," and that the Jewish state must be destroyed. But a reporter at CNN chose to call him "a moderate," while another at the Associated Press referred to him as "one of the group's more sober minds." *Time* magazine's reporter said he was "rather moderate" too, and neglected to relate the fact that Shanab had planned multiple bomb attacks on Jews. Another Hamas co-founder, Sheikh Ahmed Yassin, also directed dozens of suicide bombings. A writer at Knight Ridder, then the second-largest American newspaper publisher, merely reported that Yassin was "the elderly, partially blind quadriplegic [who] was the beloved leader of a popular movement." One at the *Los Angeles Times* went a bit further, hailing Yassin's "moral authority." *The New York Times* writer, and others, called him a "spiritual leader," and *The Washington Post*'s reporter declared that Israel's decision to eliminate the Hamas leader was "reckless."

In this adjective-rich zone, Brian Lilley and others note, where media organizations do things they would likely never do anywhere else, it's perhaps no surprise that anti-Israel NGOs have been relied on for information, often with results that favour actual terrorists. In April 2024, for example, Amnesty International—a long-time critic of the Jewish state—described Walid Daqqah as a "writer" who'd experienced an "endless nightmare" in an Israeli prison, and whose death from cancer was "heart-wrenching."

Left unsaid by Amnesty, and news agencies that regularly rely upon its reports, was that Daqqah had ordered the kidnapping and torture of an Israeli soldier, who was castrated and had his eyes gouged out. Daqqah's death, Amnesty International said to the media, was "a cruel reminder of Israel's disregard for Palestinians' right to life." Human Rights Watch, which is also frequently cited in reporting from the Middle East, has often been just as critical of Israel. As one former Human Rights Watch senior staffer noted, the organization was guilty of "years of politicization of its Israel–Palestine work that has frequently violated basic editorial standards related to rigor, balance, and collegiality when it comes to Israel." The organization defended its work to *The Times of Israel*, saying it applies the same standards with other topics.

Similarly, experienced journalists note, supposedly neutral databases like Wikipedia—which has a long and documented history of misinformation and disinformation because it lets anyone become one of its "editors"—are not much better. Online, anti-Israel and pro-Hamas hackers refer to their attempts to change Wikipedia entries as "e-jihad," and advertise generous rewards for those who would break into Israeli websites. The previously mentioned *Electronic Intifada* offered thousands to those who disrupted Israeli news and content. Two other groups, Wikipedians for Palestine and Wiki Project Palestine, removed content that cast Israel in a positive light. Called "vandalizing" in the Wikipedia demimonde, disinformation found in the online encyclopedia's entries would sometimes make its way into news reports written by unsuspecting and inexperienced journalists.

The Wikipedia manipulation effort was significant, some say. Around forty "editors" were involved in it after October 7, working to delegitimize Israel and depict Hamas and Islamic terrorist groups in a favourable light. The group also dropped fringe academic views on the Israel–Palestine conflict into entries, dramatically ramping up their efforts after October 7. For weeks after that date, the group was successful in getting the 1988 Hamas charter deleted from Wikipedia. They also promoted the Iranian regime in multiple entries, deleting hundreds of articles that documented human rights abuses by Hamas's benefactors in Iran.

Many other examples of sloppy or partisan journalism, Brian Lilley declares, are offered up by media organizations that profess to be neutral. They paint a picture that is unsettling. And Hamas has taken full and frequent advantage of the sloppy coverage by Western news agencies, he says.

In October 2000, when the two Israeli reservists took a wrong turn and were captured and lynched by a Palestinian mob in Ramallah, some Western media were present and reported on what happened. That evening, ABC's *World News Tonight* covered the murders. "This week, [Palestinians] are all angry at the Israelis" is how anchor Peter Jennings described the events of that day. *Teen Newsweek*, a magazine distributed to U.S. middle schools, affixed this caption to a photo of the Palestinians who killed the two reservists, holding up their hands soaked in blood: "In the West Bank city of Ramallah, bloodied Palestinians express their rage." *The Washington Post* profile later described one of the killers—the aforementioned one with red hands, famously leaning out the police station window—as a "calm, good-natured and athletic kid" when he was growing up.

In January 2022, when Palestinian Red Crescent worker Wafa Idris achieved the distinction of being the first female Palestinian suicide bomber—she blew herself up on a crowded Jerusalem street, killing herself and two Israelis—the Western media sounded anything but neutral. She was "charitable," said a writer at Agence France-Presse. "Sweet-natured," declared one at Knight Ridder. She "joked with neighborhood children," reported a writer at *The Philadelphia Inquirer*. A correspondent at *The New York Times*, meanwhile, talked about Idris's "chestnut hair curling past her shoulders," and how "she raised doves and adored children."

This sort of bad journalism isn't restricted to words alone, Lilley says. Images used by the media have considerable emotional impact, and have frequently been published in a manner that arguably serves neither Israel nor the news consumer. So, at a pro-Hamas protest in New York City, an Agence France-Presse photographer snapped a shot of a masked man wearing a Hamas headband and carrying a large Hamas flag. AFP described him as a "pro-Palestinian demonstrator." (After complaints, AFP changed the photo caption and specifically noted the pro-Hamas attire.)

By objective media standards, too much of the reporting of the ongoing conflict has been slanted, and clearly unfair to the Israeli side, says Brian Lilley. The world has often been fed a diet of "news" that reads like editorials and partisan cheerleading.

The solution, says Lilley, is simple: "Newsrooms need to get back to truth as first principle."

In the ongoing Israel–Palestine conflict, he says, that isn't happening enough. Or at all.

Almost a decade prior to the events of October 7, journalist and prize-winning book author Matti Friedman was raising concerns about the way the media—of which he was a respected and experienced member—was treating the Jewish state.

"The Western press," he wrote in *The Atlantic*, "has become less an observer of [the Jewish–Arab] conflict than an actor in it, a role with consequences for the millions of people trying to comprehend current events, including policymakers who depend on journalistic accounts to understand a region where they consistently seek, and fail, to productively intervene . . . the cumulative effect has been to create a grossly oversimplified story—a kind of modern morality play in which the Jews of Israel are displayed more than any other people on earth as examples of moral failure."

For half a decade, the Toronto-born, Jerusalem-based Friedman was a reporter and editor for the Associated Press. Since then, he's written many opinion pieces on life in Israel for *The New York Times*; more recently, he's been writing for *Tablet* magazine and The Free Press. But it was during his years with AP—from 2006 to 2011—that Friedman formed the opinion that the media wasn't serving its readers, listeners, and viewers in its reporting on Israel–Palestine.

Friedman is hardly what you'd call an ideologue, nor someone who without evidence routinely suggests that Israel is treated unfairly in the media. He's a vociferous critic of the Netanyahu government. And he offers multiple real-life examples to buttress his thesis about the approach of the press in his adopted home-land. Interviewed at his Jerusalem home office on a quiet cul-de-sac on a sunny day in mid-2025, Friedman recalls times when AP and other media made terrible errors in judgment, almost all of which seemed designed to make Israel look bad and its antago-nists in Hamas, Hezbollah, and the like look better. AP and others effectively became "amplifiers of the Hamas narrative," he says.

Such as, when Friedman says, when Israeli prime minister Ehud Olmert quietly made what was considered a bona fide peace offer to the Palestinian Authority at the end of 2008. The Palestinians had dismissed the offer, saying it wasn't enough. That may or may not have been so—but there can be no dispute, Friedman says, that the development was newsworthy. Yet AP refused to publish anything about it, even after getting clear confirmation from both the Israelis and the Palestinians. AP's narrative, Friedman recalls, was that Palestinians were peaceful and Israelis were warmongers. The Olmert story didn't fit the AP narrative, he says, so it was ignored. (Another former AP reporter, Mark Lavie, confirmed Friedman's account—which AP itself has never denied.)

Another time, Friedman wanted to quote Gerald Steinberg, head of NGO Monitor and considered the recognized expert on NGO activity that is critical of Israel and its Western alllies. Associated Press editors reportedly refused, telling Friedman that Steinberg's voice was banned at AP.

In 2011, an AP correspondent called Hamas "more tolerant" and approvingly quoted a Hamas leader who insisted that "we are not going to dictate anything to anyone." (It's unknown whether AP referenced the 1988 Hamas charter in that story, but it seems unlikely.) Around the same time, Friedman says he was told that AP wouldn't permit critical coverage of Hamas because Hamas might then kill someone at the news organization. The AP style guide, meanwhile, only describes Hamas as a "militant group."

Even when AP staff in Gaza City saw rockets fired at Israel— right beside their office located there—AP editors refused to mention it, Friedman says, shaking his head. So, too, when Hamas terrorists would crash into AP's newsroom and threaten journalists to get better coverage: AP wouldn't report that, either, he notes. (On Friedman's criticisms generally, AP released a blistering statement: "His arguments have been filled with distortions, half-truths, and inaccuracies, both about the recent Gaza war and more distant events.")

Hamas and their allies have been greatly assisted by the communications infrastructure they've built up, Friedman says. Immediately after October 7, they used their online platforms to push out political war-room-style rapid responses to news reports and promote more sophisticated-looking videos, at all hours. Power outages in Gaza don't affect them, leading many to conclude that Hamas has set up satellites in places like Iran, Lebanon, and Qatar. Most often—having been banned on X, Facebook, TikTok, and similar platforms—Hamas relies on Telegram because it offers an encrypted messaging service that doesn't censor their videos and is controlled by two billionaire Russian brothers in Dubai. The videos Hamas promotes look like they come from a Hollywood studio: with stirring soundtracks, professional animations and graphics, and even slow-motion sequences. Some of their propaganda—like most of the October 7 footage—is designed to recall single-player-shooter video games popular with young men.

Hamas's enthusiasm for state-of-the-art propaganda, online and otherwise, has paid dividends. Their communications teams mirror those found in the West, with their own public relations arms and TV and radio network, al-Aqsa, based in Gaza City. Gaza Now, Hamas's preferred Telegram channel, acquired nearly two million subscribers after October 7. The Telegram channel of the al-Qassam Brigades, Hamas's military wing, had two hundred thousand followers before the attack on Israel, but gained many times that number afterward. Its followers respond to the grisly videos with heart and salute emojis. The number of those who followed other Hamas accounts would triple or quadruple after October 7. Before the attack on that day, Hamas used bots and fake accounts to promote hashtags like #IsraeliCrimes, which experts now believe was to pre-condition its followers for October 7.

With Hamas and the rest having evolved into seasoned propagandists, Western news agencies have greatly underestimated their effectiveness, Friedman says. But it would be a mistake, he adds, to suggest that traditional news gatherers like AP are irrelevant in the era of TikTok and YouTube dominance. As Friedman wrote in his eye-opening exposé for *The Atlantic*, "The AP is like Ringo Starr, thumping away at the back of the stage: there might be flashier performers in front, and you might not always notice him, but when Ringo's off, everyone's off."

And AP were, he says. Among the journalistic class who gather at hotels in East Jerusalem to swap tales with actual terrorists, Friedman says, media disdain for Israel was widespread. "In my experience, a distaste for Israel has come to be something between an acceptable prejudice and a prerequisite for entry [among journalists and editors there]," Friedman wrote. "I don't mean a critical approach to Israeli policies or to the ham-fisted government currently in charge in the country, but a belief that to some extent the Jews of Israel are a symbol of the world's ills, particularly those connected to nationalism, militarism, colonialism, and racism—an idea quickly becoming one of the central elements of the 'progressive' Western *zeitgeist*, spreading from the European left to American college campuses and intellectuals, including journalists." AP, for its part, issued a statement calling Friedman's criticisms "false."

So, Matti Friedman moved on from AP. He doesn't sound as though he regrets his decision. Asked, however, if the news media's reduced economic circumstances played a role in AP's decisions on some stories, Friedman says no. "The staffing levels when I was at the AP were incredibly high," he says. "We had about forty full-time staffers covering Israel and the Palestinian territories. And that was more staff than the AP had at that time in India. And we had more people in Israel. We had more people in Israel, in fact, than we had in all of sub-Saharan Africa, which is fifty-something countries. The problems with coverage of Israel were acute at the time. And I don't think that the problems are necessarily related to shrinking [media budgets]. I'm not sure that the shrinking of media is one of the primary drivers of the problem."

Friedman says that one of the main reasons, as in the Human Rights Watch case, was the reliance of AP and others on NGOs, which were clearly biased themselves. "We have to fill a twenty-four-hour news cycle. And into that vacuum come political actors. Some of the political actors, in a big way, would call themselves human rights NGOs, like Human Rights Watch or Amnesty International. These are basically hard-left ideological organizations, and they have really big budgets. And they would come at us with these reports that we would then write up as stories. So, to make up for our shortfall in clout and prestige, we were increasingly relying on political activists. That was definitely going on."

And that was definitely a problem, he says, one that revealed itself in many examples of bias—and factual errors—over the years.

Death threats from Hamas and its fellow combatants were an issue too, Friedman says: the terrorist group doesn't ever hesitate to express its dissatisfaction with news stories emanating from Gaza. A death threat has the tendency to focus one's attention, he says. That doesn't excuse the poor media coverage of the region, however, even if it explains some of it.

"I can't remember the last permanent Western reporter in Gaza," Friedman says. "But I do remember there was a guy named Alan Johnston who worked for the BBC. He got kidnapped in 2007 by the Army of Islam. It was about that time that basically no one wanted to do coverage out of Gaza anymore, and so coverage moved almost entirely into the hands of Palestinians who live in Gaza. So, the AP bureau in Gaza—and I know people imagine it's seven guys from Wisconsin working away at their typewriters—but it's just Palestinians. The entire bureau is Palestinian. And you learn there are two kinds of people in Gaza: there are people who are afraid of Hamas—quite reasonably, I would be afraid of Hamas, too. And then there are people who actually work for Hamas. And that means that any information you're getting out of Gaza is basically dictated by Hamas."

Johnston was held for 114 days. On one occasion, a video of him wearing an explosive belt was released, and he said it would be detonated if anyone tried to rescue him. His captors told him more than once that they planned to kill him. They tortured him. When he was finally handed over to Hamas for release, his own employer—BBC—still doggedly refused to call Hamas a terrorist group. They were "militants," BBC reported. That is "our longstanding position," BBC's World Affairs editor has decreed—Hamas will not be called a terrorist group without attribution.

Since then, Friedman says, matters have gotten markedly worse. The coverage of casualties in Gaza after October 7, he says, is a prime example. "War is not a soccer match," he says, sounding exasperated. "It's not a numbers game. But too many journalists are swayed by the casualty numbers." He pauses. "The number of Palestinians being killed is awful and horrific. That's the only way to look at it. . . . But it's also true that Hamas has smart people running their [propaganda campaign]. And they are constantly being underestimated in the West. Israel, meanwhile, has been very clumsy in its communications efforts."

He adds: "I think things have become much more extreme. Absolutely. I mean, threatening people with death if they cross you [in a news story] is a pretty effective way of keeping people on message, isn't it?

"These Arab countries are not democracies. It's not just Gaza—it's also the West Bank, where you'll find that Palestinians, whether for reasons of ideology or just pure fear—they just won't flout the Hamas line. And, in the case of Gaza, I again completely understand it. I mean, if I were a stringer in Gaza, I would also be doing what Hamas told me to do, because the alternatives are pretty bad."

Friedman continues. "But there's no excuse for Western news organizations based outside Gaza playing along with this and not informing their readers [about the threats]. I mean, at the AP, really, it was very striking. In 2009 and 2010 we were basically having our coverage dictated by Hamas, with threats—explicit or implicit—against our staff in Gaza. And then, at the same time, we're running these stories telling people that Hamas was actually becoming more moderate and ready to assume the responsibilities of government!"

Those serious journalistic lapses weren't just a problem at Associated Press, Friedman says. "The conclusion with which I left the Western press, and AP, is that the biggest news organization in the world wasn't an outlier. And so a lot of it couldn't be trusted."

In recent years, and since October 7, the anti-Israel media bias has gotten worse, he says. "The new news people are activists. Their goal is not to explain what's going on, but to move people toward the correct political conclusion, like in a political campaign. So they choose the facts that they think may be true—but they certainly won't present facts that contradict their political leanings.

"And that's all very legitimate if you are an activist. But it's not legitimate if you're a journalist."

Not all share Matti Friedman's views, however. Noam Sheizaf is one—and he's dismissive of the claim that Israel is being treated unfairly in the media. To Sheizaf, Israel mostly deserves all the criticism it gets.

"Israel doesn't have a public relations problem," says Sheizaf in a Tel Aviv interview, above a bar where a suicide bomber killed scores of Israelis a few years before. "We have a reality problem. The suffering of the Palestinians is enormous, and it is visible to the naked eye. You can drive twenty minutes from this spot and see a refugee camp that has been bombed. It's horrifying and disgusting."

He acknowledges that in Israel his views, and his journalism, place him in a minority. He shrugs about that. "For me, it's very easy," he says. "I'm surrounded by a society that always tells me I'm too pro-Palestinian. I have to check myself all the time. But, as a journalist, I need to figure out what is bullshit, and what isn't."

The discussion turns to *hasbara*, which in Hebrew is defined as "explaining." A journalist's job, Sheizaf says, is to explain. But explaining what's happening in Israel—and in Palestine, he says—is very clear-cut.

"It's a cold war on steroids." Sheizaf sounds irritated. "There is a siege mentality here now. There has been a spiral downward into victimization within Israeli society. We don't consider ourselves supported anywhere."

As a journalist, a documentary filmmaker, and the founder of the left-leaning +972 magazine, Sheizaf is (clearly) a strong critic of the government of Benjamin Netanyahu, but also of Israel's treatment of Palestinians. He has strong opinions—unpopular opinions, he says, in the country. He advocates for human rights, and he refers to Israel's presence in some disputed places as an occupation. But, perhaps most of all, Sheizaf is an Israeli journalist who is truly independent.

He has always favoured peace, he says, and true reconciliation with Palestinians, many of whom he counts as close friends. He acknowledges that the atrocities of October 7 had a profound impact on everyone, however, peace-seeking Israelis included. "October 7 was a defining moment. In my circles, I know . . . it was impossible not to know someone who lost a relative, someone who had been there.

"People here are now confused. And, since October 7, they are deeply traumatized . . . we [in Israel] are stuck. We don't know what to do. Our narrative has lost its way."

The attack by Hamas greatly reduced the number of Israelis who sympathized with the plight of Palestinians, too. At the same time, Israelis came to regard themselves differently as well. Says Sheizaf: "We started to consider ourselves as victims." He shakes his head. "We've become obsessed with our own pain."

In his journalism as well as in his celebrated documentary *The Occupation Lab*—about H2, the only Jewish settlement in Palestinian territory—Sheizaf rejects left–right and us–them dichotomies as an explanation for what's happening in Israel today. It's facile, he says. That is what has gotten Israel into so much difficulty in the past.

"There's this simplistic hostile narrative, for Israelis but also Palestinians," he says, "but we have to understand that any humanization of Israelis has to be accompanied by a humanization of

Palestinians, too." In Israel, governmental and mainstream media institutions mostly aren't interested in that, he acknowledges.

Even so, as a writer, he says he will not accept the Netanyahu government's preferred narratives about the war against Hamas, or about Israel itself. "It's gotten us to a very dangerous place," he says. He concludes: "I believe in this country. I believe in its people. And I believe our future is together, with Palestinians.

"We've got to live together."

Al-Qaeda leader and 9/11 mastermind Ayman al-Zawahiri was a killer and a liar, but one thing he said could be supported by voices as diverse as Matti Friedman and Noam Sheizaf: "We are in a battle, and more than half of this battle is taking place in the battlefield of the media."

Along with social media influencers within Gaza and the Arab world, Hamas is greatly assisted by a large and professional news operation. But unlike its Israeli counterparts, Hamas's media properties are not permitted to show public expressions of dissent. Only one point of view gets communicated, as Friedman and others note, and it's the one favoured by Hamas. The terrorist group now has no shortage of platforms to push out its singular message. And it has Western-trained spokesmen and spin doctors who can speak English and many other Western languages.

There's the Hamas website, Hamas.info, and also the much-viewed news platform palinfo.com ("Palestinian Information Center"), which offers pro-Hamas news in multiple languages—English, Arabic, French, Russian, Turkish, Urdu, Farsi, and even Malaysian—reaching millions of potential supporters in predominantly Muslim countries. Hamas also maintains multiple

Arab-language sites, such as Felasteen, Shehab, Safa, and Alresalah, most of which are active online.

As they do with their social media platforms, Hamas segments its coverage according to different audiences. Shehab broadcasts to younger Palestinians. Their counterparts at Felasteen and Alresalah offer more comprehensive news commentary, all with a pro-Hamas slant. Hamas also have a television and radio network, al-Aqsa in Gaza, which dominates in Gaza and the West Bank. Despite the differing audiences, the Hamas media outlets don't ever stray from the governing party's line. Hamas is much more advanced than that, say long-time Israeli intelligence sources: "They know how to use international platforms."

The complicated relationship between online "news" and traditional journalism is easily seen in the coverage of the Israel–Hamas war around the globe. Because traditional media too often now lack the resources, and because, as both Friedman and Sheizaf note, neither side has permitted journalists or observers to enter the war zone, and finally because editors generally consider the Middle East story to be a reliable ratings winner, media often make uncritical use of untrained, unaccountable online "journalists" in Gaza and the West Bank. It has not left media audiences well served, Friedman says.

Neutral studies on mainstream media coverage of the Israel–Palestine conflict are surprisingly few, and those that do exist are limited. But all tend to document media unfairness as it pertains to the Israeli side. The Jerusalem College of Technology's Avi Rosenfeld, for example, authored a study on "user and news bias" in the 2023–2024 Hamas–Israel war using what's called natural language processing (NLP) of media reports—essentially, using computers to comprehend and interpret human language. (Google

Translate is an example of NLP technology at work, in that it takes the words of one language and substitutes them with the words of another language.)

Rosenfeld looked at thousands of Israeli and Palestinian news sources, online and off, and found dramatically dissimilar approaches to the same events. "Differences in whether Hamas had fighters, activists, terrorists or no mention at all about their actions on October 7 all indicate bias," Rosenfeld wrote. "Although Hamas is widely considered a terrorist group by many countries, we found that pro-Palestinian outlets rarely referred to their actions, and instead focused on the suffering of non-combatant Palestinians. Even the name of this conflict differs in the media. What is often referred to as the 'Hamas–Israel' war in Western outlets like CNN and Sky News is referred to as the 'War on Gaza' by Al Jazeera.

"Our thesis is that this difference is intentional and not trivial, and it highlights their implicit bias that this war is not a fight against terrorists but against all Gazan citizens."

Rosenfeld's news content analysis revealed that certain words, like *Gaza* or *Israel*, show up almost as often on both sides of the divide. There the similarities end, however. The words *genocide* and *ceasefire* were seen less often in Israeli reports—while the words *Hamas*, *hostages*, *terrorist*, *kidnap*, and *October* 7 were seen much more. The pro-Palestinian word clouds emphasized *Palestine*, *Palestinian*, *hospital*, *bombardment*, *airstrike*, and *genocide*. Those words appear in Israeli reports, too, but not as frequently; on the Israeli side, *Hamas, hostage, deal, release,* and *October* 7 were the most common. The pro-Israel media, Rosenfeld noted, was focused on Hamas's kidnapping of hostages on October 7, and the resulting desire for a hostage deal to gain their release. The

Palestinian side was focused on a ceasefire without any mention whatsoever of hostages, Hamas, or October 7.

When Rosenfeld and his colleagues examined bias within individual Western news agencies, some organizations did better than others. "The BBC and RT (formerly Russia Today) were deemed to be classified more . . . pro-Palestinian." CNN and the *Telegraph* were found to be slightly more favourable to Israel—with Sky News and Fox News being the most positive. As Rosenfeld put it, "There seems to be a correlation between political orientation (e.g., anti-Western and left-leaning) and conflict coverage, almost to an obsessive level."

Donald Trump has infamously denounced journalism he dislikes as "fake news." At his campaign rallies, he's called the media "among the most dishonest people on earth." Regrettably, many news consumers now agree. Around the time of the Watergate scandal, trust in the media was at 72 per cent. It is now half that, or less. For those engaged in the propagation of lies and misinformation—as Hamas and their axis now clearly are—that media trust gap is highly beneficial. News consumers are now much more willing to accept "news" from terrorist organizations, says Matti Friedman and others, as well as from Iran, China, or Russia, as long as it reinforces their own biases and beliefs.

Khaled Hassan, the Egyptian-born Muslim who converted to Judaism and is now an analyst of foreign policy and media policy, says the fake news problem is traditionally even more pronounced in the Middle East, and particularly since October 7, 2023. "What we're facing is media outlets, across the West and the Arab world—with the assistance of Russia and others—who are predominantly willing to accept the Hamas narrative," Hassan says. "It is a well-established fact."

In September 2024, following several months of research, Hassan released the results of analysis done on stories produced by the BBC's Arabic service. These results were disturbing to many. Out of 160 randomly selected interviews quoted by the BBC, 45 had what Hassan calls reportable affiliations to Hamas or Palestinian Islamic Jihad. Fully 14 were found to be directly tied to Hamas. None of the affiliations were disclosed by the BBC, however—instead, the interviewees were presented as neutral observers and commentators. Says Hassan: "BBC Arabic is an excellent service . . . for representing the views of a society that supports Hamas. This is not okay." (Contacted for comment, the BBC Press Office acknowledged receiving this writer's questions about Khaled's claims—but did not provide any answers.)

Others have attempted to analyze the media coverage of the Israel–Hamas war, endeavouring to be as objective as they could. In July 2024, for instance, the media analysis firm Betaworks reviewed coverage of Israeli military actions in the war and their corresponding treatment in the media. They quickly identified a cluster of pro-Palestinian reports coming from a number of Western mainstream and left-leaning sources. Major media organizations and official UN accounts were also clustered near the pro-Palestinian side.

That, Betaworks said, meant that those embedded within the pro-Palestinian side were "interacting far more with mainstream media Twitter accounts than pro-Israel ones." As Betawork's chief of data analytics Gilad Lotan put it when analyzing his firm's data, "The cluster of bloggers, journalists and international media entities is closely connected with [a] group of pro-Palestinian activists, which means that information is much more likely to spread amongst the two." The result, Lotan noted dryly, "reinforces general Israeli sentiment regarding international media bias"—namely, that international media are unfair to the Jewish state.

Reporters Without Borders concluded in their Press Freedom Index in 2023 that Hamas-run Palestine ranks only slightly above Russia for press freedom, but around the same level as Cuba and Iraq. As Reporters Without Borders has said, "Both Hamas and Fatah run roughshod over press freedom and arrest journalists without justification . . . Hamas has become a real press freedom predator." Notwithstanding that, many Western media still rely on Hamas and its allied organizations for information.

Hassan nods when asked about the reception received by studies such as his. "I get that sort of thing: 'You're a Mossad agent. You work for the Israelis. You make money out of this work.' None of that is true.

"To me," says Hassan, "that is an indication of how successful [Hamas, etc.] have been in their propaganda campaign. They've changed the foundations of the narrative. They've changed the foundations of the discourse to basically intimidate people and prevent them from stating the obvious, which is that the media are behaving in a terribly destructive manner. And we are entitled to be critical of that."

Within newsrooms across the West, the anti-Israel tilt was affecting readers, listeners, and viewers. But reporters and editors were affected, too. Canada's taxpayer-subsidized broadcaster, the Canadian Broadcasting Corporation, provides an interesting case study.

For example, the CBC has refused to call Hamas terrorists what they are, which is terrorists; they have routinely accepted Israel–Hamas war casualty counts that come from Hamas; and they have established a secretive internal group—"Middle East

2023"—to oversee coverage of Israel, leaving Jewish CBC journalists saying they feel isolated and victimized. As one Jewish
former senior producer said in an interview about the CBC's treatment of the Jewish state, "It's extremely one-sided and is only
leading to more misinformation and hatred towards the Jewish
community in Canada." The chief CBC spokesman refused comment, saying only, "Respectfully, whatever meetings or sessions
we may be having with employees are just that, they're internal."

Since the attack on October 7, Jewish reporters and editors
currently employed at the CBC will only speak on the condition
that they're not named, saying that the problem has grown worse.
To cite just one example, a writer and producer for CBC's digital
team had repeatedly come to work in the Toronto newsroom
wearing a keffiyeh—and, more significantly, had posted online
that Israel is "an oppressive, destructive" country and "you're a
vile human being if you still defend or excuse Israel." Employees
who complained to CBC bosses were told to mind their own
business. CBC's spokesman, Chuck Thompson, said the news
organization does not police its employees' social media.

The pervasive antisemitism at the taxpayer-supported network left another respected CBC journalist feeling marginalized.
Said the reporter, speaking on condition of anonymity: "Many
of us Jewish journalists have spent our entire careers committed
to fairness and making sure that the work we put out is balanced,
and that it's backed up by journalistic ethics. And what we've
seen within the last number of years is a pivot within the CBC
from journalism to activism." A closer look at the CBC coverage
seems to support this view.

In the lead-up to the first anniversary of the October 7 attack,
the CBC promoted a man it called its "eyes and ears" in Gaza,

Mohamed El Saife, who it paid to work as a videographer. An extensive essay about El Saife was posted on the main CBC website on the first anniversary of October 7. On that same day, a flattering profile of him was broadcast on CBC's main news programs, on both CBC News Network and its main network. What El Saife had published on his social media was left unreported by the CBC, however.

It was relevant, say the Jewish journalists employed by CBC. El Saife had said "Israel"—he put the Jewish state's name in quotation marks, perhaps to suggest that it's a fiction—has an "occupation army that violates the dignity of the bodies of martyrs." He also accused Israel of deliberately "massacring" citizens in the Gazan city of Khan Yunis, and published an AI-generated image of monstrous-looking weapons-toting IDF troops chasing a Palestinian child wearing wings.

Clearly, some of its own reporters say on condition of anonymity, the CBC has a problem with anti-Israel bias. But it's not alone. Jewish reporters and editors say they're being targeted or stigmatized at other news organizations throughout the West. Documenting the extent of the bias and the unfairness became important to those reporters and editors. So, Trevor Asserson stepped forward to provide hard evidence.

Asserson is an experienced litigator, an Oxford-trained scholar, and an award-winning member of the bar in both Israel and the U.K. In the fall of 2024, he released a report on the British Broadcasting Corporation that found "a deeply worrying pattern of bias and multiple breaches by the BBC of its own editorial guidelines on impartiality, fairness and establishing the truth."

Asserson and a team of data scientists and lawyers, carefully selected for their objectivity, examined nine million words produced by the BBC across television, radio, the web, and podcasts in the weeks following October 7. They found an "overwhelming disparity in the perception of the two sides, with sympathy for Palestinians vastly outstripping sympathy for Israelis, even shortly after the massacre of October 7th, 2023."

Key findings of the Asserson report included revelations that the BBC's major TV newscasts favoured the Palestine/Hamas side more than 90 per cent of the time, and that BBC web stories favoured the Palestine/Hamas side nearly twice as much as the Israeli side. In addition, Asserson detailed how the BBC accused Israel of war crimes 592 times—and Hamas only 98 times. Its Arabic service, he noted, even broadcast Hamas propaganda videos, and some there expressed sympathy for the terror group. (When the BBC received the report, they swiftly announced that they would look into Asserson's findings. They later said they strongly questioned Asserson's methodology.)

Hamas terrorism was consistently downplayed, the study's authors concluded, and Israel's "aggression" was repeatedly emphasized by the BBC. As a result, Asserson says, the BBC's reporting was found to have breached its own policies for impartiality, accuracy, editorial values, and public interest no fewer than 1,553 times in the four-month, post–October 7 period examined. The group's research showed that Hamas was described as a terrorist organization just 409 out of 12,459 times—only 3.2 per cent of the time during that four-month period.

In a wide range of BBC reports, the term *war crimes* was associated with Israel 127 times, but with Hamas only 30 times. Israel was tagged with the word *genocide* 283 times—but with Hamas only 19 times. *Breach of international law*, too, was associated with Israel in BBC news reports 167 times—and with Hamas only 27 times.

The results of his review were disturbing, Asserson agrees, adding that publicly supported broadcasters like the BBC and the CBC need to be held to different standards than private broadcasters. "Israel is being reported on by media organizations that have authority [and that are] obliged to be impartial. So people therefore assume they are." But they're often not—and that bias needs to be challenged, he says.

"I'm less interested in private broadcasters being very anti-Israel or very pro-Israel, because they're allowed to be. They don't get any public money. You can just switch them off and watch something else. I believe in freedom of speech."

Concludes Trevor Asserson: "But I don't believe that a public body that's obliged to be impartial should be allowed to get away with unfairness."

It's well known that traditional media platforms like newspapers—as well as TV and radio news—are in steep economic decline, mainly because of the loss of advertising to online sources. This downturn has been going on for a while, with long-established media migrating to online channels, some with more success than others. Some have simply gone out of business.

Online news is faster than the old ways of reporting, and much more competitive. The internet is awake 24/7, with millions of news and opinion channels for people to choose from. So news reporting isn't nearly as profitable as it once was, meaning that media organizations are trying to cover fast-moving stories with fewer resources while hoping not to get scooped by online outlets, many of which don't observe traditional journalistic standards regarding facts and ethics.

Foreign correspondents, one 2008 analysis observed, have become a vanishing breed. And Israel has been hurt by this change in the news business arguably more than most. Traditional news bureaus have shut down, leaving "reporting" to partisans and the inexperienced.

Whenever there's a crisis in Israel, the ranks of international media can grow to the thousands. It does not attempt to censor what they write or broadcast from within Israel. But those who are posted to cover the latest crisis, as many were after October 7, frequently lack knowledge about the intricacies of the ongoing Israel–Palestine conflict—a lack that too often reveals itself in their coverage. The result is a "meagre one-dimensional news product" that reflects "pack journalism," observed Martin Kalb, the legendary *Meet the Press* host.

Coverage of the October 7 Hamas attack on Israel perhaps demonstrates why. "Networks have been scrambling" to cover the aftermath of the massacre, *The Washington Post* admitted after the attack, noting that news agencies simply did not have enough reporters and editors on the ground in Israel to cover the story. So, when Israel commenced its ground incursion into Gaza weeks after October 7, no major news organization had a presence there. As Matti Friedman noted, "The press has been gutted. The bureaus have shrunk, and into that vacuum have come ideological voices."

Other problems abound. There are the physical dangers in reporting from a war zone. As well, reporters have to contend with being denied physical access to that war zone by Israel, Hamas, and Egypt. The power goes out; infrastructure is limited. And in the Israel–Hamas war, "embedded" reporters also have to contend with wartime censors on both sides.

All of this—threats from terrorists, economic pressure, fewer experienced correspondents, online competitors without training or transparency—has combined to create an environment rife with misinformation (false or inaccurate information) and disinformation (deliberately false and inaccurate information). In 2023 and 2024, the Israel–Hamas war was one of the biggest news stories in the world, quickly eclipsing other conflicts like the war between Russia and Ukraine. But to cover that story news organizations had to make a Faustian bargain, Matti Friedman and others say: they started using locals—"stringers," as they are known—to file words and pictures about the war.

In too many cases, critics like Friedman say, it was a serious mistake. The reports being generated by these untrained, unsupervised freelancers were often neither objective nor accurate. In some cases, the news organizations became conduits for propaganda coming directly from Hamas, some critics say. Hassan Eslaiah, to cite just one example, was a freelancer who supplied CNN, *The New York Times*, and Agence France-Presse with photographs. He was later revealed to be a close friend of Yahya Sinwar, the now-deceased supreme Hamas commander who planned the October 7 massacre. A photo of the pair circulated online, with Sinwar planting a kiss on a smiling Eslaiah's cheek. Photos taken by Eslaiah, since deleted, showed him side by side with Hamas while the October 7 attack was still underway. Red-faced Western news agencies scrambled to fire him.

Another example: an AP stringer, Issam Adwan, posted support for Hamas online, writing "the Palestinian revolt against the Israeli oppression will be a triumph." Initially, the Associated Press did not terminate him, however. Yet another stringer, Fayq Abu Mustafa, was seen laughing in a video as a Palestinian mob lynched an Israeli soldier at a breach in the Gaza border on October 7. Meanwhile, two Al Jazeera stringers were killed in fighting in Gaza; both were shown to be members of Hamas. AP issued a statement about their Gaza-based freelancers, saying, "AP uses images taken by freelancers around the world. When we accept freelance photos, we take great steps to verify the authenticity of the images and that they show what is purported. The role of the AP is to gather information on breaking news events around the world, wherever they happen, even when those events are horrific and cause mass casualties." AP no longer works with the freelancers.

The fact that neither Israel nor Hamas gives media access to the battlefield increased reliance on such freelancers, often with little to no editorial oversight. Errors and disinformation quickly became widespread, media critics have noted. For example, in March 2024, Qatari-owned Al Jazeera reported that Israeli soldiers had raped and then killed women in the al-Shifa Hospital. The story was made up, however. It had only one source, and she later admitted that her story was entirely fictional. Al Jazeera was forced to retract: "The woman who spoke about rape justified her exaggeration and incorrect talk by saying that the goal was to arouse the nation's fervour and brotherhood." It was not much of an apology given that the damage had been done, some said.

Hamas controls the media narrative by regularly denying reporters access, Matti Friedman and others observe. It controls it, too, by flooding the landscape with misinformation and disinformation. And, as Friedman and others can attest, it exercises media control with actual threats.

But Hamas excels in other media-control strategies as well. Cyabra's vice-president, Rafi Mendelsohn, describes two: using social media content to legitimize favourable news reports and carefully scheduling military attacks to achieve maximum news coverage. The Israel-based cyber watchdog found plenty of evidence of both types of manipulation on October 7, 2023.

Says Mendelsohn: "Telegram was the destination for the content of the GoPros that Hamas were carrying on October 7 and for the recordings they wanted to pump out. So, news crews and TV crews picked up on that, and they started covering it. And then the fake accounts Cyabra uncovered would take the clips and re-broadcast them. Here's an example: Al Jazeera was covering an interaction between a hostage and a terrorist that had been recorded on the camera of the terrorist and then published on Telegram. That video wasn't AI. It was just simply cut, so only a portion of that video was shown, and that portion of the video was the hostage interacting with the terrorists. It didn't show any aggression. They posted it to say: 'Look at how we are interacting with each other and speaking to each other. Look at our compassion and humanity. Look at the way we are looking after the hostages.'

"And that's an incredibly powerful and successful technique because when you see it later on CNN or BBC or Al Jazeera, right, you're seeing the same footage. But you might not realize, at that point, that the video has been edited and that the narrative accompanying the video is completely false. It takes a level of sophistication to run a successful disinformation campaign like that. That tactic involved monitoring, editing, deciding what the narrative is, and then distributing that amongst thousands of fake social media accounts in a matter of hours. You can't plan that weeks ahead because you don't know what the footage is going to be. So that's very powerful and very effective media manipulation."

The other way Hamas have dominated news coverage comes from their understanding of how Western media organizations work—most particularly, that if it bleeds, it leads. Journalists are drawn to conflict, and will always focus on conflict. Hamas knows this, Mendelsohn says.

He cites a tactic that terrorist groups mainly in Gaza have used for years, marvelling at how successful they've been. "This is one of those moments where you have to give credit where credit's due," he says, emphasizing that he's speaking only for himself and not Cyabra. "Hamas understands media schedules. So, for example, there are sometimes quieter periods—let's put that in quotation marks—between Gaza and Israel. When those periods of calm happen, occasional barrages of rockets would come from Gaza into Israeli territory. And they would happen a few minutes, or within half an hour, of the evening news. And so in Israel, the attack would always make the evening news. And that would form part of their psychological warfare—even on New Year's Eve. On New Year's Eve, Hamas will launch a barrage of rockets exactly, precisely at midnight.

"And that was to achieve two things," he says. "One, yes, we have the capability to attack you whenever we want. And two, the news stories will be that Israelis were ringing in the New Year, at exactly midnight, with rocket attacks. It was a stark reminder of their media effectiveness.

"It shows their appreciation for the importance of the media narrative."

The media image that is most difficult to forget is found on a bed at the kibbutz called Nir Oz.

It is a child's clothing, fresh out of the laundry: a stack of tiny, carefully folded underwear, toddler-sized, placed on the corner of a bed. The child's clothing is covered in ash and dust and dirt, as if frozen in time. There's a Cookie Monster shirt, and what looks like some little dresses. All unused, all untouched since October 7.

The room that it's in resembles the inside of a long-unattended pizza oven—blackened and blistered from the Hamas attack. Bits and pieces of a former life are seen everywhere: broken dishes, a melted television, charred children's toys.

No shell casings or bodies can be seen. Those are long gone. But dozens of people were slaughtered in Nir Oz, some still in their beds. Children, as well. More than seventy were taken hostage. In the abandoned homes of the four hundred people who once lived there, visitors wonder if the shadows on the walls and the floors are bloodstains.

Months later, and at an undisclosed location, the Son of Hamas shakes his head, recalling what happened at Nir Oz and the other kibbutzim. Early in 2024, he travelled to the farming communities destroyed by Hamas. He will never forget it, he says.

"It's a tragedy," says Mosab Hassan Yousef when asked about Nir Oz and Gaza. "It's a tragic situation. First of all, we have to acknowledge that what is happening [in Gaza] is a tragedy, too. The collateral damage is huge—even though the numbers have been faked. But this is the first time in modern history that we see a war on social media—where people are being killed, butchered, annihilated by mobs. We have never experienced this before. Even in World War II, people died but not everybody saw it." He pauses, his dark eyes scanning the wall.

"It's understandable to oppose war. We don't want to take that away. People should oppose war—it's not a natural state.

But now? Hamas is capitalizing on the tragedy. They had a sense of how the public was going to respond, and that there would be public pressure on Israel to surrender. And they've succeeded this time. Their violence has become legitimized—and they are getting global recognition as a resistance movement."

The former Hamas member shakes his head in disgust. The media, he says, have much to account for. In many cases, he adds, their coverage has been complicit in the information war of Hamas and its axis.

"Son of Hamas" isn't a name that most would accept willingly, but Mosab Hassan Yousef does. Because that's what he literally is: the first son of Sheikh Hassan Yousef, one of the men who helped create the terrorist organization in 1987. Yousef was the eldest son, and therefore always expected to embrace Hamas and its methods—which he did. In 1988, he was arrested for throwing rocks at Israelis. He was just ten years old. From the start, he was groomed to one day lead the organization, which by the 1990s had devolved into what Yousef now calls "death culture."

As a young man, he enthusiastically embraced Hamas's dogma of hate, and was imprisoned because of it. But it was in those Israeli prisons that he started to turn against the murderous ideology of his father. He had witnessed men being tortured and killed by Hamas for being collaborators. Few, if any, were. Their innocence did not matter to Hamas, which he says regards all human life—Jew or Muslim—as subordinate to the establishment of a global Islamist caliphate. One built in a house of blood, he says, atop the corpses of Jews and non-believers.

In 1996, Yousef agreed to become an informant for Israel's Shin Bet. He told the Israeli intelligence agency that he'd help them if they jailed terrorists and didn't simply kill them. Shin

Bet agreed. Befitting his lineage, he was given the code name Green Prince, and would ultimately be credited with saving the lives of hundreds of civilians, Israeli and Palestinian.

Not long after he started to inform on Hamas, a missionary gave Yousef a Bible. A year later, he quietly became a Christian. He now lives somewhere in the United States, where he's been accepted as a refugee—but where he must remain in hiding to avoid being assassinated. He can never return to the place of his birth, where his father has renounced him, and where many have pledged to kill him. He travels now with an army of private security, speaking about Hamas and trying to alert Western audiences to its propaganda campaign. Which, he says, has been wildly successful, particularly with Western media.

"It's not just propaganda," Yousef says. "It's indoctrination. It's ideology. Hamas relies on systematic indoctrination in order to create these very strong individuals who will actually fight to the death. Their training is sophisticated."

So, too, their media effort. Says Yousef, "This is where people need to pay attention. [Hamas's media manipulation] attracts the masses to a false idea of heroism, freedom, fighting and sacrifice. . . . It's very, very sophisticated."

The effectiveness of Hamas's media effort is readily seen among young people in the West, he agrees. But experienced journalists have fallen under the spell of Hamas, too. "This is what the West is buying into. The claim that Muslims are the actual owners of the Holy Land, not the Jewish people," says Yousef. "So, when you have 1.6 billion believers of this false version of history, via their [media] machine, it becomes true to a certain degree. Hundreds of millions of people repeating the media narrative that this is Palestinian land, this is Islamic land.

"It's the big lie," he says. "Hamas have nothing to their side of the argument. No facts at all. But they have a media narrative—which the majority of people are now repeating. And they are winning."

Atrocities like the ones that happened at Nir Oz, he concludes, are going to happen again if the West doesn't wake up and if the media continue to present a version of reality that is wrong.

"Hamas," says Yousef, "should not be in power. They should not decide the destiny and future of humanity, and the future of Palestinians. But that is what they want.

"If we do not go after them," he concludes, "they are going to come after all of us."

FIVE

FOLLOW THE MONEY

Following the money is Garon Amuk's job.

Anonymity is essential if a discussion about the funding of extremism and terrorism is to take place. So, the Hebrew synonym is suggested, which roughly translates to Deep Throat.

The source is a very senior operative within Israel's intelligence firmament. Along with a group of others at Mossad (Israel's foreign intelligence agency) and Shin Bet (the country's internal intelligence service), Garon Amuk has followed the money for years—preventing terror attacks and disrupting the economies of Hamas, Hezbollah, and their allied terrorist organizations.

"Iran is the greatest funder of extremism, of terrorism," he says. "And what's interesting about Iran, even though it is a Shiite state, is that they are indifferent about who they are funding." As long as it harms Israel and Israel's allies in the West, Amuk says, Iran will usually fund it. That is happening with Hamas (which is Sunni) and Hezbollah (which is Shia), he adds, and with multiple anti-Israel groups in the West.

"They are funding all of the Muslim Brotherhood (allied) organizations, yes," says Amuk. "So, whatever they can do to support terrorism, or support extremism, they will do. Iran is always there, either directly or indirectly."

Qatar is the oil-rich country that many allege is the main banker for Hamas—having provided a home base for much of the terrorist group's leadership. The source is asked: Does Iran fund all the anti-Israel agitation and extremism, or does Qatar contribute as well? Garon Amuk muses. "I'm hesitant to talk about Qatar," he says, "because Israel has discussions with Qatar."

After a pause, he continues. "I can say that Iran funds the extremists [in the West]. But what is the why? It is not necessarily for terrorism. It's not always designated as terrorism. What we [in Israel] are obviously very focused on is terrorism, and terrorist-funding channels." Iran is funding anti-Israel, antisemitic, and anti-Western protests, groups, and extremism, he says. And Israel is limited in what it can do about that extremism and antisemitism: "If they are not officially sanctioned [by a state], we can't act." They are "sanctioned" when shown to be funding terrorism. Not extremism.

But as other contacts within the Israeli government make clear, Israel is gravely concerned about what is happening online, in the streets, in academia, and within NGOs. Extremism is widespread, they say, because of a well-resourced propaganda campaign in Europe and North America. And extremism, if left unchecked, often leads to radicalization and then acts of terror, Amuk notes. As on October 7.

Over two decades, Amuk says, Israel has developed intelligence strategies to follow the money flowing into the coffers of Hamas and Hezbollah and the like, and to choke it off. Often, he says, Israeli intelligence receive a surprising degree of cooperation from Western banking institutions and state agencies.

Amuk explains: "When there is a sanction [issued by Israel for terrorism], we present it to the financial institution. They can then act upon it. They can explain [to the target] that they don't want to do business with someone Israel is sanctioning. But when it comes to the extremists, not the terrorists, if you want to effectively deal with it, you have to sanction the entire funding chain. You don't have to sanction the extremists directly, but you can find the one who pays them, right? Such as Iran. They are the ones who transfer the money, who use the wire services, the banks. [They are] the ones which hold the accounts, and so on. So, that is one way of stopping extremism."

Israel has successfully done so in the past, Amuk continues. The benefits are obvious. "You don't have to necessarily go to Iran in order to stop [the funding of propaganda and extremism]. For instance, if Iran uses a company or uses an agent, and this agent uses additional agents, or transfers money to a few financial institutions? Then sanctioning their agents will not only stop Iran's efforts, but also has a deterrent effect on others. And this is why the sanctions are very effective, with either terrorism or extremism.

"One way or another, we get the solution that we want."

One of Israel's most successful efforts against the funding of terror and extremism was called Operation Harpoon. Harpoon was secretly set up by Mossad, Shin Bet, and other Israeli government intelligence operatives in 1995. It was led by Israeli counterterrorism legend Meir Dagan, who told his peers at the time that cash fuelled the suicide bomber machine. Harpoon would become a means to disrupt and destroy the financing of terrorism, Dagan believed. So Dagan and Harpoon operatives took down Hezbollah-connected institutions like the Lebanese Canadian Bank, which held $5 billion in accounts controlled by terrorist groups. After 9/11, Harpoon's successes attracted the interest and support of the CIA and the FBI, who recognized that they too needed to eliminate terrorist financial networks.

Asked about Operation Harpoon, Amuk is modest. "What was Harpoon? Harpoon was five people. They would approach financial institutions abroad and provide them with intelligence and ask them to do whatever they saw as appropriate. That was Harpoon. The effect of Harpoon was not so big. If they had information on some guy in a certain country, they would approach a financial institution and say, 'Look, this is the information that we have. He's connected to terrorism.' And wait for a response."

Given the huge sums that were still pouring into the accounts of Hamas, Hezbollah, and their axis, financial institutions were too often willing to look the other way in exchange for enormous service fees, he says. So, at the urging of Amuk and a few others, Harpoon was moved to the Ministry of Defense in Israel—and equipped with the power to issue enforceable sanctions against individuals and organizations. And even though the sanctions were being issued by little Israel, Amuk says, laughing, other countries paid attention. Like former Israeli intelligence officer Avi Melamed, Amuk emphasizes that many Arab and Muslim countries oppose terrorism and radicalization.

"I know how things work, and I know that financial institutions abroad—even in Muslim countries, and with law enforcement agencies abroad—will respect Israeli sanctions. So we started applying Israeli sanctions on the basis of our anti-terrorism laws. . . . Now, in the U.S., in European countries—even in Turkey, in the Emirates, and in the East—our sanctions are respected." That is because the intelligence the Israelis share is always backed by hard evidence, according to Amuk.

The fact that other countries are cooperating with Israel's

efforts to stop the financing of terrorism, he says, is the good news. The bad news, he adds, is that the beneficiaries of funding—the extremists and propagandists, mostly in the West—are still benefiting. Moreover, the sums ending up in their hands are significant, and largely beyond the reach of Israeli sanctions because it doesn't meet the dictionary definition of "terrorism."

Garon Amuk concludes: "We see the [propaganda] funding—globally or community funding—is much, much greater since October 7. We see it in Hamas, we see it with the PFLP [Popular Front for the Liberation of Palestine], we see it with Hezbollah, and with other such organizations.

"And the money, if you follow it, is getting through."

Gerald Steinberg also follows the money, but in a different way. He works with what is mostly in plain view, however, and then shares the results for all to see.

He's a professor, sixtyish, with an easygoing laugh and a friendly manner. Born in the United Kingdom, Steinberg was (perhaps ironically) educated at some of the current hotbeds of anti-Israel campus activity, Berkeley and UCLA—but before they got that way, he laughs. He obtained a doctorate in politics at Cornell and then started teaching in Israel. In 2001, after observing what was happening in the powerful world of non-governmental organizations, Steinberg founded NGO Monitor, which is focused on transparency for these organizations. As such, it's open about its own objectives and bias on its website: "NGO Monitor is the leading source of information on political NGOs active in delegitimization campaign[s] against Israel and [on] the role of both government and private funders-enablers."

Steinberg and his organization are regularly attacked by NGOs and governments alike, mainly because they're effective at exposing wrongdoing and shady connections. He makes no apology for that. From its beginnings, NGO Monitor has been attempting to pull back the veil on the funding of Islamist terror and extremism, he says.

"I use the term *soft power*," Steinberg says. He's speaking in his modest Jerusalem office on a day when sirens are warning of a missile attack by Yemen's Houthis, an Iranian proxy. "The NGOs are in many ways the engine—along with United Nations bodies and academic frameworks—for a systematic demonization of Israel. And they have been responsible for an explosive resurgence of antisemitism."

The propaganda effort against Israel and the West has been happening for a long time, Steinberg agrees. But it has never been as effective as it is now, following the atrocities of October 7. To do that, you need people, he says. But you need something else as well: lots of money.

"These are major players," he says. "They're huge now. They're almost superpowers. And they have a huge amount of money. Just to give you the order of magnitude: Amnesty International's annual budget is about 350 million U.S. dollars. And what's common with all these organizations is there's no checks and balances. They are closed. There's really no oversight. The board members are chosen by the heads of the organization, and vice versa. And these organizations promote campaigns claiming that Israel commits war crimes, that Israel is genocidal, that Israel commits apartheid, that Israel is starving people. And NGOs are always at the forefront of that."

Amnesty International, Human Rights Watch, even OXFAM,

says Steinberg, have budgets of hundreds of millions, and they too often use them to "join in on this demonization of Israel. When they're supposed to be about humanitarian aid."

Amnesty International has suspended its Israeli branch for its criticism of the organization's treatment of Israel. Human rights icon Natan Sharansky has accused Human Rights Watch of anti-Israel bias—which its leadership has strongly denied— and has claimed Israel is leading a smear campaign against it. OXFAM, meanwhile, says "Israel is inflicting mass death, forcible displacement, starvation and deprivation upon more than two million people, and reducing Gaza to rubble." But it, too, denies it supports boycotts against Israel.

The NGOs have more than money, according to Steinberg: they also have credibility bestowed on them by Western media, governments, and the United Nations. "These organizations are out in front," he says. "They are the ones cited at the United Nations, not the other way around. When the UN says that Israel is doing terrible things, they are citing reports of these NGOs."

At one time, Steinberg acknowledges, the NGOs conducted themselves very differently. They were mainly led and staffed with decent, fair-minded individuals. "These organizations were really created for altruistic reasons, by altruistic people," Steinberg says. "But when the Cold War ended and the original people retired— whether it's at Amnesty or Human Rights Watch—well, NGOs are very easily susceptible to takeover. And because their structures are somewhat ambiguous, there's a lack of transparency."

And with that came huge budgets and spending power. Take, he says, Students for Justice in Palestine (SJP), which is active across North America and overseas. "SJP, they claim three hundred branches. We've tracked about a hundred that are active in the United States, and now more and more seem to be springing up in Canada. Whether they were there before or not, I don't know, but they're certainly active now. And they report no funding whatsoever. None. They tell journalists they are totally voluntary. But the projects that they run, the scale of their activities? All that makes it completely untenable that they are [organic and spontaneous]. On October 9, SJP issued a detailed handbook, with dozens of pages—with posters to use, and slogans, and how to organize rallies, and all these other things that they ended up doing. It didn't just come out of nowhere." (Asked repeatedly for comment about the criticism, SJP does not respond.)

Money, Steinberg says, is the key. It is the glue that has kept the anti-Israel, pro-Hamas propaganda machine running. He points to the university and college encampments assisted by SJP and others. "To maintain those organizations," he says, "you're going to need staff members, because students come and go. But when you look at the names of the people in SJP, they don't come and go. They often go from one campus to the other again, sure, but they don't disappear."

None of that organizational clout comes for free, he says. "When you do it for months, even as a student, and let's say you do it for a longer period of time, year after year. That's got to be a salaried position. There's got to be benefits, there's got to be somebody paying the rent, somebody's paying for food. But they don't tell you where their money is coming from.

"So when you look at the finances, you see that their donors are not public. It's a huge amount of money, too, in what is a very amorphous framework.

"It's a problem," Gerald Steinberg says. "A big problem."

The protestors didn't even wait for Israel's army to go into Gaza. IDF troops moved into the Gaza Strip on October 27, 2023, but the anti-Israel protests started many days *before* that, when it was still widely accepted that Israelis were the victims of that day. That was noteworthy.

There have always been protests against Israel in Western countries—and there is nothing antisemitic about protesting the policies of the government of Israel. In years past, however, the protests were typically smaller, disorganized, and ineffective. Not many people came out, and public opinion was seldom changed. But following the atrocities of October 7—even after it became known that twelve hundred Israeli men, women, children, and babies had been slaughtered, and that hundreds had been taken hostage—the protests were dramatically transformed, and became much more aggressive. They were bigger and they were better structured; dozens of them around the world took place before Israel even knew how many had been killed. Quickly, protests against the Jewish state, and even Jews themselves, started springing up everywhere.

In Algeria, the protests began on October 19, and in Nigeria it was October 21, when fifty thousand marched, holding signs accusing Israel of "apartheid." In South Africa, they started earlier, on October 13—the "Day of Rage"—with protestors carrying seemingly professionally rendered signs proclaiming BDS NOW. In Afghanistan, it was also October 13, as it was in Bangladesh, India, and Bali, where hundreds died in the ensuing violence. And in Kuala Lumpur, where thousands protested that same day, signs reading CRUSH THE ZIONISTS were indicative of what was to come.

France prohibited protests but they happened anyway, such as one in Paris on October 12, when police were obliged to step up security at synagogues. Protests continued there for several days before the IDF entered Gaza. Germany also banned protests, but they still took place across the country, and as early as October 12 as well. In Greece, on October 13, thousands marched on the Israeli embassy carrying professional-looking signage bearing anti-Israel and antisemitic themes.

In Ireland, where antisemitic sentiment is seen as pervasive, marches took place in multiple cities throughout mid-October. Italy witnessed protests on October 14, where calls were made to "Free Jerusalem." On October 17, one happened outside the Israeli embassy in Oslo, Norway—another country that has been an anti-semitic hotspot. There, protestors chanted "Allahu Akbar." In Spain—where, as in Ireland and Norway, antisemitism has become almost normalized—anti-Israel protests occurred just forty-eight hours after October 7, when much of the world was still express-ing sympathy with the Jewish victims, not their killers. Most seriously, in Russia in October, a mob stormed the airport in Dagestan to prevent Jews from disembarking from a flight from Tel Aviv. Two dozen people were injured, some seriously.

In North America, anti-Israel protests happened throughout the month of October, in multiple cities. In the Toronto suburb of Mississauga, dozens celebrated Hamas's attacks on the evening of October 8, waving the Hamas flag and cheering at major inter-sections, screaming "Allahu Akbar!" Similarly, on the same date, hundreds also gathered in New York's Times Square to cheer and chant "Resistance Is Justified" and "Globalize the Intifada."

The most revealing protest of all, perhaps, happened in Britain. Not because it happened: there were many protests there—some antisemitic, some not—in the days immediately following October 7. It was significant because of its timing. At around noon London time on October 7—while the massacres in Israel were still underway, and when Hamas was still occupying some kibbutzim—an organizer from the Palestine Solidarity Committee (PSC) called the city's Metropolitan Police Force (MPS), asking for a protest permit for the following week.

Said a spokesperson for the Met, as the Greater London police force is called: "The [Met] were contacted on Saturday, October 7 at approximately 12.50 hours via telephone call and informed of the intention to protest. The MPS committed this to our systems on the same day and are satisfied being contacted by telephone was a sufficient means in which to notify the MPS as the event was taking place seven days after notification." When a director from Britain's Jewish Leadership Council discovered this, he was outraged: "[At 12.55 p.m.] on October 7 was when I finally found out my family had been rescued from the house set on fire hours earlier by Hamas. Many others were still being killed and kidnapped. Five minutes earlier, those who hate Israel were making their plans to march against the victims." The head of policy at the Community Security Trust was equally shocked: "It's hard to comprehend that, while Jews around the world watched with horror as a pogrom took place in Israel on October 7, the ghouls at PSC saw the exact same images and thought, 'Let's have an anti-Israel demo.'"

What could the PSC be protesting while Israel was still under attack? At that point Israel had done little, militarily. As noted, no troops had yet entered Gaza. The PSC, when asked about the timing, was defiant: "Those who seek to demonize the organizers of and participants in protests for justice for Palestinians do so to deflect attention from the crimes against humanity that Israel has committed. We shall not be deflected by their apologism for genocide." The spokesperson added: "It is entirely appropriate, therefore, that PSC would call for a protest that would seek an immediate ceasefire and call for the root causes of Israeli occupation and apartheid to be addressed."

Calling for a "ceasefire" while Hamas was still killing Israeli citizens struck many in Britain as unseemly, to say the least. To a few, it suggested something even worse: prior knowledge.

As noted, before October 7, rallies against Israel genuinely seemed to be spontaneous. Protestors carried homemade signs and banners. Most demonstrations were chaotic and disorganized, and broke up quickly. But many of the post–October 7 protests were different, Jews and Israelis and others noted. Some protests—and this became the case, more and more, as the days went by—looked like they'd been planned. They had organizers who clearly had experience. They also had slickly rendered signs and banners, lots of food and drink, transportation, and even designated spokespeople using what sounded like professional talking points.

As former ambassador Marc Ginsburg noted, the post–October 7 protests were highly disciplined and structured events, which he believed had been planned long in advance of Hamas's attack. And, as *Tablet* magazine would later state in a lengthy probe of the protests, they "bore a striking resemblance" to the protests that far-left groups had once put together with military precision.

Between October 7 and November 30, 2023, the Institute for National Security Studies (INSS) think tank at Tel Aviv University counted 3,891 protests in 92 different countries. In the first week of the war, 69 per cent were anti-Israel. But once the global Day of Rage was announced by Hamas for October 13, demonstrations against Israel multiplied and soon accounted for up to 95 per cent of the total worldwide. As the INSS put it, "[Our] analysis shows that pro-Palestinian demonstrations were held in no fewer than 88 countries. While most of the demonstrations against Israel take place in Arab countries, they occur in Western countries as well. The countries where the highest number of pro-Palestinian demonstrations were held are Yemen (486 demonstrations), the United States (402), Turkey (355), and Iran (275)."

They continued: "The demonstrations against Israel, immediately following the most terrible massacre against Jews since the Holocaust, reflect a disturbing trend. In many cases these demonstrations include expressions of support for the killing of Jews, damage to Jewish communities, and the destruction of the State of Israel. These statements are not confined to rhetoric, but are reflected in a wave of antisemitic incidents and the murder of Jews that recall dark periods in history."

The early protests—the ones where antisemitic chants could be heard, and around which antisemitic vandalism and criminal acts were often taking place—were seemingly happening at all levels, in every time zone: locally, nationally, sub-nationally. Soon enough, stories started to spread about shadowy figures, and perhaps even governments, funding and organizing the protests. Who, some started to ask, was behind it all? Individuals who legitimately opposed Israeli policies, to be sure. That had always been the case. But, as reporters began to document, generous funding was also now coming from a network of progressive non-profits, pro-Palestinian and leftist charities, and offshore bank accounts.

Canada, which has notoriously lax standards for tracking the movement of possibly illicit funds, provided many early examples of this. At the local level, anonymous sources started to reach out. It didn't take long for it to be revealed what many had suspected: many protestors were indeed being paid to protest in towns big and small. They were being compensated generously, in fact, to show up. In some cases, the protestors—paid and otherwise—were blocking highways and roads, blockading Jewish neighbourhoods, and intimidating people going into synagogues. Along with the professional-looking signs and banners, the protests usually had organizers who wore reflective vests and controlled the crowds using whistles and bullhorns and walkie-talkies.

Early on, one of the smaller anti-Israel groups behind the protests slipped up. They left a website portal open, and it was discovered that the Victoria, B.C., organization was handing out tens of thousands of dollars to anti-Israel protestors. The Plenty Collective, as it called itself, had created what it referred to as a "Solidarity Fund" for Victoria-area individuals and groups to pay for "costs related to supporting or organizing actions in solidarity with Palestine and Palestinian people."

In a message to their followers, the Plenty Collective wrote: "This fund is to help cover costs incurred when organizing or participating in local actions. This can include, but is not limited to, the costs of lost wages, supplies, items for fundraising, paying speakers, etc." Priority was given to Palestinian, Black, or Indigenous people. And thousands had been paid out since October 7—as much as $20,000 every month. (The Plenty Collective refused repeated attempts to seek comment.)

Few were willing to speak about the scheme, fearing retribution. One who did said this of the Victoria-area protestors: "They are highly organized. I've watched them. A van pulls up, and they've got flags, signs, and they've got organizers from the Plenty Collective wearing orange vests controlling the crowds."

Much of the money was being generated locally, some sources suggested, but not all of it. The Plenty Collective, which had organized multiple anti-Israel protests for months, received $28,000 from the Victoria Foundation, a long-standing and respected registered charity in British Columbia. The foundation, in turn, received hundreds of thousands in funding from Canada's federal government through its Investment Readiness Program. In 2023, the Victoria Foundation was supplied with more than $500,000 by the federal government. It later passed along thousands to the Plenty Collective for what was described as "gender equity." When the paid-protestors story broke, however, the Victoria Foundation was reportedly furious and announced it had initiated a "review process" to see how that money was used. After the review concluded, the money received by the Plenty Collective was quietly returned to the foundation.

Some groups were also using the non-profit or charitable status of other organizations to finance their activities. The Plenty Collective, for example, benefited from its relationship with the Victoria-based Belfry Theatre. That theatre group was a not-for-profit, putting on half a dozen plays a year. But—for reasons that were unclear—the Belfry Theatre also passed along monies received from the government-supported Victoria Foundation to the Plenty Collective. On its website, the theatre claimed that "through the Victoria Foundation Community Grants Program the Belfry similarly assisted the Plenty Collective to implement queer community building, with an intersectional lens, through nourishment, art, and connection."

After it was reported that the collective was funding anti-Israel protests, however, the theatre company hurriedly announced: "We have been assured by the Plenty Collective that the Victoria Foundation grant is being used for community arts-based projects. Together with the Victoria Foundation and the Plenty Collective, we are reviewing the grant activities undertaken by the Plenty Collective." Those monies were also returned to the Victoria Foundation.

The money wasn't being used only for protests. Pressure was being applied in other ways as well. Revealingly, the Belfry Theatre group cancelled a showing of a play called *The Runner* after the Plenty Collective angrily objected to it—apparently because the play sympathetically depicted an Orthodox Jew who works for ZAKA, an organization that collects the remains of Jews killed by terrorists. Meanwhile, another Victoria-area group, much more hardcore than the Plenty Collective and the Belfry Theatre, also revealed itself. The Anarchist Network of Vancouver Island had made a plea on X for "support (for) Palestinian anarchists defending their community from genocide and apartheid against the settler-colonial state of Israel."

The group—whose appeal was titled EMERGENCY FUNDS FOR FAUDA, PALESTINIAN ANARCHISTS with what appeared to be blood dripping off it—then shared a cryptocurrency address for donations, and made the mistake of naming the location of the crypto bank. Thousands in equivalent U.S. dollars were being transmitted. The ultimate address was for a cryptocurrency exchange in the Middle East—and the anarchists' "wallet," as it's called, was in the middle of three sanctioned Iranian cryptocurrency exchanges associated with the terrorist-designated Iranian Revolutionary Guard. The anarchists on Vancouver Island also publicized their channel on Telegram, the encrypted platform favoured by Hamas. One of the threads there was titled, in Arabic: "How to make a Molotov cocktail."

Experts were contacted to look at what was happening on Vancouver Island. Neil Schwartzman, an anti-spam investigator, examined the documents showing cryptocurrency transactions to and from Iran. "It's very, very dirty," said Schwartzman. "And it raises the possibility that Iranian entities are funding some protests." He adds, "What we are seeing is financial interactions between local Canadian activists and groups who are potentially adjacent to, or are even actual terrorist groups. It is clear they are taking steps to prevent the origin of the funds from being seen."

These were all small-scale scandals, perhaps, all happening in a smallish city in a distant part of the country. But the funding controversies weren't unique to Victoria. Honest Reporting Canada simultaneously discovered that the federal government had supplied another small Western organization—the Pride Centre of Edmonton—with $138,000 in funds. They did so despite the centre having signed an open letter calling the fact that Israeli women and girls were raped and subjected to extreme sexual violence by Hamas on October 7 "unverified accusation[s] that Palestinians were guilty of sexual violence." That letter referred to Canada as "so-called Canada" and called on politicians to resign for their "complicity" in genocide.

Other examples of anti-Israel (and sometimes pro-Hamas) protestors being paid to protest, and agitate, started to bubble up across North America and Europe. In some cases they were using government funding, directly or indirectly, to stage those protests. Said one British Columbia–based critic who tracked the groups' activities, "As long as politicians refuse to condemn antisemitism, and stall on a needed call for investigations into funding, we will continue to see our cities held hostage and our democracy under threat.

"These organizations are paying people to be the face of their movement. And it's all organized by a lot of the same individuals and groups who have been arrested at past protests. They're linked. And we know they are getting money from outside."

Beryl Wasjman looks out the window at the Montreal neighbourhood where well-organized anti-Israel and pro-Hamas protests have been taking place on a near weekly basis.

Wasjman is the dapper and articulate editor of an award-winning Montreal newspaper, *The Suburban*, and a long-time politico in Quebec, with contacts in every party. Asked if the practice of paying anti-Israel, pro-Hamas protestors by governments and foreign nationals is indeed happening in Montreal, Wasjman sadly nods his head. Antisemitic activity in Montreal is among the worst in any major Western city, he says. So, too, antisemitic crime. In the much-read December 2024 essay cited earlier, Terry Glavin described Montreal as "North America's most dangerous city for Jews." After an antisemitic riot in Montreal happened in November 2024, even then prime minister Justin Trudeau condemned what was happening in his home city: "What we saw on the streets of Montreal last night was appalling. Acts of antisemitism, intimidation, and violence must be condemned wherever we see them."

In the days following October 7, however, as frequently violent anti-Israel and pro-Hamas protests took place in Montreal's streets, hate crimes surged. And for much of late 2023 and early 2024, the protests and the crimes seemed to be happening in a coordinated fashion. A Montreal Jewish school for young children had been shot up twice; another Montreal Jewish school, for children as young as grade one, had also been sprayed with bullets; a Molotov cocktail had been thrown at a Montreal synagogue while Jewish community centres and other synagogues were firebombed; a Montreal Muslim cleric had spoken at an anti-Israel rally and called for God to kill Jews "and spare none of them"; and scores of Montreal Jewish businesses had been targeted for boycotts, threats, and graffiti—including Nazi swastikas.

In the majority of the crimes, no arrests had taken place, Wasjman noted. "[There's a] reason Montreal's pro-Hamas crowd feels they have a licence to do what they're doing. There's a lack of political will here. We have not heard the right words from our mayor.

"The reason that Montreal is the only city in North America that has had multiple violent targeted attacks against Jewish institutions and people—from gunshots to Molotov cocktails—is because there is no condemnation of jihadist behaviour taking place on the streets of Montreal. None. We need a political voice to say, Enough! But we don't have it."

According to police sources, protestors in Montreal could get at least $50 for each anti-Israel, anti-Western protest they attended. Groups—ranging from anti-Israel to pro-Hamas, Wajsman alleged—had reportedly divided the city up into grids, with leaders or "captains" responsible for quickly staging protests in each grid. Most of the protestors, Wajsman added, were non-residents and students from outside Canada. In France, Germany, Austria, and other European countries, he noted, any non-citizen who openly promoted antisemitic messages—whether it be "Intifada" or "From the River to the Sea"—was facing swift deportation. Canada needed to consider doing likewise, he said.

In the meantime, he added, it was critical to expose who was funding the protests. "Follow the money," said Wasjman.

Following the money, in any political scandal, is standard operating procedure. And as the anti-Israel and antisemitic protests became more intimidating, following the money became imperative, he agreed. But, Wasjman says, it's not always an easy thing to do.

In other places, the funding of extremism wasn't always hidden. In the United States, for instance, protestors were also getting paid to protest, in some cases many thousands of dollars. Multimillionaire tech mogul Neville Roy Singham and his wife, Jodie Evans, were shown to be bankrolling pro-Palestinian protests long before October 7, 2023. They dramatically ramped up their involvement after the attack on Israel, American media reported. Their People's Forum organized multiple anti-Israel protests, including dozens of efforts designed to "shut down," as they put it, public and private sector offices and infrastructure. In November 2023, they posted on X: "Are you ready to disrupt business as usual? No celebrating in peace while genocide takes place!"

And on Craigslist in New York City, a now-deleted November ad read: "Needed for November 24th, evening, 2-3 hours, paying $30/hour." The ad called for "actors." Notable, too, was that November 24 was the same day the People's Forum had set aside to "shut down" Western governmental and corporate offices. On that occasion, thirty-four people were arrested trying to disrupt the Macy's Thanksgiving Day parade and Black Friday sales.

Meanwhile, on the other American coast, Amnesty International—long one of the NGOs with a stated antipathy toward Israel, NGO Monitor has said—started hiring people to "demand a ceasefire in Gaza now." On a Seattle, Washington, jobs board, Amnesty International offered "$20 to $30 an hour," about double the state minimum wage, to raise yet more money for the cause. Amnesty even offered dental and vision benefits to those they brought on. The positions were to be full-time, part-time, or weekends, and would include "paid training."

Said Amnesty International: "Make up to $30 an hour standing up for human rights with Amnesty International! The unparalleled escalation of hostilities between Israel, Hamas and other armed groups has taken a devastating toll on civilians. We are demanding that Congress and the Biden administration call for an immediate ceasefire to end civilian suffering. Apply today to fight back as part of our door-to-door canvassing team. You can start immediately!" (In December 2024, Amnesty went even further, concocting a new definition for the word *genocide* in a report on the war in Gaza. It said the accepted 1948 definition is an "overly cramped interpretation of international jurisprudence and one that would effectively preclude a finding of genocide in the context of an armed conflict.")

After the news broke about paid protestors in British Columbia and Washington state, more revelations about paid protestors started to appear. The *New York Post* revealed that anti-Israel "fellows" at Harvard, Yale, UC-Berkeley, Ohio State, and Emory in Georgia were getting paid via Hamas advocate Students for Justice in Palestine (SJP), which was itself getting funding from assorted charities, non-profits, and various far-left groups. Wrote the *Post*, mockingly: "Though most of the campus occupiers are themselves plenty privileged, the charitable giving helps explain why the demonstrators get to protest in style:

sleeping in Amazon-ordered tents, enjoying delivery pizza, coffee from Dunkin', free sandwiches from Pret a Manger, organic tortilla chips and $10 rotisserie chickens."

Organizers, meanwhile, were being paid by the U.S. Campaign for Palestinian Rights (USPCR)—in some cases getting thousands of dollars a week in exchange for just a few hours of agitating. The organizers were showing converts how to "rise up to revolution," they said. Meanwhile, in their confidential Fellowship Info Slides, hires were told they would get "paid organizing time," aimed at "mentorship from [USPCR] staff, peer coaching and fellows workshops." The focus of the workshops, the USPCR told recruits, was to "end the deadly exchange [and] demilitarize" Israel.

In their organizational slides, USPCR emphasized "building up local infrastructure" to aggressively oppose Israel. Their main audience, they said, were those "age 15-35" who were "ready to build a campaign targeting a government, institutional, or corporate target"—and who are "committed to an abolitionist vision of the future." To do all this, there would be check-ins with mentors, monthly "fellowship workshop calls," coaching calls, and "intensive and public network trainings." Training sessions would happen four times a year, the USPCR said, with local and in-person training happening at least once a year. Trainees would be taught how to "mobilize around key mobilization dates"—mainly protests and shutdowns.

USPCR told recruits that protests and anti-Israel activities were directed at exposing "white supremacy, settler colonialism, capitalism." They would achieve this with "revolution," the group declared.

The revelations about the anti-Israel (and, increasingly, pro-Hamas) activity in the United States and Canada were followed by the British *Daily Mail* publishing a report authored by the Institute for the Study of Global Antisemitism and Policy (ISGAP). That report alleged that the main group behind the occupation of dozens of university and college campuses had received more than US$3 million a year from organizations that included charities reportedly linked to Hamas. In the seventy-three-page report, ISGAP revealed that Students for Justice in Palestine—with chapters across Canada and the United States—had been funnelling millions via myriad non-profits such as the Westchester People's Action Foundation (WESPAC), Tides, American Muslims for Palestine (AMP), its parent organization Americans for Justice in Palestine (AJP), and Jewish Voice for Peace (JVP). Unsurprisingly, all these organizations consider themselves independent and have explained their involvement in the protests as motivated by concern for Palestinian rights and not any support for terrorism.

The report stated: "It is clear that individuals who previously worked for Hamas-linked charities are now a driving force behind [campus protests]. The Department of Education (DoE) should carry out an immediate investigation into which universities are funding and/or supporting SJP activities and instruct those universities to cease such funding and/or support . . . ISGAP calls for SJP (and its affiliated organizations) to be banned and for Jewish students to be protected." SJP, for its part, simply claims that it is "grounded" in "safety" for students.

The practice of paying for protestors, while unethical and dishonest, was not strictly illegal. So said Adam Swart, who runs a Beverly Hills firm, Crowds on Demand, that openly acknowledges it pays for protests. In an interview, Swart said he has no doubt that the practice of paying people to show up at protests is much more widespread than anyone realizes. Operating his firm in Canada as well as the United States, Swart has been providing paid-for crowds for everything from red carpet events to audiences at speeches since 2012—although he won't say for whom. Swart said "extremely lucrative offers" had been made to Crowds on Demand to provide bodies in North America after October 7. So far, he had declined, he said.

Swart says it's clear that the anti-Israel side has considerable resources. "There's obviously money in these protests. In my business, I know that some of the professional banners that these [anti-Israel] people have—those are $200 and $300, and the signs can be up to 100 bucks. Someone's paying for that, here in the United States. So you have essentially an unlimited amount of money coming in to potentially violent organizations that are tax-exempt non-profits here and are social advocacy groups in Canada."

As more reports started to appear about paid protestors and organizers, a sprawling *New York Times* investigation revealed that Neville Roy Singham had also funded a group called Code Pink, which in turn had passed along hundreds of thousands of dollars to anti-Israel protestors. Reported the *Times*: "The groups are funded through American nonprofits flush with at least $275 million in donations. Singham, 69, himself sits in Shanghai, where one outlet in his network is co-producing a YouTube show financed in part by the city's propaganda department. Two others are working with a Chinese university to 'spread China's voice to the world.' . . . He and his allies are on the front line of what Communist Party officials call a 'smokeless war.' Under the rule of Xi Jinping, China has expanded state media operations, teamed up with overseas outlets and cultivated foreign influencers. The goal is to disguise propaganda as independent content." Singham, for his part, denies he works at the direction of China.

But China, Russia, and Iran were indeed actively involved in providing rhetorical and material support for anti-West and, often, antisemitic protests, the *Times* reported. The amounts involved were significant, watchdogs like NGO Monitor noted—and the impact was felt at all levels, in multiple countries. The April 15, 2024, series of orchestrated shutdowns—called A15 and proclaimed by its organizers to be a "Coordinated Economic Blockade to Free Palestine"—was the most dramatic example of this, they said. The shutdowns had been promised on the A15Action website, ostensibly put together by an anarchist collective in the United States.

AMP and SJP chapters across North America aped the Strike4Gaza materials and called for mass disruption of American infrastructure on that day. Metadata showed that the blockade websites had been purchased and created many weeks before then.

On that day, the anti-Israel and anti-Western groups—an unlikely mix of Islamist and Marxist extremists, plus assorted agitators from both the far left and the far right—combined to "shut down" locations across the globe. It was highly effective, all agreed. All around the world, just as the groups had threatened, global trade and movement were blocked on April 15.

Traffic into Chicago's O'Hare airport, one of the world's busiest, was blocked, as it was along the busy I-880 mega-highway in Oakland, California, on San Francisco's Golden Gate Bridge, and on the Newburgh-Beacon Bridge over the Hudson River in New York. It was similarly blocked on a Vancouver bridge leading to a critical container port and outside a major federal government facility in downtown Ottawa.

The A15 Action site was more professional-looking than what some governments or political parties offer online. A video greeted visitors with an unidentified woman's voice: "In each city, we will identify and blockade major choke points in the economy, focusing on points of production and circulation with the aim of causing the most economic impact.

"Escalation has become necessary: there is a need to shift from symbolic actions to those that cause pain to the economy. As Yemen is bombed to secure global trade, and billions of dollars are sent to the Zionist war machine, we must recognize that the global economy is complicit in genocide, and together we will coordinate to disrupt and blockade economic logistical hubs and the flow of capital." The video called on pro-Palestine groups to "block logistical hubs to stop the flow of capital worldwide" and to create "a global economic blockade, answering the call from Gaza to fight for a liberated Palestine."

And tens of thousands of protestors did so, the media documented, with almost military precision. Lawyers were provided for those who got arrested, at no cost. "Graphics and flyers" were offered for download. Contacts were listed in just about every major city on earth, along with talking points and media kits. The claim that it was all the work of a "grassroots" pro-Palestine effort seemed unlikely. The reason: the existence of a campaign manager for April 15—and many of the other staged protests—began coming to light.

It was Iran.

That Iran was covertly organizing protests in the West—using propaganda to "enter the hearts of Western societies," as one Hezbollah leader had put it—was long suspected, but always officially denied. In the spring of 2024, however, the curtain was pulled back and Iran's role was revealed by the most senior intelligence source of all: Avril Haines, director of National Intelligence (ODNI) in the United States.

In July 2024, Haines took the extraordinary step of officially and clearly identifying Iran as the mastermind behind the protests. In her written statement—issued on behalf of the ODNI, the Federal Bureau of Investigation (FBI), the Cybersecurity and Infrastructure Security Agency (CISA), and a number of other U.S. intelligence agencies—Haines confirmed that Iran was the author of many of the protests, and had covertly stage-managed them to hurt Israel and its Western allies. In some cases, she confirmed for the first time, Iran was indeed providing financial support to protestors.

"I want to be clear that I know Americans who participate in protests are, in good faith, expressing their views on the conflict in Gaza—this intelligence does not indicate otherwise," Haines said, acknowledging the strong First Amendment protections afforded speech in the United States. "[But] Americans who are being targeted by this Iranian campaign may not be aware that they are interacting with or receiving support from a foreign government. We urge all Americans to remain vigilant as they engage online with accounts and actors they do not personally know."

Said Haines, "As each of us has indicated in prior public statements, Iran seeks to stoke discord and undermine confidence in our democratic institutions. Iran has furthermore demonstrated a longstanding interest in exploiting societal tensions through various means, including through the use of cyber operations. . . . We have observed increasingly aggressive Iranian activity [in 2024], specifically involving influence operations targeting the American public and cyber operations."

Haines's statement was unprecedented. Never before had the United States directly linked Iran to the protests and occupations that had swept Western democracy since October 7. Never before had anyone in government confirmed what just a few Western journalists had been reporting: protestors, and organizers at various anti-Israel protests, were getting organizational support—and they were getting paid by powerful interests bent on the destruction of Israel as well as of the West.

Immediately after Haines made her statement, Joe Biden's White House press secretary stepped up to her microphone in the James S. Brady Press Briefing Room. Speaking to the assembled reporters, Karine Jean-Pierre cautioned that critics of Israel needed to "guard against efforts by foreign powers to take advantage of—or to co-opt—their legitimate protest activities." And, just as Haines had, Jean-Pierre acknowledged the constitutional protections afforded political speech, including speech that causes hurt and outrage.

"Americans across the political spectrum, acting in good faith, have sought to express their own independent views on the conflict in Gaza. The freedom to express diverse views when done peacefully is essential to our democracy," she said. "At the same time, the U.S. government has a duty to warn Americans about foreign malign influences. . . . We will continue to expose attempts to undermine our democracy in our society just as we are today."

Iran needs to understand, Jean-Pierre said, that "meddling in our politics and seeking to stoke division is unacceptable."

Before the day was over, anonymous intelligence officers fanned out across the U.S. Capitol to speak anonymously to media and emphasize what Haines and Jean-Pierre had said. One officer in Haines's employ said that Iran had hoped to take advantage of controversial issues in the run-up to elections, both to embarrass the United States and to "inflame social division." As a result, said the officer, "we are monitoring Iranian actors who are seeking to exacerbate tensions on the Israel–Gaza conflict." Those who did so would be facing severe consequences.

Just before the confirmation of Iran's role was revealed by Haines, President Joe Biden spoke about what those consequences might be.

"There's a right to protest, but not the right to cause chaos," Biden said. "Destroying property is not a peaceful protest—it's against the law. Vandalism, trespassing, breaking windows, shutting down campuses, forcing the cancellation of classes and graduations—none of this is a peaceful protest."

He added, "There should be no place on any campus—no place in America—for antisemitism or threats of violence against Jewish students."

For decades, Iran has sought to influence—or destabilize— Western politics. That is well known. As the years went by, however, not as many knew how successful Iran had become in its anti-Western campaign. Iran has invested considerable resources stage-managing protests in democratic nations, intelligence agencies say. And it has paid many dividends.

After October 7, more media started to take note. "The Iranian regime is funneling money and its influence into anti-Israel college campus protests across the US, often through buzzily named organizations—and many who join the protests don't realize who is really behind them," wrote Isabel Vincent in the *New York Post* in August 2024. She went on to quote the director of Middle East Forum's Islamist Watch project: "For decades, the Iranian regime has worked closely with far-left, far-right and Islamist groups across Europe and North America. . . . Following the October 7th attacks, Tehran has poured money and logistical support into anti-Israel and pro-terror rallies, encampments and civil disorder.

"We've uncovered evidence . . . where the Iranian regime appears to operate mosques, activist and student groups that are deeply involved in pro-terror demonstrations, alongside Hamas-aligned groups," the Middle East Forum said.

As noted, Iran's involvement in promoting extremism and terrorism in the West—or simply stirring up trouble—was not new. As the CIA stated in 2018 in a partially declassified analysis about "radical cooperation" between Iran, Libya, and Syria, these countries were "hostile to Israel's existence" and working "to encourage the emergence of revolutionary, anti-Western" groups around the planet. Of the three, the CIA's prescient analysts wrote, "Iran is the most implacable foe and will remain the most effective and dangerous state sponsor of terrorism over the next few years." Iran's activities ranged from small-scale operations to ones on a global scale.

For example, in the years prior to the October 7 massacre, members of a fringe orthodox Jewish sect called Neturei Karta—which numbers in the low thousands and opposes the State of Israel—have been front and centre at protests across North America and Europe. They wear obvious religious garb, and are often caught by the television cameras. Iran has a long and documented history of supporting the sect. Most recently, Neturei Karta members acted as spokespeople on Iranian state television during the summer 2024 university encampments.

More recently in 2024, Canadian investigative journalist Nagar Mojahedi—who, along with her family, has received multiple threats from the Iranian regime—revealed that Iran had funded protests on the McGill University campus. Mojahedi reported on scores of fake online accounts that were "coming from Iranians inside Iran linked to the regime and [the Islamic Revolutionary Guard Corps (IRGC)], fuelling the campus protests at McGill." It was "a massive, funded, coordinated and organized" effort by Iran designed to influence public opinion and government policy, Mojahedi stated. In all, more than five hundred thousand posts were traced to Iran. All were designed to cause further unrest at the storied Canadian university, she reported.

There are multiple examples of Iranian agitation on a much larger scale, however. Cotton Sandstorm, for example, is the code name for an infamous Iranian Revolutionary Guard cyberwarfare group that uses fake accounts online, such as Jewish Peace Advocate, to spread anti-West and anti-Israel propaganda. Microsoft's Threat Intelligence team discovered the existence of the fake accounts in early 2024.

Said the Microsoft Threat Analysis team, "As the Israel–Hamas war broke out on October 7, 2023, Iran immediately surged support to Hamas with its now well-honed technique of combining targeted hacks with influence operations amplified on social media, what we refer to as cyber-enabled influence operations. Iran's operations were initially reactionary and opportunistic. By late October, nearly all of Iran's influence and major cyber actors focused on Israel in an increasingly targeted, coordinated, and destructive manner, making for a seemingly boundless 'all-hands-on-deck' campaign against Israel. Unlike some of Iran's past cyberattacks, all of its destructive cyberattacks against Israel in this war—real or fabricated—were complemented with online influence operations."

Microsoft's cybersecurity experts added: "[Iran's] influence operations grew increasingly sophisticated and inauthentic, deploying networks of social media 'sockpuppets' as the war progressed. Throughout the war these influence operations have sought to intimidate Israelis while criticizing the Israeli government's handling of hostages and military operations to polarize and ultimately destabilize Israel. Eventually, Iran turned its cyberattacks and influence operations against Israel's political allies and economic partners to undermine support to Israel's military operations. We expect the threat posed by Iran's cyber and influence operations will grow as the conflict persists, particularly amid the rising potential for a widening war. Increased brazenness of Iranian and Iran-affiliated actors coupled with burgeoning collaboration among them portends a growing threat ahead of the US elections in November."

Around the same time, in late 2024, Meta—the company that owns and operates Facebook, Instagram, and WhatsApp—shut down a sophisticated Iranian influence operation run by the dictatorship's Islamic Revolutionary Guard. Meta's Threat Disruption Center revealed that Iran, aided and abetted by Hezbollah, was running multiple fake accounts across Meta's platforms as well as on TikTok, X, and others. An IRGC-controlled front company had been flagged by Israeli cyber intelligence as the source of threats, via emails and texts, against Israeli athletes at the Paris

Olympics. Iran had also fabricated a website purporting to be *The Jerusalem Post* and was using artificial intelligence to push out fake narratives about Israel. Iran-supported Hezbollah, they said, also created fake sites and even purchased thousands of dollars of advertising on Facebook and Instagram. Hezbollah's propaganda, which originated with its media outlet in Lebanon, promoted stories suggesting that Israeli society was breaking up and that the Jewish state was experiencing food shortages.

Several examples of Iran's involvement—in the protests, in the attacks, in the campaigns of intimidation and discord— became more widely known in early 2024. But few of the Iran-affiliated operations were as big, or as successful, as the global shut-down effort that took place on April 15, 2024.

Indications that something big would be happening that day had leaked out just a few weeks earlier. And immediately after the April 15 protests, Iran's supreme leader, Ali Khamenei, also openly encouraged the global anti-Israel protests. Khamenei, the Grand Ayatollah of Iran and previously the country's president, posted in English on X alongside videos of Western student protestors: "See what is happening in the world. In Western countries, in England and France, and in states across the U.S. itself, people are coming out in huge numbers to chant slogans against Israel and America. U.S. and Israel's reputation has been ruined. They truly have no solution."

In June 2024, as the student encampments were spreading across North America and Europe, Iranian proxy Hezbollah also confirmed that support was flowing to Western students. Hezbollah legislator Mohammad Raad appeared on Russia Today and said, "I believe we should rely on the ability of Arabs and Muslims to invest in the changes we are witnessing, specifically the Western students in the demonstrations in the West. There are Arab students who are demonstrating in the West, and this is something we can understand. But the Western students who are demonstrating in support of Palestine—we rely on our ability to invest in this positive activity into the future. . . . We should invest in the students.

"We need to enter the heart of Western societies."

Qatar has supplied Gaza—and its government, Hamas—with millions upon millions of dollars for years. Over a billion dollars, in fact, had been sent to Hamas by Qatar for slightly more than a decade.

The funding was not public knowledge, but the government of Israeli prime minister Benjamin Netanyahu knew, and even secretly encouraged the practice. The Netanyahu regime believed the funds were a way of "buying quiet" with Hamas, *The New York Times* revealed in an extraordinary report in December 2023. Incredibly, as the *Times* reported, "for years, Israeli intelligence officers even escorted a Qatari official into Gaza, where he doled out money from suitcases filled with millions of dollars." The idea, apparently, was to make Hamas strong enough to govern, but not strong enough to wage war. It was a legitimate scandal, one that would have grave consequences for Israelis.

The money, meant to be untraceable by Western nations, wasn't all used to support terror. Some of it was ostensibly legitimate and aimed at humanitarian support, such as paying salaries for bureaucrats in the Gaza Strip or paying for important infrastructure like power utilities. But millions also ended up with Hamas's military wing, which would use the funds to prepare for the attack of October 7, 2023.

The story in the *Times* was shocking, shaking Israel's politics to its foundations. In the years to come, when the wars against Hamas and Hezbollah end, Netanyahu and his circle will face many questions and inquiries about their willingness to let money flow to terrorists. But in years past, Netanyahu and his supporters angrily defended the approach without indulging in too many specifics. In December 2012, Netanyahu confided to an Israeli journalist that keeping Hamas strong was useful because it offset the power of the Palestinian Authority. And in 2015, Bezalel Smotrich, who has been finance minister in Netanyahu's far-right government, said, "The Palestinian Authority is a burden. Hamas is an asset." Disaffected members of Netanyahu's regime, meanwhile, bitterly called the funds "protection money." If that was what the money was for, some grimly observed, twelve hundred Israelis were not protected on October 7, 2023.

Qatar is where the bulk of the funding for Hamas and terror groups has come from. But there has been funding of the pro-Palestinian and anti-Israel cause, too, in substantial amounts from several other sources, on a lesser scale. In 2023, for example, the Princeton-based Network Contagion Research Institute (NCRI)—one of the world's leading experts in identifying and stopping the spread of disinformation on social media—issued a detailed report on how Shut It Down for Palestine (SID4P) has overseen sophisticated anti-Israel and arguably anti-democracy campaigns online and offline. As SID4P writes itself about its mission, "We must keep building momentum and increase the pressure with more marches, walk-outs, sit-ins, and other forms of direct action directed at . . . political offices."

SID4P emerged immediately after October 7, rapidly establishing itself as a significant opponent of Israel and nations like the United States, using protests, "direct action" attacks, and effective propaganda campaigns. Like many other such groups, SID4P is a hybrid, using internet-based and real-world tactics to whip up anti-Israel sentiment. It also, says NCRI, has paid for and organized "gradually escalating direct-action campaigns targeting critical infrastructure and public spaces." SID4P pays what it calls "convenors" to oversee these disruptions—which are ultimately underwritten by the so-called Singham Network, founded by the aforementioned Neville Roy Singham.

One such group is the Chinese Communist Party, intelligence sources noted. Singham's organization, *The New York Times* also reported in an expansive December 2023 investigation, mixes "progressive advocacy with Chinese government talking points." (As mentioned earlier, Singham denies he works at the behest of China's regime.) The Singham Network is, the *Times* and others have said, part of a massive influence operation that "works closely with the Chinese government media machine" and was also "financing its propaganda worldwide." The network relies on a mélange of non-profits, fiscal sponsors, and "alternative" news sources to do this, the *Times* revealed, and, as the NCRI alleges, it exploits loopholes in American non-profit rules to flow millions to "organizations and movements that actively stoke social unrest at the grassroots level." One of those is SID4P, which the NCRI says has links to extremists who favour violence to end Israel— and one of SID4P's "endorsers" is Samidoun, now a designated terrorist group. Samidoun has been promoted on, and linked to, SID4P's website. (Singham has generally denied violating applicable laws through his activities and related networks.)

"We mobilize in the belly of the beast because we understand that we have a unique role to play in combating material support for Zionism and weakening the handmaiden of U.S. global imperialism," Singham's People's Forum declared immediately after October 7. In November 2023 a complaint was filed with the Internal Revenue Service against the People's Forum, alleging that it had "been advocating in support of the U.S. designated foreign terror organization Hamas in its war on Israel and Jews and also advocates for the overthrow of the United States." Between 2012 and 2022, People's Forum donations worth more than $20 million were funnelled to a New York "philanthropy fund" that NCRI calls "a dark money clearinghouse, obscuring the identity of donors while facilitating the transfer of substantial sums to American non-profits." Asked for comment, Manolo De Los Santos, spokesperson for the People's Forum, said: "Nothing will deter our commitment to continue fighting for Palestinian self-determination and statehood. . . . For us, Zionism is synonymous with colonialism and racism." The People's Forum has not, however, responded to various requests for comment on the IRS allegations.

It is a model seen elsewhere. In August 2024, for example, questionable funding was reported coming out of Canadian pro-Palestinian charities. Their names—as with SJP, AMP, and a hodgepodge of others—are almost irrelevant. What is important is what these groups did to support the larger pro-Palestine, anti-Israel effort.

Some of the charities had been funding, or have possible links to, Palestinian extremist or terrorist groups. As with the lobby effort, they were mostly doing so in the open. All had been accepted as legitimate charities by the federal government, and all had the ability to provide tax receipts for donations, which together add up to millions. And all had been sending large amounts to Gaza and the West Bank for years. The details were seen in the charities' filings with the federal charity regulator. The filings showed links, or possible links, with entities in the Middle East that have long been associated with terrorism. This information was found through searches of open-source charity databases, their required filings, corporation searches, and evidence found openly on social media.

One charity described its objectives as "allocating donations and funds" to "victims of violence" in Arab countries. In one of its most recent filings, from 2022, the charity admitted it sent nearly $14,000 to An-Najah University in Nablus, in the northern West Bank, even though it's not considered an approved recipient. The problem: according to the Middle East Forum, An-Najah University has been alleged to be a terrorist recruitment ground, with even Hamas calling it "a greenhouse for martyrs." The university has student groups directly associated with Hamas, and Israel has accused several students there of belonging to terrorist cells. According to charities watchdog NGO Monitor, the university had also held ceremonies honouring Palestinian terrorists.

The charity, like others, had previously sent thousands to Palestinian charity Inash El Usra, which the federal government has said is connected with Hamas. While Inash El Usra's website stated that it supports families of "martyrs," resisters, and detainees, it had also been funded by another charity, IRFAN-Canada, which had its charitable status revoked by Canada a decade ago for its links to terrorism. Meanwhile, Inash El Usra's website shows videos of a children's concert, uploaded to its YouTube account. In one video, a child is dressed up as a Hasidic Jew—complete with *payot*, or side curls—and he shoots a toy machine gun at girls wearing Palestinian flags. In 2022, the same charity provided more than $400,000 to Community Abdel Shafi, which NGO Monitor says was founded and is directed by leaders of the Popular Front for the Liberation of Palestine (PFLP), a listed terrorist entity throughout the West.

There were many other such examples, with many other such charities. A forty-year-old charity associated with the Palestine Red Crescent Society, now defunct, had objectives that appeared to be inconsistent with the rules. For example, the charity listed zero dollars in expenses in nearly every single category for things such as office supplies, transportation, salaries, staff training, research, and rent—but listed most of their expenses, which added up to hundreds of thousands of dollars each year, in the category called "Other." Charity law experts say it's unusual that an active charity that's spending hundreds of thousands of dollars on anything has "zero expenses" in all the normal categories that most charities spend on.

Also unusual: the charity's filings provided no details on how they used donations, which were substantial. Even though it claimed to be focused on medical aid for Palestinians, the charity told government its only external activities in 2018 and 2019 were in the African nation of Tanzania. Meanwhile, a registered British charity with a nearly identical name also had a controversial past. The U.K. charity had worked with Abdel Shafi Community Health—which, NGO Monitor has alleged, had ties to the PFLP. In addition, the charity boasted that it enjoyed an "excellent relationship" with Hamas's health agency and yet emphasized its "independence" and support for "democratic values."

Asked for comment about its relationship with possible extremist or terrorist groups, the charity merely challenged the notion that it had changed its original charitable objects. It did not answer questions about how it uses donations, why a Palestinian charity was active in Africa, or any relationship with groups like the PFLP.

———

Antisemitism—some of it funded by Iran and Qatar, some by NGOs, charities, and non-profits—was being seen on hundreds of campuses across North America and Europe in the spring and summer of 2024.

Most agreed: Yale, Princeton, NYU, UCLA, and Northwestern had it bad. But Columbia University had it the worst. Columbia, on Manhattan's Upper West Side, had become the Western epicentre for college antisemitism and hate. What President Biden had called "antisemitism and threats of violence against Jewish students" had been commonplace at Columbia since mid-April 2024, when hundreds of students (and non-students) set up what they called the Columbia Gaza Solidarity Encampment—an "autonomous zone" in which to demand divestment from Israel and, often, to oppose what they called Western "imperialism." Tents were pitched, generators were secured, water and food was purchased, and Palestinian flag signs were erected around the perimeter, reading WE STAND WITH PALESTINE. In other places, banners proclaimed COLUMBIA FUNDS GENOCIDE. At the start, the "encampment" seemed mostly peaceful.

In the days and weeks that followed, however, attacks on Jews and Jewish students surged. There were clashes with police and security. Scores of students, mostly Jewish, reported being spat on, punched, and mobbed on or near Columbia's grounds. Some Jews started hiding jewellery and insignia that showed their faith; some simply stopped going to class. Israeli flags were regularly set ablaze, and American flags as well. Classes were cancelled, as were commencement ceremonies. A rabbi who was part of a learning initiative at the university told Jewish students to stay home for their own safety. Some professors, meanwhile, reportedly told Jewish students that Jews "control the media," *The Jewish Chronicle* reported.

Shai Davidai, an Israeli professor lecturing at the university's business school, was even barred from campus "for the safety of the community," a Columbia official said. "It blew me away," Davidai said in an interview, many months afterward. "Everyone was welcome at Columbia—unless, of course, if you're quote unquote Zionist. All I wanted to do is read out the names of the hostages. They wouldn't let me."

Davidai said that what he experienced reflected "a concerted effort" in the West by Israel's enemies. "[The antisemites and pro-Hamas allies] were prepared," he alleged. "They may not have known exactly in advance what Hamas was going to do. But they were prepared for it, and the head of the Iranian Revolutionary Guard specifically thanked the students in Canada and the United States."

There were multiple confrontations at Columbia as well. Masked anti-Israel protestors screamed "Yehudim [Jews] fuck you!" and "Go back to Poland!" at Jewish students who came too close. At one point, riot police were called in to remove anti-Israel, pro-Hamas protestors who had occupied—and blockaded and vandalized—the university's administration building, Hamilton Hall. Hundreds were arrested. Later, it was learned that the occupation had been meticulously planned—and that some participants had been trained by professional "protest consultant" Lisa

Fithian, a veteran of some Occupy and Black Lives Matter clashes in the past. Fithian, the author of a 2019 book called *Shut It Down*, instructed the protestors on how to barricade themselves within Hamilton Hall. For this sort of work, media reported that Fithian is paid hundreds of dollars a day.

Chants were heard across Columbia's campus in mid-2024, some openly celebrating murder. One anti-Israel activist posted a video: "Al-Qassam [Hamas Brigades], make us proud, take another soldier out. . . . We say justice, you say how? Burn Tel Aviv to the ground! Go Hamas, we love you! We support your rockets, too!" A second video featured students chanting "Kill another soldier now." The Jewish Chabad Columbia group, meanwhile, were heckled when they gathered outside: "Go back to Europe! You have no culture! All you do is colonize!" In another video, on Instagram, a poster of the PFLP's secretary general can be seen in the background while the Columbia anti-Israel protestors sing, "Oh Hamas, our beloved, strike, strike Tel Aviv."

At Columbia, things were very bad, but then a single video made things dramatically worse. It was a video that would be seen by many. In it, Khymani James—one of the leaders of the group that had seized control of the university's main lawn—is seen speaking to someone in the school's administration.

Weeks before James and dozens of other students set up their encampment site, James had filmed the video and posted it on Instagram. His words would end up damaging the Columbia anti-Israel, pro-Hamas campaign more than anything else had to date. "Zionists don't deserve to live comfortably, let alone Zionists don't deserve to live," James told Columbia administrators. "The same way we are very comfortable accepting Nazis don't deserve to live, fascists don't deserve to live, racists don't deserve to live, Zionists, they shouldn't live in this world."

He went on: "Be grateful that I'm not just going out and murdering Zionists."

People were shocked, including some of those in the Columbia encampment. James was suspended after he posted his video on Instagram. He later insisted that he "misspoke." But, for the Columbia anti-Israel protestors, the damage had been done. Their movement started to lose momentum because one of their leaders had gone too far. (In the fall of 2024 James reversed himself and said he wasn't sorry for what he said, doubling down on it. Meanwhile, Columbia University Apartheid Divest supported him and called for more resistance "by any means necessary.")

The chaos and antisemitism continued at dozens of other university campuses. In the United States, these included Emerson College, the University of Southern California, the University of Texas at Austin, New York University, Ohio State, Yale, Princeton, and Emory. Similar problems were reported at Canadian universities, among them McGill, York, McMaster, Western, Concordia, and the University of Toronto.

The university encampments were always anti-Israel, and too often antisemitic. And they proved to be powerful fodder for propaganda, including in unexpected places. In March 2025, for example, a lawsuit was filed in the Southern District of New York that named leaders of Within Our Lifetime, SJP, and other groups as defendants. In one section, the lawsuit detailed how a hostage taken by Hamas on October 7, Shlomi Ziv, described how his captors "bragged about having Hamas operatives on university campuses" and "showed him Al Jazeera stories and photographs of protests at Columbia University."

The occupation at Columbia attracted the most attention worldwide because New York City is the centre of America's media, and because it had been the scene of many arrests and lots of violence and confrontations. When police tried to arrest masked wrongdoers, they would often encounter a wall of people, arms linked. When someone was arrested, the masked anti-Israel protestors would converge to "de-arrest," effectively swarming police officers and rescuing their comrade. Sometimes, police would even find themselves doxxed and threatened by the protestors at Columbia and other university encampments. And at UCLA a video showed masked men providing training in hand-to-hand combat for those who were facing off against police.

Soon enough, the media started to uncover yet more evidence of money flowing to the protesting students and the organizations supporting them. The *New York Post*, for example, reported that hard-left interests—such as the Campaign for Palestinian Rights and the George Soros–funded Students for Justice in Palestine—had supplied protestors with significant amounts, much of it run through non-profits. The *Post* reported that a campus-based "fellow" could receive close to US$4,000 a week for devoting eight hours to "organizing campaigns led by Palestinian organizations."

Elsewhere, a plan for anti-Israel campus protests was provided to this writer. Previously unseen by most, the document had been authored by a shadowy group that refers to itself as Ill Will. The manual, written by Anonymous, is titled "First We Take Columbia"—which, for months, the anti-Israel students effectively had done. The manual had been translated into French, Spanish, Turkish, Japanese, and Chinese for use at other campuses abroad. Said the document's authors: "Occupations are effective because they are disruptive. . . . An occupation needs to spread in order to survive. New buildings need to be taken on campus, throughout the city, and across the country. Take the enemy by surprise."

It went on: "Every occupation is a commune. By shutting down the normal flows of capitalist society, they open up space for something new to emerge. Occupations draw strength from the spectre of a riot." The manual concluded: "This is only the beginning. . . . Pushing the university struggle to its limit might contribute in a similar way to producing a constellation of revolutionary forces in the city today."

The manual was similar to another one circulating on campuses in Europe. That booklet was much more direct, however. It suggested that some of the anti-Israel student groups needed to embrace violence and terrorist tactics to advance their cause. Provided confidentially by a source, the "underground manual" was created by Palestine Action, a network of groups that used what they called "direct action" against individuals and organizations who are believed to support Israel. Palestine Action would be designated a terror group by the British government in 2025.

Founded in 2020 and most active in Britain, Palestine Action had been at the forefront of an increasingly radicalized global movement, mainly populated with Generation Z, Millennials, and university students. Its "underground manual" suggested that groups that oppose the Jewish state were willing to use violence and vandalism to do so. Asked for comment, the group admitted that it authored the manual but refused to discuss its contents, citing criminal prosecutions it was facing.

The manual would go on to form part of the police actions against Palestine Action members in the United Kingdom. Like terrorist groups of the past—such as Germany's Red Army

Faction, Abu Nidal, and the Irish Republican Army—Palestine Action members were strongly encouraged to form "cells" of just a few members to reduce the chance of police infiltration and "to make it more secure." The manual urged the cells to "pick your target," which it identified as anyone who "enables and profits from the Israeli weapons industry." Specific companies were suggested, such as Elbit Systems, Rafael, and Teledyne.

The manual then called on cell members to "prepare for action" and do what it refers to as "recce" (reconnaissance), even advising agitators to "borrow someone's dog" for a walk to avoid looking suspicious. Extremists were counselled to map out the location of closed-circuit cameras as well as fencing, barbed wire, access points, alarms, and how far the police were from the target. After that, cells were advised to "plan action." Among the suggested actions were "smashing windows and exterior equipment," blocking companies' external pipes, even using concrete. This "will cause disruption for the target," the manual stated.

The manual further advocated for break-ins. Those work, Palestine Action declared, because "breaking into your target and damaging the contents inside is obviously a very effective tactic." Cells were counselled to map out escape routes well in advance, using a variety of means. Cells were also told to use only cash when "buying equipment, whether it's spray paints or sledgehammers," and never to leave a "paper or digital trail." And as seen at the campus protests across the West, "face coverings are key," Palestine Action declared. "Do not have your face [visible] at any point during the action. Balaclava is best for this. This might seem pedantic, but cops are obsessed with [shoes]. Don't wear shoes that you've worn when arrested on an action or at a protest, or that are all over your social media."

The manual also urged followers to cover their entire bodies to ensure that tattoos or birthmarks weren't observed. As elsewhere in Europe and North America, the "protestors" were urged to wear similar clothing to promote anonymity. Extremists were also advised to methodically videotape every "action" and share the results with other extremists for propaganda purposes. Only untraceable "burner phones" should be used, they wrote, with all digital identifiers removed. And, naturally, Palestine Action should be sent a copy.

Finally, in all caps, Palestine Action warned: WHEN TAKING ACTION, NEVER LEAVE ANYTHING BEHIND. ABSOLUTELY NOTHING APART FROM PAINT AND DESTRUCTION. THE POLICE MAY TRY TO FORENSICALLY ANALYZE ANY ITEMS WHICH ARE LEFT, SO DON'T LEAVE ANYTHING. But, if they were caught, Palestine Action members were given the names of lawyers to represent them, apparently at no cost, and offered the assistance of "our dedicated support team throughout the legal process."

Lawyers, usually, are not free. Who was paying them to represent students and non-students who had broken the law?

It was an important question. To some, it was *the* question.

Alex Gandler was the one who said it first: "the hidden hand." The hidden hand is Iran, Hamas, and Hezbollah, plus others, who have long been staging and funding anti-Israel and anti-democracy protests and activity in the West. So, too, say Avril Haines and others now. And what with the campus encampments the upheaval in the streets, and the hate being spewed online, Gandler acknowledges that the problem is widespread and cannot be easily dismissed.

Gandler, deputy spokesman for Israel's Ministry of Foreign Affairs, is under no illusion about the nature of the protests, the global rise in antisemitism, or the desire to delegitimize the State of Israel. After October 7, he says, little of it seems to be either spontaneous or homegrown. "This is not organic. This is not a coincidence," he says. He is not alone in this view.

As the CIA acknowledged in their classified analysis released in 2018, entities that consider Israel and America their sworn enemy—Iran and its proxies now, Libya and Syria in the past—have been reliable sources of funding for extremist groups in the West. To Gandler and others in Israel, that is beyond dispute. "This has been going on for years, and the infrastructure for the existence of these protests was set up pre-Hamas," he says.

"State-driven voices have been pushing these messages and investing a lot of money [in the rallies and protests]. And not just money, but time—and they have been shaping what they want the response to be when the day comes."

Money is key, according to the experts. Foreign interests are giving material and rhetorical support to the anti-Israel side, they say. And, as many have now reported, protestors are even being paid to show up in cities across North America and Europe. Concludes Gandler: "This is even more than that. There has been heavy investing in changing or rearranging the political map of other countries. It is a political push.

"It is Western liberal democracy that is on the line. That is, Western democracy that is represented in Canada and the United States and Western Europe and also in Israel. The aim, at the end of the day, is to change all that into something else.

"We need to protect ourselves from the worst—by being the better."

SIX

THE HIDDEN HANDS

The woman turns, calls someone off camera a "Zionist pig," then spits on him. On a different day, a masked pro-Palestine protestor is at the centre of a near riot outside a riding association meeting, seen attacking police and media with her fists, over and over. Another day: a pro-Palestine group scream obscenities at a City Hall skating party as terrified-looking children reach for their parents. Yet another: a mob of anti-Israel protestors smash through a wall of fencing at the University of Toronto, having earlier surrounded and blocked a Jewish professor trying to move through the area. Multiple video clips show other protestors—masked with keffiyehs—blocking roads into a predominantly Jewish neighbourhood, defying police. At Union Station, Canada's busiest transportation hub, a large group of masked protestors loudly cheer news that Iran is firing rockets at Israel. And on and on.

All these moments, and many more, have been captured on film by Caryma Sa'd and her videographer, who goes by Lee. Sa'd's videos have been seen around the world, in many media reports. Since October 7, in fact, she has witnessed more anti-Israel—and sometimes antisemitic—protests than just about anyone. She's been up close with the anti-Israel protestors thousands of times. Asked why she does this work, she gives a small smile.

Sa'd is a prolific writer, a cartoonist, a notary public, and a busy litigation lawyer. But generally, she is now best known for filming protests. For years she's been documenting and reporting on all types of demonstrations. And since the terrible events of October 7, Sa'd, with Lee, has been present at hundreds of them—pro-Palestine, anti-Israel, antisemitic, pro-Hamas, pro-Hezbollah. Sometimes she even finds the capacity to document more than one protest in a single day.

She makes a point of being fair to all sides. As a result, her footage—with her name watermarked in the bottom right corner—often shows up in the news coverage of many mainstream media organizations. She scrupulously maintains her neutrality, too, and only objects—in a dry, lawyerly fashion—when someone is clearly breaking the law.

And Caryma Sa'd, it should be noted, is half Palestinian.

That's on her father's side; her mother is Indian. She was born in 1989 in Mississauga, Ontario, where there's a large expat Palestinian population. She studied law at the University of Ottawa, graduated *cum laude*, and was called to the Bar in 2016. She articled at a Bay Street law firm, then worked at one of the top litigation firms in Canada. From there, she went off on her own.

During the pandemic Sa'd became well known for her many filmed reports on members of the anti-vaccination movement who, among other things, opposed the lockdowns. She amassed a formidable online following—on X she has tens of thousands of followers, on Instagram ten thousand—and she and her work started to appear regularly in mainstream media.

More recently, she's become even more widely known for

documenting the various Palestinian protests. Some—like the one where a Toronto police officer ferried coffee and doughnuts to some masked anti-Israel agitators blocking access off a superhighway to a predominantly Jewish neighbourhood—ended up being seen around the world, leading to many red faces among the leadership at the Toronto Police Service. As a result Sa'd has become a target: death threats have forced her to move three times in as many years. She's had to make multiple complaints to the police about the abuse and violence she experiences, too. On the job she's been sworn at, spit at, and assaulted by protestors more times than she can count. She knows them, many by name.

"I'm not looking to suppress the good or the bad about any particular group, and that is what I believe sets my work apart from what a lot of other people are doing," Sa'd says. "You can have a camera, and you can be out and record incidents, or whatever, at a protest. But I have worked really hard to not put a slant on it—apart from focusing on what's the impact of these tactics."

What has made impartiality so hard to maintain since October 7 is the inclusion at these protests of the most extreme elements of the far left, Sa'd says. They've wormed their way into the pro-Palestinian, anti-Israel groups, and the results have been unhelpful to the Palestinian cause at best and—at worst, she says—turned it into something dark and hateful. "It's as if there is an Antifa-like, anarchist element to it. That has hijacked the Palestinian cause."

Some of the behaviours Sa'd has observed—among the leaders, organizers, and grassroots alike—share characteristics with the far-right anti-vaxxers she spent three years tracking and filming, she says. Among other things, they don't always advocate a specific solution, although they share a propensity for anger and are sometimes openly violent, she adds.

"I could speculate as to why. All I can say for sure is that I see how it's happening. Everyone in this [protest movement] is a cog to some degree, in service of what end I don't know. Political power, money, the prestige of media? Those are all motivating factors."

Sa'd stresses that the pro-Palestinian cause has "real grievances," and she won't denounce them (or anyone, apart from lawbreakers). But she believes other forces are at work that have clearly made effective use of internet-based propaganda to rally their troops—and that have led to what she euphemistically calls bad behaviour. The protestors are victims of the unseen algorithms at TikTok or Meta or X, she says, adding that those she films sometimes don't seem to know what's real and what's not.

For Sa'd, money has clearly played a role in the protests, although she admits that it's almost impossible to quantify. "There is some money that flows around protests. We see it with the signs, with the speakers, with the truck rentals, sometimes having snacks . . . you can see that there's things that have expenditures. There's union money; there's likely some discretionary funds from politicians that flows. There are non-governmental organizations [from which] money will flow.

"I'm not going to be shown a pay stub," she adds. "It likely happens in greasy old cash. But there are people whose behaviour just does not make sense logically, unless there is some kind of external motivator, which could be money. It's inconceivable, in fact, that there isn't something influencing them to act in the ways that they do. [They act like] paid provocateurs. I'm confident that that exists."

While there's money flowing in, the crowd sizes often vary, she says. Different people show up to protest Israel or celebrate Hamas, and sometimes they even let the keffiyehs slip off their faces. But one constant for Sa'd is how the pro-Palestine side has alienated many potential supporters. The presence of aggressive and violent far-left agitators has made all that markedly worse.

"So," she says, "we now have Palestinian protestors mixed in with Antifa protestors and adopting the Black Bloc–style protocol—wear this mask, wear this keffiyeh. And that creates a certain visual impression. Add to that the fact that police are failing to keep the peace there. Police will say that a lawful assembly, a protest, is a protected right. Sure. But there's a line between one's own constitutional rights and where it becomes criminal activity—like blocking [neighbourhoods]. And the police have not been proactive in addressing that or nipping it in the bud. And so there's constant escalations."

At one protest—now the subject of a criminal prosecution— a woman approached Sa'd as a police inspector stood nearby. She slammed her megaphone into Sa'd's face repeatedly, all the while shouting into it. Eventually the woman was arrested and charged with assault with a weapon.

"The only reason that lady did that, I think, was because she was egged on by someone else standing shoulder to shoulder with her, and they said I was a Zionist, and that I was there for bad reasons. And 'Go get her.' And so this lady attacks a fellow Palestinian woman based on the word of another Palestinian woman, and it's just like . . . it's dangerous.

"So yeah," says Sa'd. "I do kind of worry for my safety. But I also think that there is value in documenting what I can."

And what Caryma Sa'd has been documenting, as she herself knows better than just about anyone, is a movement that is increasingly willing to push the limits of tolerance, and of the law.

Hamas fights in two ways, most agree. It fights with bombs and bullets, and it fights with words and images. It's better at the latter than the former. By the time Donald Trump's ceasefire took effect in October 2025, some claimed Hamas had been militarily reduced to a shadow of what it had been.

The facts of October 7, 2023, are not in dispute, however. On that day, Hamas and other Palestinian terrorist groups attacked Israel by ground, air, and sea in what they called Operation Al-Aqsa Flood. More than 3,800 were part of Hamas's Nukhba force and al-Qassam Brigades; 2,200 belonged to other designated terrorist groups. Hundreds of Palestinian civilians joined them to loot or participate in the documented acts of violence. They entered Israel through 119 breaches in the fences bordering Gaza.

In all, they killed 1,182 people—some Jewish, some not— and over 4,000 more were treated for gunshot wounds, grenade injuries, and burns. They took 251 civilians hostage; 210 were alive and 41 were declared deceased. At least 100 Israeli women and girls were subjected to extreme sexual violence. All of this has been meticulously documented by NGOs that are arm's-length from Israel—and, in many cases, strong critics of the Jewish state.

More than 90 per cent of those killed or taken hostage were Israeli citizens, and included Jewish Israelis, Arab Israelis, and Bedouins. Many were dual nationals, and citizens of forty-four different countries were murdered or kidnapped. The largest group of foreigners came from Thailand, most of them farm workers hired to help out on *kibbutzim* and *moshavim*.

Hamas's violence and sadism are well known by now; many of its generals and commanders have been eliminated by Israel. Less known, however, is who, exactly, is ultimately behind their global propaganda effort. Even less is known about the names of many of the generals overseeing that worldwide disinformation campaign.

Within hours of the attack on Israel, when the Jewish state and the West were still reeling, Hamas issued a worldwide call. It ordered its allies to commence pushing out disinformation and denial, and to start spreading chaos and division throughout the West.

In sworn legal filings made in U.S. courts, Hamas's propaganda team is alleged to be centred in that country, and to have been for many years. The leaders of the anti-Israel, anti-Western propaganda effort have different names: American Muslims for Palestine, Students for Justice in Palestine, the Palestinian Youth Movement, and the Council on American-Islamic Relations. Others in the mix include Jewish Voice for Peace and Within Our Lifetime. All these groups dispute allegations that there is central control and planning in their movement. All of them—the ones that claim to be Jewish, in particular—dispute that they are antisemitic.

It's all organic and spontaneous, they claim. But that seems disingenuous at best. Their Google Doc manuals, their "toolkits," and—most of all—their actions show an impressive degree of centralization, organization, and focus. And their efforts appear closely connected and coordinated.

As *Tablet* magazine observed in the detailed investigative 2024 report cited earlier, "It is a mistake both to view the campus protests as a 'student' movement and to regard the outsiders as 'infiltrators' or somehow separate from the movement. Rather, student activists have been working together with outsiders, with whom they are linked via overlapping activist networks and nationwide organizations. The 'student' revolts, in turn, exist on a continuum with the broader anti-Israel protest movement."

As a result, in May 2024 an extraordinary lawsuit was filed against Hamas's alleged proxies in the West by American Jewish victims, and family members, of the October 7 attack in the District Court for the Eastern District of Virginia. It described, with forensic detail, who makes up Hamas's propagandists in the West. It's a complex picture. For years, Hamas has relied on the AJP Educational Foundation, Inc., also known as American Muslims for Palestine (AMP). According to lawsuits filed in American courts, AMP is alleged to be Hamas's disinformation arm in North America. It was created out of the ashes of other pro-Hamas official groups, which had been banned after being found criminally or civilly liable for providing financial support to Hamas and other terrorist groups. (AMP has refused to comply with demands by Virginia's attorney general to provide internal and financial documents, and has issued a statement about the Virginia action: "AMP operates for the lawful purpose of educating the Muslim-American community and others here in the United States as to the rich culture and history of Palestine." It calls the lawsuit "baseless" and "misdirected.")

In 2010, AMP turned its attention to one key audience—college and university students and their professors across North America—by creating the National Students for Justice in Palestine. The NSJP, in turn, would effectively go on to control literally hundreds of Students for Justice in Palestine (SJP) chapters—clubs, associations—across the continent and even overseas. The U.S. government has alleged that AMP "disseminates information/propaganda," often aimed at receptive university and college students, in order to recruit them as foot soldiers or (in the case of Jewish students) to intimidate and threaten them. For more than a decade, AMP's two creations, NSJP and SJP, successfully built up a lot of capacity and members.

Then, on October 8, the day after Hamas's terrorist attack, AMP and NSJP sprang into action. Hamas had issued a "call for mass mobilization," an important part of which would involve disseminating its manifesto and plan of attack. Much of that manifesto, called the NSJP Toolkit, was prepared long before October 7. It included what it termed "resistance materials"—a call for mass mobilization of supporters, plus celebrations of what Hamas had done, which the toolkit called "a historic win." The toolkit also identified AMP and NSJP as part of a Unity Intifada, which would be seemingly controlled by Hamas's "unified command" of terrorist operations in Gaza.

In the toolkit, AMP and NSJP openly embrace what they call "armed struggle." As part of that struggle, both organizations state that they are seeking "liberation." They then go on to define liberation as "a real process that requires confrontation by any means necessary," and which necessarily involves "armed struggle." Say AMP and NSJP: "All [resistance] is legitimate, and all of it is necessary." And all of it was to become active—coincidentally or not—on October 7, 2023.

One lawsuit filed against leaders of SJP and Within Our Lifetime in March 2025 in the Southern District of New York made startling new allegations about what the anti-Israel groups knew and when they knew it. As the lawsuit alleged, "Three minutes before Hamas began its attack on October 7, Columbia SJP posted on Instagram 'We are back!!' and announced its first meeting of the semester would be announced and that viewers should 'Stay tuned.' Before the post, Columbia SJP's account had been dormant for months." The SJP Toolkit was released while the Hamas attack was still underway in Israel. Its cover featured Hamas terrorists landing in Israel—on motorized paragliders. SJP would not disavow the attacks, stating on October 8 that they encouraged "not just slogans and rallies, but armed confrontation with the oppressors."

Meanwhile, in the Virginia lawsuit, the plaintiffs stated: "The AMP and NSJP have intentionally instigated a mass culture of fear, threats, violence, and overt hatred to intimidate politicians and institutions for Hamas's substantial benefit. AMP and NSJP are coordinating the occupation of dozens of college campuses across the country to 'force' government and academia to bend to Hamas's will. There is a legal chasm between independent advocacy and knowingly serving as the propaganda and recruiting wing of a Foreign Terrorist Organization. AMP and NSJP are the latter. They are not innocent advocacy groups, but rather the propaganda arm of a terrorist organization operating in plain sight."

As of this writing, the case is still before the courts. Responding to the Virginia lawsuit, the defendants stated: "AMP (and AJP) remain nonprofits in good standing in the eyes of the United States government. These entities simply exercise their First Amendment rights to free speech and operate well within the laws of the United States." NSJP did not respond to media requests for comment.

AMP is described as a "501(c)(3)" non-profit corporation, meaning it's tax-exempt. It was incorporated in California, but its main place of business is Falls Church, Virginia, in Washington's suburbs. The NSJP, meanwhile, is an unincorporated association—but it doesn't have a main place of business or even a publicly available leadership structure.

The origins of both organizations (and, ultimately, SJP) can be traced back to 1988. In that year, Hamas's founding organization, the Muslim Brotherhood, set up the Palestine Committee: a network of smaller groups, some incorporated and some not, with all focused on raising funds for the cause. Their chief policy objective was to derail any normalization of relations between Israel and moderate Arab nations. In 1993, the committee held a conference in Philadelphia where the attendees discussed ways to disrupt talks leading to peace and diplomatic relations. The committee decreed that they would assist Hamas on all matters "financial, information[al] and political." Leaders of Hamas—not yet designated a terror group—were present at the event, along with Islamic Association of Palestine (IAP) staffers and future members of the Council on American-Islamic Relations (CAIR).

Along with the IAP, others were in attendance in Philadelphia. Among them: the Holy Land Foundation for Relief and Development (HLF) and the American Muslim Association (AMS). The HLF would fundraise in North America for Hamas and serve as its propaganda arm. The AMS was initially separate but would eventually merge with the IAP.

This alphabet soup of organizations and associations ultimately met an unhappy end. In 2001, the U.S. Office of Foreign Asset Control designated the HLF a "global terrorist" group and convicted five of its leaders of providing support to Hamas. They went to prison. Three years later, IAP and AMS were found civilly liable for the same type of offences, and as such both were dissolved. The directing minds behind these organizations kept trying, however: in 2002, they founded something called KindHearts for Charitable Humanitarian Development, based in Toledo, Ohio. A decade later, it too was dissolved for fundraising for Hamas.

The pro-Palestine activists were determined: they didn't give up. In 2006, the leaders of the various dissolved entities started AMP. Its goal, as with all its predecessors, was alleged by the lawsuit plaintiffs to fundraise for Hamas and to assist it in disseminating its propaganda. Six members of AMP's leadership were IAP members, or active in the HLF and IAP. One had been involved with KindHearts. Many of those who led the banned organizations were again brought together to run the new one, AMP. Unlike its predecessors, however, AMP was much more careful. It had learned from the mistakes of the past. It openly addressed this at its 2014 annual conference, where it discussed—as AMP itself put it—the importance of "navigating the fine line between legal activism and material support for terrorism."

It's a distinction without a difference, said the plaintiffs in the Virginia District Court action. "AMP is a reincarnation of IAP and AMS, and continues to operate with the same core people and endeavors to achieve the same goal: acting as Hamas's propaganda division."

AMP purports to be its own organization. But it uses the corporate status of its fiscal supporter, AJP Educational Foundation, Inc. (AJP), which it founded in 2008. AMP and AJP have identical leadership structures and even share the same business address in Falls Church, Virginia. In October 2023,

Virginia's attorney general started to investigate both organizations for "potential violations of Virginia's charitable solicitation laws," including "benefitting or providing support to terrorist organizations." Namely, Hamas. For its part, AMP claims that it "always [has] been . . . operating for a legal purpose." AJP, meanwhile, pointed to the statement of the American-Arab Anti-Discrimination Committee, which said the lawsuit was "deeply troubling and echos [sic] a resurgence of McCarthyite tactics aimed at silencing support for Palestinian rights."

SJP, in legal filings, is alleged by the plaintiffs to oversee anti-Israel and pro-Hamas activity on campuses across North America—an allegation SJP has rejected in court. It had its first national convention in 2010 at the University of California at Berkeley, where it successfully brought together its various chapters. SJP was mostly the brainchild of Hatem Bazian, a Berkeley professor who founded the very first SJP chapter. There, AMP announced the creation of NSJP in order to control the management, financing, and messaging of SJP branches across the country. Some of those chapters chose to remain unaffiliated on paper, but they still receive aid and materials from NSJP—particularly the messaging to be used on campuses.

Every association and non-profit needs financial support, and NJSP, AMP, and SJP are no exception. NSJP's official "fiscal sponsor" is Westchester People's Action Committee Foundation (WESPAC), a non-profit organization that describes itself as "a leading force for progressive social change in Westchester County, New York, since 1974." It is, however, quite a bit more than that. As one of the main fiscal sponsors of NJSP, it "lends" its tax-exempt status to NJSP and other groups like Within Our Lifetime. WOL are effectively the anti-Israel, pro-Hamas shock troops in and around New York City. "Long Live October 7th!" some shouted at WOL-led protests in New York City. "The Zionists Are Not Jews and Not Humans!" WOL has been banned by Meta for violating the platform's "dangerous organizations and individuals policy." It has led protests at New York City's Grand Central Station, has shared a video calling for the bombing of Tel Aviv—which it later deleted—and has even orchestrated a protest to, as they put it, "cancel Christmas" at Rockefeller Center.

WESPAC receives and administers donations on behalf of groups such as NSJP and Within Our Lifetime. WESPAC then keeps a small percentage of the donations and passes along the remainder to groups it supports. The problem with that arrangement, critics have noted, is that it lets NSJP collect and distribute funds without any real transparency. As the plaintiffs in the Virginia lawsuit stated, "The financial interactions between WESPAC and its clientele [are] intentionally opaque to largely shield from public view the flow of funds between and among them . . . [meanwhile] NSJP, through its leadership and recruited grassroots supporters, has regularly identified itself as a supporter of, and sometimes even part of, Hamas and its affiliates. . . . [It has] disseminated instructions from Hamas and others, hosted speakers that are 'Specially Designated Global Terrorists' or affiliated with them, and provided direct aid to [specially designated terrorists]."

WESPAC has used the Virginia legal action to fundraise, stating: "The well-funded forces of darkness are now waging legal warfare against us. . . . The threat to WESPAC's survival is real. Please give generously." NSJP, meanwhile, has not responded to requests for comment. Media inquiries sent to WESPAC's White Plains, New York, headquarters went unanswered.

Early on the morning of October 7, AMP's message to college campuses—through NSJP, and then disseminated by SJP—was not subtle. Violent attacks, such as those occurring hours before in Israel, were a justifiable response "to Zionism as an idea, to Israel as an entity, and to Zionists as people." Their purpose, the plaintiffs alleged, was to defend the actions of Hamas and its affiliates in Gaza, within Western academia and society at large— but also to establish an environment where violence against Jews (and anyone else associated with Israel) "could be construed as acceptable, justified, or even heroic." These groups, they alleged, are "dedicated to sanitizing Hamas's atrocities and normalizing its terrorism."

Hamas's propaganda strategy has had two main objectives: influence public opinion and justify its violence. Article 29 of the Hamas charter is clear about this. It calls on Hamas support- ers to work toward these objectives "through the convening of solidarity conferences, the issuing of explanatory bulletins, favor- able articles and booklets, enlightening the masses regarding the Palestinian issue, clarifying what confronts it and the conspira- cies woven around it. They should mobilize the Islamic nations, ideologically, educationally and culturally, so that these peoples would be equipped to perform their role in the decisive battle of liberation."

On October 7, the effectiveness of Hamas's strategy—and their team—was there for many to see. As the American anti- hate group Coalition for a Safer Web observed in a report, "Within hours of its attack on October 7th, Hamas' Qatar-based politburo web operatives flipped the switch on a slickly produced global social media disinformation campaign calculated to trig- ger an outpouring of pro-Palestinian/anti-Israel sentiment across global social media platforms to amplify (and justify) Hamas' terror. The initial disinformation flood was in Arabic directed at Arab social media sites to create sympathy for Hamas for its 'defence of Jerusalem's Muslim holy places' and its 'justified' struggle to free Palestinian prisoners jailed in Israel. But its second phase unleashed tens of thousands of fake [disinformation] bots in other languages to push the Hamas anti-Israel/ antisemitic narrative. When Hamas launched its attack against southern Israel on October 7, it not only caught Israel off guard—it also caught Israel and its global supporters flat-footed in the all too crucial information wars."

As the Coalition for a Safer Web, Cyabra, CyberWell, and many others have noted, Hamas and its propaganda team deployed disinformation bots on October 7 to push the narrative in Arabic that Hamas's terrorist attack, specifically its hostage-taking, was justified. These bots are designed to grow and interact in the way that real people do online.

Hamas and its axis iniated this first wave of propaganda using servers in Pakistan, Qatar, and Iran. The second wave was conducted in English by Hamas's PR team in the West: AMP, NSJP, and their allies, the plaintiffs in the Virginia lawsuit alleged. The plaintiffs summed it up this way: "Hamas relies on its propagandists around the world to do its bidding, spreading its falsehoods about Israel and the Jews far and wide, and to instigate a culture of violence and fear to sway global institutions to behave in Hamas's favor. Global propaganda, particularly directed at the West and the United States, is not just one small part of Hamas's broader strategy: it is Hamas's grand strategy."

Some of the post–October 7 propaganda effort was quite subtle and hidden. Other parts were out in the open. Now-deceased Hamas leader Ismail Haniyeh, for example, called for Hamas's "resistance abroad" to "join this battle any way they can," adding: "let us be partners in creating this great victory." Then, just three days later, IAP founder Khaled Mashal called on Hamas's global supporters to be "part of this battle." Within hours of the attack, prose identical to that used by the Hamas leadership appeared in NSJP material across social media and on college and university campuses. On October 8, NSJP released the Day of Resistance Toolkit to hundreds of college campuses. The toolkit reads: "Today, we witness a historic win for the Palestinian resistance: across land, air, and sea, our people have broken down the artificial barriers of the Zionist entity. . . . As the Palestinian student movement, we have an unshakable responsibility to join the call for mass mobilization."

The toolkit goes on, demanding that pro-Hamas supporters "not only support, but struggle alongside our people back home . . . and above all normalize and support our fearless resistance." The toolkit came out a few days before the massive October 2023 Day of Resistance took place on multiple campuses to support Hamas. The document makes no mention of the rapes, kidnappings, and murders. It simply states that "settlers are not civilians." The implication, to Israelis and their allies, is that civilians are legitimate targets. "We reject the distinction between 'civilian' and 'militant.' We reject the distinction between 'settler' and 'soldier,'" the George Washington University SJP wrote: "A settler is an aggressor, a soldier, and an occupier even if they are lounging on our occupied beaches."

Like other "toolkits" for which it would become a model in the coming weeks and months, the October 7 NSJP Toolkit provided graphics and advertisements for SJP chapters. Some of the material included images of motorized paragliders, which Hamas used to attack young people at the Nova Music Festival. The toolkit insists that anti-Israel—and, presumably, pro-Hamas—activists endorse the Towfan Al-Aqsa Statement, part of which reads, "We display our unwavering support of the resistance in Gaza and the broader occupied Palestinian lands" and "We honor Palestinians who are working on the ground on several axes of the so-called 'Gaza envelope' alongside our comrades in blood and arms, and what is coming is greater. Victory or martyrdom." The phrase *comrades in blood and arms* seemingly means organizations in the West operating as part of the so-called Unity Intifada, which is under Hamas's "united command." The phrase is lifted directly from a Hamas-affiliated Telegram chat called Resistance News Network. It was first used by the Martyr Abu Ali Mustafa Brigades of the PFLP on October 7 to refer to Hamas. The next line: "We stand with our brothers in the Al-Qassam Brigades and with all the resistance forces, and we merge with them in this battle that will be recorded in history."

All of it, the lawsuit alleges, meant that Hamas was the prime beneficiary of propaganda efforts in the West. Hamas's spokespeople were candid about this, as well. In a December 2023 Hamas TV discussion, for example, senior Hamas official Sami Abu Zahri called on the terrorist organization's allies in the West to engage in domestic terrorism to support Hamas's terrorist activities. The toolkit urged supporters to move "beyond symbolism and rhetoric" and embrace "confrontation by any means necessary." This led, the Virginia lawsuit noted, to an orgy of "trespass, assault, vandalism, robbery, destruction of property, harassment, and intimidation." Riots and protests commenced at university and college campuses across North America and Europe, just as the erstwhile hidden hand had commanded.

Because it's considered a terrorist entity, Hamas is prohibited from hiring a public relations firm in the United States, Canada, and many other Western countries. AJP, AMP, SJP, and the others, stated the Virginia plaintiffs, "fill this critical gap by providing invaluable communication services that Hamas cannot receive or pay for elsewhere . . . [they] do not just parrot Hamas's talking points. [They] regularly adopt [Hamas] propaganda language and framing." They also act quickly on urgings by Hamas and its cabal, the lawsuit states—all of which AJP and AMP vigorously deny.

On October 30, 2023, Hamas, the PFLP, and other terrorist groups stated that they intended to continue their terrorist campaigns. The very next day, NSJP responded by advertising a Week of Action for Gaza. Then, on November 9, Hamas announced on their Telegram channel a call for supporters to protest in its name and to "escalate their demonstrations" to put pressure on the U.S. government. That very day, NSJP held a nationwide Shut It Down for Palestine event and revealed a training session for how to create new SJP chapters.

All of it suggested close coordination of messaging between Hamas and its axis in the Middle East, and their propaganda network in the West. So, on or about May 12, 2021, an interview with Saleh al-Arouri was broadcast on Hamas's al-Aqsa TV. (Al-Arouri was a senior leader of Hamas until he was assassinated by Israel, in the West Bank, in January 2024.) In it, al-Arouri was direct, stating that Hamas's objectives were military in nature. But he also said that Hamas wanted "to hit deep in the enemy's own turf, and to shatter the enemy's morale and the morale of its people."

Al-Arouri added: "The resistance is designed to last for a long while."

Over and over, the same Arabic name was showing up all across North America and Europe: Samidoun. In the United States, Britain, France, Sweden, Belgium, Greece, Spain, Lebanon, Palestine, and Canada: just about everywhere, it seemed, Samidoun had chapters and was at the forefront of the anti-Israel protests and agitation.

In Canada, it had been active since March 2021. It had three directors: Charlotte Lynne Kates, Vancouver; Dave Diewert, also of Vancouver; and Thomas Gerhard Hofland, of the Netherlands. Its name meant "steadfast" in Arabic.

As a registered non-profit corporation, Samidoun didn't pay taxes. Being a non-profit isn't the same thing as being a charity, however. A charity has to observe its charitable purposes, and these are regulated. But a non-profit can do almost anything it wants to do. Which Samidoun—full name: the Palestinian Prisoner Solidarity Network—effectively did, for years. Their philosophy was public, in plain view. It included openly advocating for the listed terrorist entities Hamas and the PFLP. The government of then prime minister Justin Trudeau let them do so for several years. With few restrictions, Samidoun would regularly show up at campus occupations or shutdowns across North America.

In August 2024, Charlotte Lynne Kates travelled to Iran to receive a human rights award from a country that is considered to have the worst human rights record in the world, second only to Yemen. There, she covered her crewcut with a modest scarf and beamed as she was lauded by the Iranian regime representatives. Other winners of the Eighth Annual Islamic Human Rights Award included Ismail Haniyeh, the head of Hamas's political bureau until Israel ended his life in July 2024. Also honoured was Mohammed Reza Zahedi, a top officer in the banned Islamic Revolutionary Guard Corps, who was killed by Israel in April 2024.

In that same month, Kates and Samidoun supporters gathered on the steps of the Vancouver Art Gallery, facing the courthouse. Kates was filmed shouting through a megaphone: "Long live October Seventh! Long live October Seventh!" She also said, "We stand with the brave Palestinian resistance, and their heroic and brave action on October Seventh." And: "The beautiful, brave and heroic resistance of the Palestinian people"

Samidoun's co-founder in Canada is Kates's partner, Khaled Barakat. Barakat has been referred to as a "leader" of the Popular Front for the Liberation of Palestine, a listed terrorist entity in many Western nations. The U.S. government stated in October 2024 that Barakat was part of the PFLP central committee, and designated him as a supporter of a terrorist entity. The Americans had earlier deported him when his residency permit expired, and he somehow relocated to Canada.

Samidoun has been removed from Instagram and YouTube for violating the latter platform's "violent criminal organizations policy," and has been banned in Germany. It's considered a terrorist group by Israel. The Dutch Parliament, too, has voted to designate Samidoun as a terrorist group. In Canada, however, Samidoun for years openly received money from an organization called the Alliance for Global Justice, whose website boasts that it supports "political prisoners" who are allegedly affiliated with Hamas, al-Qaeda, PFLP, and others. Asked about its relationship with Samidioun, an Alliance spokesperson said: "It is being claimed that one of our sponsored organizations, Samidoun, that exists to support Palestinian political prisoners and their families, broke the law. That is untrue."

In October 2024, following years of complaints and expressions of concern, the Canadian and U.S. governments finally moved against Samidoun. Along with the U.S. Treasury Department, Canada designated Samidoun as a terrorist group, and Barakat a supporter of terrorism. This meant that banks would be required to freeze Samidoun's property, and no one would be allowed to enter into any financial transactions with it. Travel would be severely limited as well, particularly when done to propagandize or recruit new supporters.

How could a group that openly supported terror—a group led by a woman who received "human rights" awards from Iran—be permitted to carry on, openly, for so long? No one seemed to have an answer. Nor did anyone seem to know why many other supporters of extremism and terrorism were being allowed to operate, more or less without any consequences, legal or otherwise. In the fall of 2024, Capital Research Center, a U.S.-based think tank, issued a voluminous report making clear that Samidoun was just one Western pro-terrorist group of many.

Authored by researcher Ryan Mauro, the thirty-one-page report was titled *Marching Toward Violence: The Domestic Anti-Israel Protest Movement.* Capital Research concluded that there are now more than 150 campus groups like Samidoun in the West, including political warfare groups, inciters, supporters, and domestic terrorists. To those who'd tracked antisemitic movements over the years, it was a familiar spectrum: at one extreme were those engaged in acts of violence and crimes; then there were those, Mauro said, who would engage in incitement and propaganda but avoid getting their hands dirty—an identical model to, say, far-right hate groups, neo-Nazis, and others of that ilk.

As Mauro and Capital Research noted, there is in fact considerable overlap between the two types of groups. Both the neo-Nazis and the jihadists favour revolution. Both embrace violence and violent rhetoric. And both are united in their hatred of Jews.

"These revolutionary goals are held by the two different factions of anti-Israel extremist groups. The first faction combines Islamists, communists/Marxists, and anarchists. The second faction consists of groups with white supremacist/nationalist ideologies." For example, white supremacist promoter Nick Fuentes said he favours Hamas "over all these tricky Zionist Jews"; a pro-Hamas Minnesota imam has allegedly promoted Nazi propaganda; and an editor of the far-left outlet *The Grayzone* used the white supremacist term "Zionist-Occupied Government" to allege that Israel controls American foreign policy. It was arguably what Libya's Muammar Qaddafi had called "The Third Position"—an anti-capitalist, anti-Western, antisemitic alliance of the far right and the far left.

There was one key difference, however. As Capital Research observed in their report, the anti-Israel, anti-West movement has become much bigger and much more successful since Qaddafi's time. They have achieved in a year what the neo-Nazis and white supremacists couldn't achieve in over a hundred years of trying, going back to the founding of the Ku Klux Klan.

In its study, Capital Research reached three main conclusions. One, "the current anti-Israel protest movement on and off the college campuses is driven by over 150 pro-terrorism groups, with the vast majority supporting Hamas and/or the October 7 terrorist attacks. The actual number of pro-terrorism groups involved in protests is certainly higher. [Two,] the backbone of the protest movement can reasonably be characterized as Hamas. [Three,] the movement is increasingly militant and criminal, with significant elements pushing it to escalate into a wider domestic terrorism campaign aimed at forcibly dismantling the infrastructure of the U.S.–Israeli alliance."

Those allied against Israel and Western countries—which these groups sometimes refer to as an "empire"—have become the main draw for an alliance of "revolutionaries who advocate radical forms of socialism, communism, Marxism, anarchism and Islamist extremism." It's a new unholy alliance in the West, Ryan Mauro and the Capital Research Center concluded, and "they are increasingly willing to take more aggressive actions."

On a campaign-style flowchart, Iran's regime would be the campaign manager of what some call "the resistance." China and Russia are the campaign's co-chairs, seen less often but providing assistance and support when it's required. Qatar's been the principal campaign's banker, with other entities—NGOs, charities, non-profits—also providing critical financial assistance. Hamas, Hezbollah, and the Houthis are the campaign's hardcore, the ones executing the campaign's bloody strategy in the Middle East. And, far from the front line, there are the others—those who will never pick up a weapon—who are members of the global anti-Israel, anti-West campaign.

They are now found throughout the West, in the Americas,

in Europe, and elsewhere. They operate mostly in the open, and usually within the confines of the prevailing law. If Hamas and Hezbollah and the Houthis are the campaign's most extreme members, the remainder are the campaign's relative moderates. They are found throughout the Muslim world's *ummah*. They are the campaign's diaspora, the ones who support the "Free Palestine" effort around the world.

Arsen Ostrovsky is a human rights lawyer, CEO at the International Legal Forum, and a senior fellow at the Misgav Institute for National Security and Zionist Strategy. Born in Ukraine, Ostrovsky and his family fled the USSR when he was a child to start a new life in Australia and escape Soviet-style persecution and antisemitism. These days, he uses his legal skills to take on the myriad manifestations of antisemitism and anti-Israel extremism in court. That extremism—also manifesting itself in lobbying, fundraising, and public relations campaigns—has been quite successful, he says. And it has been a more challenging fight than Israel's military effort against Iran and its proxies.

"The war of narratives is a far more difficult battle," says Ostrovsky. "At the end of the day, it's also a pure numbers game. There's nine and a half million people in Israel, of maybe fifteen million Jews globally. And, granted, we have some of the most incredible and brave friends and allies in the U.S. and Canada and Europe as well. But the reality is, those who loathe us, those who despise us, hate us, and refuse to see Israel as a Jewish state exist as it does? There are far too many of them."

He pauses before citing just one example of how Israel is presently losing the information war. "When you look at that in the context of social media, just that, it's a cesspool of hate and vitriol. It's very difficult to compete in that in this battle, but we have no choice. We cannot, we do not, have the luxury to stay silent. We cannot allow the other side to claim the narrative."

The other side is pushing that narrative at multiple levels, Ostrovsky says. There has been the effort of South Africa—aided and abetted by Iran—to have the International Court of Justice (ICJ) find Israel guilty of genocide in Gaza. And for Ostrovsky, the ICJ case was about more than the legal precedent.

"People ask me, for example, Should Israel have attended the ICJ hearings on genocide or not? Knowing the likely outcome in advance, should we? And I said from the beginning, Yes, absolutely. Because we weren't just speaking to the fifteen judges. We were speaking to the entire world. I think it was one of the most highly televised cases ever. So we were speaking to politicians. And diplomats. We were speaking to the world at large—not just to the judges. We needed them to know what a gross perversion of justice occurs, for example, with the weaponization of the term *genocide*." Ostrovsky holds up the ICJ decision, which artfully found that Israel hadn't committed genocide but warned the Benjamin Netanyahu government about actions that could lead to genocide. "It is a long, difficult battle, and one in which we need to make the case [for our side]. Because this isn't just the war between Israel and Hamas, between good and evil. This is a war of narratives, across every arena."

One such arena, Ostrovsky knows, is at the local level. At this level, the anti-Israel, pro-Hamas side has been more successful than many know, he says. Take, for example, the U.S. Campaign for Palestinian Rights' City Council Palestine Organizing Toolkit, which the USCPR insists it doesn't hide—possibly because lobby laws prohibit operating in secrecy. Even to critics, the multi-page toolkit is one of the most professional-looking lobby and PR blueprints around. And it's been effective in places one would not expect.

The document says it's a "guide on organizing for ceasefire resolutions in local city councils." It contains draft anti-Israel resolutions for city councils to pass and a media plan on how to manipulate news coverage. It offers guides for calling and emailing voters to apply pressure on city councillors and maps on how to increase what it calls "grassroots advocacy capacity with digital tools, such as mass mailers, text alert systems, etc."

The toolkit also describes, in detail, how to host "weeks of action" to paralyze cities and towns that don't comply—and offers advice on how to "create narratives" that "ending genocide is a moral issue." It talks about how to track votes. And it contains slick, professional talking points, graphics, and leave-behind documents for the anti-Israel, anti-West lobby effort.

City councils and municipal governments don't set foreign policy; governments at the national level do that. The USCPR, however, has apparently embraced the old political truism that all politics are local. They seem to know that if they can get enough sub-national governments to embrace their main messages, then those governing at the national level—and representing their countries at the international level—will be obliged to pay attention. And, possibly, sign on.

So, the USCPR—like similar organizations found in Canada, Britain, France, Germany, and other countries—conduct quiet but effective lobby campaigns. The USCPR's toolkit reports on the many cities where they've been successful: Dearborn, Providence, Akron, Detroit, Seattle, Oakland, Kalamazoo, Portland, St. Louis, and Chicago, plus a score of smaller towns and cities. The toolkit gives the anti-Israel campaign's troops tips on how to obscure their online presence so that it will be more difficult for politicians and their staff to learn more about their real backgrounds. The plan also describes how to effectively push reluctant politicians into submission. Or, if they're opposed, how to isolate them.

The U.S. Campaign for Palestinian Rights, like other such groups, is no church bake-sale outfit. It has a multimillion-dollar budget, a website that is more impressive than those of many established political parties, scores of full-time staff, field organizers, and steering committees and advisory boards aplenty. Its message, as with other such groups, is quite clear. It accuses Israel of "apartheid," "ethnic cleansing," "genocide," "war crimes," and "colonialism." It promotes anti-Israel Boycott, Divestment, and Sanctions efforts, going after companies that include McDonald's, Google, Airbnb, and Volvo. Most seriously, USCPR helps fund the Palestinian BDS National Committee—which, Israel alleges, shares members with Hamas. The group's leader has stated that "we're not ashamed to have armed resistance as well as peaceful resistance."

Arsen Ostrovsky is too familiar with BDS and the other "anti-Zionist" campaigns, because he fights them using the law. Often the other side prevails, he says. Ostrovsky points to another way in which the anti-Israel, pro-Hamas effort has been successful: money. Raising it, disbursing it. Ostrovsky alleges that Qatar and Iran have been the principal source of funds for the war effort. While international law prohibits the funding of terror groups like Hamas and Hezbollah, the campaign's bankers have been undeterred. They are highly creative, he says.

"It's very difficult, in reality, to hold Iran and their proxies accountable when you're dealing with legal issues of sovereign immunity. How do you hold a state accountable? Does that effort ever hold them accountable? And that has happened in the United States, many times. How are you ever going to enforce [a judgment], and receive any compensation?"

Some still try. The Virginia lawsuit, for example, targeted the main anti-Israel campus organizers in North America in May 2024, because the university encampments had become the centre of anti-Israel agitation. The lawsuit, all forty-nine pages of it, lays out the ways AMP and SJP "serve as Hamas's propaganda divisions" in Canada, the United States, and elsewhere. AMP and SJP, as noted, deny its allegations.

In some places, SJP chapters have taken slightly different names, like Students Against Israeli Apartheid (SAIA) or Solidarity for Palestinian Human Rights (SPHR). But they're all branches of the same anti-Israel tree—about which the Anti-Defamation League has said: "Students for Justice in Palestine (SJP) and many of the organization's campus chapters explicitly endorsed the actions of Hamas and their armed attacks on Israeli civilians. . . . SJP chapters issue pro-Hamas messaging and/or promote violent anti-Israel messaging channels." SJP has been present and very active on hundreds of campuses, and have helped oversee hundreds of protests and "actions" that have often devolved into antisemitism. In the days following October 7, SJP called the attack a "historic win for the Palestinian resistance." They also stated that "this is what it means to Free Palestine: not just slogans and rallies, but armed confrontation with the oppressors."

It is significant, then, that the Virginia lawsuit was brought by other young people. Many of them were those who somehow survived the slaughter at the Nova Music Festival on October 7, or the mass murder of innocents at Kibbutz Holit on the same day. Fifteen people were killed at that kibbutz, Israelis and non-Israelis alike. At Nova, the site of the worst atrocities, 364 mainly young people were killed.

The lawsuit was detailed and well argued. It meticulously laid out the ways in which SJP and its allied organizations lobby, fundraise, provide public relations, and "provide on-campus management and control hundreds of university chapters of SJP." They do so, stated the plaintiffs, "to operate a propaganda machine for Hamas and its affiliates across campuses." The lawsuit was brought by five of the biggest and best law firms in the United States. It is seeking a jury trial and unspecified damages for the plaintiffs.

In the statement of claim, the victims wrote: "[The anti-Israel groups] provide ongoing, continuous, systematic and material support for Hamas and its affiliates . . . by operating and managing Hamas's mouthpiece for North America, dedicated to sanitizing Hamas's atrocities and normalizing its terrorism."

Arsen Ostrovsky agrees with that allegation. The other side in the information war isn't hard to see: often, they're not hidden at all. That makes it all the more imperative that Israel and the West fight back, he says.

Ostrovsky concludes: "I would actually say it's more of a duty. It's an obligation. For those who believe in these values that we all hold dear—including outside of Israel, including our friends and allies—we must speak out against this multifaceted campaign against us. But don't be under any illusion: it's a tough battle, and it's one that will take many years for us to win."

Hillel Neuer is a humble man. But it's a fact that he's almost single-handedly taken up the fight against the most important part of the pro-Palestine, pro-Hamas, anti-Israel, antisemitic global propaganda campaign: the people who seek to legitimize it. The individuals—and organizations, and countries—who seek to demonize Jews and the Jewish state at the international level. They do so from within associations, think tanks, non-governmental bodies, and (most of all) the United Nations itself, just as Gary Wexler was warned, long ago, that they would.

Neuer is the executive director of UN Watch, an NGO that fights antisemitism at a global level. No other person or organization is doing that, really. Certainly no one is doing it as effectively. He reflects on this writer's question: Why is the United Nations so important to the global propaganda effort against Israel and its Western allies?

"It is certainly true that the United Nations applies, systematically, a double standard against Israel, even though it's founded on universal standards," says Neuer. "For example, the whole point of the Universal Declaration of Human Rights is that they're meant to be universal standards. But, sadly, the way that they are applied undermines the very idea that they are standards at all. So, for example, we see in New York at the UN General Assembly, there is one resolution every year criticizing Iran. There is one on Syria, there is one on North Korea, maybe a couple of other countries get criticized.

"And then there's fifteen on Israel. Every year."

In theory, the United Nations makes sense: an international body that promotes peace and security and that fosters better relations between countries. A place to coordinate the actions of nations, to ostensibly create a better world. The UN was born from the ashes of the Second World War, phoenix-like, with the initial aim of preventing future world wars. Four dozen nations met in San Francisco in June 1945 and hammered out the broad principles that formed the UN Charter. There are 111 articles in the charter, collected in 19 separate chapters.

This is the very first one: "To maintain international peace and security, and to that end: to take effective collective measures for the prevention and removal of threats to the peace, and for the suppression of acts of aggression or other breaches of the peace." Those are the first words one sees: that the United Nations would always strive to maintain peace and take action to prevent and remove "threats to peace." In practice, it hasn't always worked out that way, and particularly when Israel is the subject matter.

Neuer laughs about how he's disliked by many at the United Nations. One anti-Israel activist, for example, has claimed that he leads a "small, right-wing organization" that is "hardly known outside of UN headquarters," but that isn't quite true. The *Tribune* in Geneva, where Neuer presently lives, has said he is "feared and dreaded" by the world's dictators, all of whom have a vote and a bully pulpit at the UN. Others have celebrated what he does with just a small staff of about six people. The City of Chicago, for example, declared a Hillel Neuer Day in 2016, noting that he is "one of the world's foremost human rights advocates" and applauding how he has "promoted peace, justice and human rights around the world." Meanwhile, when McGill University gave him his honorary degree, they said he was "a voice for those without one."

Hillel Neuer shrugs about all that. He doesn't like to talk about his awards and accolades. He and his staff are more focused on the singular anti-Israel bias that permeates the United Nations, which its critics say is getting dramatically worse. Neuer and his organization have had many successes, but perhaps none as important as how they have effectively exposed antisemitism at the highest levels of the institution. There are two notable cases.

One is that of Francesca Albanese. Albanese is Italian, telegenic, and elegant. She's also an international lawyer and an academic, and holds a Ph.D. in international refugee law. She has many academic awards and distinctions. And she is, Neuer has alleged, a bigot.

Albanese's title is the United Nations' "special rapporteur" on Palestine. As Neuer notes, however, she's not just an advocate for Palestinians—she's also, he says, an advocate against the Jewish state who has devoted herself energetically to that unwritten part of her job description. After the atrocities of October 7, Albanese stated: "Our collective obliviousness to what led, 100 years ago, to the Third Reich's expansionism and the genocide of people not in conformity with the 'pure race' is asinine. And it is leading to the commission of yet another genocide." She vigorously denies, however, that she is antisemitic.

The facts seem to suggest otherwise, Neuer says. In the fall of 2024, for example, Albanese conducted a North American "campus tour" sponsored by none other than the Students for Justice in Palestine (SJP), previously described as the "mouthpiece for [Hamas in] North America, dedicated to sanitizing Hamas' atrocities and normalizing its terrorism" by the survivors of the Nova Music Festival in their lawsuit filed in Virginia's District Court. Neuer has catalogued some of Albanese's alleged antisemitism in a compendious report. She has stated, he notes, that "America is subjugated by the Jewish lobby"; that the victims of October 7 were "not killed because of their Judaism" but because of Hamas's "reaction to Israel's oppression"; and that Gaza is "the largest and most shameful concentration camp of the 21st Century."

Francesca Albanese is objectionable enough, Neuer says—but UNRWA, the United Nations Relief and Works Agency, causes far more damage. UNRWA is the only UN humanitarian body preoccupied with a single group of people, the Palestinians. It has become a major focus for Hillel Neuer and UN Watch. (UNRWA's leadership would not provide comment.)

For some time, UN Watch has documented how UNRWA's leaders and staff have promoted antisemitism and hate. They have issued multiple reports: on UNRWA applauding Adolf Hitler; on UNRWA's open teaching of antisemitism to Palestinian children; on UNRWA glorifying the violence of Hamas, the Taliban, terrorist attacks on Jews, and even the Holocaust; on how UNRWA demonizes Judaism and Christianity with impunity; on its embrace of hateful and antisemitic conspiracy theories; on many, many UNRWA staff cheering on Hamas murders and rapes on October 7; and, most often, on flatly denying Israel's right to exist. UNRWA does all these things, he says, but it still receives about $1.5 billion annually from the United Nations and countries like the United States, Britain, Canada, Germany, France, Italy, Sweden, Japan, and Australia. It accepted that some of its members participated in the October 7 attack. "UNRWA is upholding the values of the United Nations and has a zero-tolerance policy for hatred. The Agency takes each allegation seriously," it claims.

In January 2024 came the most shocking news of all, although Hillel Neuer and UN Watch were perhaps less shocked than most: in the last week of that month, it was confirmed that as many as a dozen UNRWA employees had been active participants in the atrocities of October 7. Multiple nations immediately announced that they were suspending funding of UNRWA; the employees were fired or suspended. Neuer, meanwhile, already had their names and published profiles of the men, their social media history, and even their UNRWA employee numbers. As he said on Israeli's ILTV about his group's discovery: "You don't need to be in Gaza. Their Telegram group is online. Very quickly, within an hour or two, we were able to identify individuals, who they were, their UNRWA contract ID numbers. Numerous details of the people posting, including the fact that several of them were the admins of the group, the leaders of this Telegram group, and who work for UNRWA."

One kidnapped an Israeli woman. Another participated in the massacre at Kibbutz Be'eri, one of the worst places to be on October 7, where ninety-seven were slaughtered. Another distributed rocket-propelled grenades he had stored at his home. Another stole the remains of a murdered Israeli back to Gaza, to be held for ransom. One directed Hamas vehicles and helped coordinate the attack. Most of them, it turned out, were teachers at UNRWA schools. They were clerks, social workers, a storeroom manager, as well. And all worked for the United Nations agency called UNRWA, and all were ultimately paid by Western nations.

It was a shocking story, one that—perhaps coincidentally, but likely not—came out on the very same day the International Court of Justice ruled that Israel had not, in law, committed genocide in their war against Hamas. It was a useful distraction: it drew attention away from the scandal that had enveloped the UN organization.

Philippe Lazzarini, UNRWA's controversial commissioner-general, said he "condemns in the strongest terms" what happened to Israeli civilians on October 7, and offered up a few words asking for the return of all remaining Israeli hostages. UNRWA and the United Nations knew the damage had been done, and that it was likely irreparable. At least twelve of their employees helped to murder, maim, and kidnap Israelis. The Israelis had been raising the alarm about UNRWA for a long time. But their objections seemingly fell on deaf ears at the United Nations.

In particular, the UN did not heed the many warnings from Neuer, who—days before the story broke about UNRWA staff participating in the murders and rapes of October 7—reported that three thousand UNRWA employees were active on a Telegram feed, "replete with praise of the Hamas massacre of October 7th."

Neuer is certainly aware of the pro-Hamas, anti-Israel agitation taking place across Western democracy but admits that its funding and organization are not the main focus of his work. He does, however, agree that Iran and its proxies clearly made use of the loose alliance of antisemites that existed before October 7, turning them into a formidable force: "The Islamic Republic of Iran has openly embraced [the anti-Israel protestors], and that raises questions. Iran has openly taken responsibility. It has been proud to show its support for Hamas and its proxies, publicly. The story begins with Iran, and how it is obviously coordinating with its proxies. Hezbollah is a major proxy. The Houthis in Yemen. The various Shia militias in Iraq and Syria. And it all starts with coordination, major coordination, coming from the Iranian regime. This anti-Western alliance has rallied behind Hamas and the others, I think it's very worrying."

Hillel Neuer adds, "It's certainly worrying for people who care about peace."

Palestine, Inc.

That's what Guy Goldstein calls the hidden hand—and the not-so-hidden hand—that makes up the many who are now agitating and propagandizing against Israel and, often, Western democracy itself. It's an unholy alliance of sorts, a new web of hate, he suggests, of "institutions and players," ranging from international legal and academic institutions to human rights organizations, social media platforms, non-state actors like Hamas and Hezbollah, NGOs and non-profits and charities, diplomats and politicians, individuals in the West, and—now—even what Goldstein calls "press freedom organizations."

On September 1, 2025, Goldstein says, the world saw an example of the latter at work. That day, more than 150 media outlets in more than 50 countries launched a simultaneous multilingual campaign ostensibly designed to advocate for journalists reporting in and around the war zone in Gaza. Goldstein, an Australian now living in Israel with his family, saw it coming before it happened: Reporters Without Borders and the online activism portal Avaaz, he wrote in August on his Substack platform, were planning it. It would go on to include PBS in the United States and *The Independent* newspaper in the U.K.

Goldstein observed that the campaign's coordination included very detailed tactical instructions for print, digital, and broadcast platforms. They were, he said, "using the exact operational methods we identified in the Hamas [propaganda] warfare campaign . . . and the messaging is designed for maximum emotional impact."

That was true. In their materials, Avaaz and the journalist group did not hold back: "At the rate journalists are being killed in Gaza by the Israeli army, there will soon be no one left to keep you informed," they proclaimed. It was hyperbolic, but it was likely designed to saturate global media in the same month that multiple states would formally recognize Palestinian statehood at the United Nations General Assembly, Goldstein observed. Was it linked? "The timing could be coincidental," he acknowledged. "[But] it could also represent strategic coordination for [a] maximum delegitimizing effect against Israel."

And, on September 1, 2025, that is indeed what happened: headlines were seen around the world about journalists being killed by Israel, just as representatives of dozens of nations were gathering in New York. Gathering to recognize a state run by a terror group, as accepted by those very states: The timing, Goldstein says, was perfect.

What Reporters Without Borders and Avaaz and others were doing wasn't actually about journalism, he says. "It's systematic information warfare using press badges as camouflage," he observed, condemning the campaign. "[Their] planning document reads like a military operations manual with unified messaging protocols, multi-language asset distribution, and synchronized hashtag deployment. These organizations function as coordination hubs for influence campaigns while masquerading as neutral advocates. . . . The strategic implications are catastrophic. Every international proceeding now faces identical manipulation through coordinated influence campaigns disguised as human rights advocacy. Democratic societies are being systematically exploited by organizations that masquerade as neutral advocates while executing anti-democratic objectives."

As much as he condemns it, Goldstein acknowledges how effective the September 1 campaign—and campaigns like it— have been since October 7. "Hamas [isn't just] winning a single campaign. They have tapped into a template for systematic institutional exploitation that operates across multiple conflicts and diplomatic cycles."

What is critical to its success, says Goldstein, is the timing of it all. The "systematic information warfare" used by Hamas and the rest of their axis, he says, always follows a pattern. Whenever Israel ramps up a military effort in Gaza, what he calls Palestine Inc. simultaneously accelerates its propaganda efforts. All of it, he says, is clearly designed to hijack the global discourse by systematically delegitimizing Israel. All of it is meticulously arranged to conclude with global recognition of Palestinian statehood.

It's working, he says. Since October 7, 2023, the propaganda campaign has become "permanent, operational, and [is] executing the next phase of a multi-year strategic campaign," he writes. The evidence is everywhere.

In this new type of war, writes Goldstein, "every dead Palestinian child becomes ammunition. Every destroyed building becomes evidence. Every civilian casualty becomes a weapon in cognitive warfare." Hamas, he says, knew Israel would respond to the horrors of October 7 with overwhelming force. They were, in fact, counting on it. "They needed casualties to feed their [propaganda] warfare machine," he alleges.

That has been Hamas's modus operandi for a long time, Goldstein says. They haven't hidden it; it's a war—and not just on the traditional battlefield. Hamas has always had one strategy, he continues: "To create a cognitive war, a war where the only front that they seek advantage is in our minds."

There have been many losses. Even if Israel's calculations are wrong, there have been far too many civilian deaths, and Israel is accountable for at least some of that. Thousands of innocent lives lost to a war that Hamas itself started on October 7. Deliberately, Goldstein says, to "lure Israel in"—and to thereby seize control of the global narrative about Jews and the Jewish state. "Hamas doesn't care about its people. It has never cared about its people," he says, sounding disgusted. They're sacrificing pawns that they don't care about. And Israel is losing their key strategic allies." Because, while Israel may be good at traditional warfare, Hamas and its axis are far, far better at the information war.

The longer the Hamas–Israel war went on, too, the worse it got for Israel's international reputation, he says. "So, Israel declares an escalation in the war. They're going into Gaza, and there's no one waiting there to stop them. They meet no resistance. They just encounter some [improvised explosive devices]. They clear buildings, they clear hospitals, right? And, at the same time that Hamas's narrative escalation is happening, there's a famine. It's the fifth famine that's been declared this war, I think." He pauses again. "Why was no one ready in Israel with a narrative response to that? Because, again, Israel has a 'narrative comes last' doctrine. Both sides make massive gains very quickly, and then—it saddens me to say—Israel is left trying to figure out how to recover. Because the [wartime] losses don't harm Hamas. It doesn't care about the territory, because the world has guaranteed that it'll get the territory back at the end of the conflict anyway."

Israel has brilliant battlefield commanders, he says, ones who've been battling Hamas and its antecedents for decades. But Israel's old soldiers are schooled in traditional warfare, "counting tanks and planes and boots." Not the warfare of now. Not the propaganda warfare in which Hamas is expert. The fact that the "ceasefire now" protests continued after a ceasefire was in place is proof, he says. The haters were never really for Palestine, he adds. They were just against the Jewish state

Most people in Israel and the West have dramatically

underestimated Hamas, Goldstein says, and adds that he used to count himself among them. "The Islamists are not seventh-century barbarians. They're very sophisticated, in a lot of ways. They understand a lot of things about Western society that the West probably still doesn't understand about itself. So, the idea that Hamas are irrational and crazy people, and that barbarians just do barbaric things? Well, I've never been a fan of underestimating the enemy. I asked myself: How can what they do be rational? How can it be sensible, be smart?" He came up with the answer: "Hamas knows the math. It knows the math of the propaganda battlefield far better than Israel does.

"[Their] digital advocacy campaigns are incredibly sophisticated," he continues. "I come from a background in digital communications and digital engagement, so it's something that I've got familiarity with. And they are really, really sophisticated. They understand algorithms incredibly well . . . research shows us that there's a fifty-to-one ratio of pro-Palestine posts to pro-Israel posts. [These weren't] coming from a disparate number of creators, either. It was algorithmic selection. So, on the one hand, you have the bad guys making [promotional] things that destabilize the West. And on the other side you have the good guys, who think that the most important thing is free speech—and therefore allow more destabilization to get through."

Added to those many challenges, he notes, are Israelis themselves: they're so accustomed to being hated by the rest of humanity that they regard Israel's growing pariah status as nothing new. "This is one of those things which is tragic: Israel, as a country, is used to being the whipping boy of the of the world," says Goldstein, himself a recent migrant to Israel. "This has been going on since well before the 70s. And since the 70s, that's been accepted doctrine at the United Nations. You know, that Zionism is racism. And so there is delegitimization of Israel with [international organizations], over and over and over again. And Israel is preconditioned to dismiss what the world says. Because, of course, the world is complaining about Israel again."

Guy Goldstein sums up. "What we're seeing is Hamas and [their axis] pushing this narrative, to destroy the fundamentals of Western society." He pauses one last time.

"And the people who live in Western society do not understand that the fundamentals are being destroyed."

Kfar Aza was a farming community. Just under eight hundred people lived there. It was always a peaceful place, with modest single-storey homes arrayed around a central dining hall, which—along with a synagogue—was the centre of Kfar Aza. Residents subscribed to the socialist and Zionist ideal of communal living, plus shared ownership and responsibility. It's doubtful that any of them ever voted for Israel's conservative prime minister, Benjamin Netanyahu.

Kfar Aza is about five kilometres from the border with Gaza. Before October 7, 2023, many Palestinians would commute to Kfar Aza to work. On this day, it's mostly quiet. A few nightingales are singing in the untended olive and cypress trees and many cats are slipping in and out of shattered, burned-out homes. But there are no people. Today, there are just a few visitors from Canada listening to Eilon Kutler.

Kutler is a young man, slender, with dark hair. He's wearing jeans and running shoes and a black T-shirt, and he looks so, so sad. His English isn't perfect, but he makes himself understood.

Kfar Aza was created in the 1950s, he says. Jewish refugees from Egypt and Morocco came first. Then others, from Europe and other places. At Kfar Aza, the people farmed the land and developed irrigation systems for agriculture. They were teachers, mechanics, social workers. Lots of kids and older people. It was a place of love, he says.

On the morning of October 7, Kutler remembers, no one warned them that Hamas was heading toward them—from the air, from the land. The killers surrounded the kibbutz and came in from four directions. "We received no warning from the government or the IDF," says Kutler, standing in front of Kfar Aza's civil guard building. "There was no contact. We had no clue what was going on." Hamas descended on the place shortly after 9 a.m., he recalls, when the residents started hearing the sounds of gunfire.

"It was so sudden. It was total chaos. It was like a war zone."

On the side of the tiny civil guard structure someone has hung up a banner showing the faces of seven men, most of them smiling. All are dead, killed by Hamas or another terrorist group, the Maoist National Resistance Brigades. One of the murdered men, Avi Hindi, was the deputy security coordinator, and Eilon Kutler's best friend. "We lost so many people here," Kutler says, placing a hand beside Hindi's picture. "One in eight." Just off to one side, one can see the white concrete wall has been sprayed with bullets.

Inside the small building, the bodies and the blood have been removed by ZAKA, the Israeli organization that retrieves remains of the dead so that proper burials can take place.

"There was a pyjama party happening the night before," he recalls. "The kids were sending text messages to our civil guard members in the morning, saying, 'The terrorists are outside our house. Please save us. Please come and save us.'" But they didn't come because they were among the first to be killed.

The terrorists knew where to go first, Kutler says. "[They] had the right intelligence. They knew where the important buildings were. They got it from the people, the Palestinians, who had worked here. We had lots of workers from Gaza. I'd run into them in the mornings when I would take my dog for a walk, and I'd say good morning to them. But in the days before October 7, they wouldn't say good morning. They wouldn't look at me." Pause. "We just feel betrayal now."

Just past the civil guard building is the home of an elderly man who repaired bicycles. "His name was Elijah," says Kutler. "He built a beautiful garden, too." He looks up at the front door where Elijah had affixed a sign saying LIFE IS GOOD. The wheels of a bicycle form the O's. Beside the door are dozens of bullet holes. Through the window the sky can be seen, but no roof. Hamas set fire to the place after they killed the old man.

Kutler keeps walking. He goes past a home, largely untouched, where a flag of Israel is flying alongside a rainbow Pride flag. "That's something you don't see in Gaza," someone says.

Everywhere, there is total destruction. Kutler stops beside the rubble of one shattered place where someone has sprayed some numbers on what's left of a wall. "I knew the people who lived here," he says. "The woman managed our cultural committee. The father was a great guy, a very positive guy. He grew up in an agricultural environment. One of the neighbours called them to check on them. She said: 'I can't speak. The terrorists are in my house.'" Hamas set fire to their home, he says. To speed it up, they blew up a propane tank. It took ZAKA three weeks to find all the couple's remains. "They were burned alive."

Over on the western side of Kfar Aza, there is just a chain-link fence. No wall separates the kibbutz from Gaza, which can be easily seen on this day.

Directly across from the fence, in some newer one-storey structures, are the places where the kibbutz's younger residents lived. The homes weren't big: a door at the front, windows at the back. Outside, on the ground, are scorched mattresses and furniture and some ruined bicycles. Almost everyone in this part of Kfar Aza was kidnapped or killed, Kutler says. The terrorists flooded through a gate that is about a hundred feet away. On the doors of many of the small homes ZAKA has left behind stickers certifying that human remains had been found there. On a piece of concrete, however, there is a spray of what looks like blood. ZAKA may have missed that.

"The people who survived," says Kutler, "they survived because of luck or coincidence. That's all. I don't think those who lost someone will ever come back." His sister, he says, has left for Europe.

Outside the small homes, hung on whatever is available, there are photographs of the people who lived there. There are yellow photos (for those who were kidnapped) and red photos (for those who were murdered). There are many red photos. In the end, it took Israel's army almost twelve hours to arrive at Kfar Aza, and almost two weeks to clear out the last terrorist. They had fortified themselves inside the homes.

Kutler keeps walking, then stops near another shattered building. He looks like he might cry, but he doesn't. "What happened on October 7 didn't change my opinion about living here," he says. "To care for our neighbours, to love them. That will not change. This is how this community was. This is how we are."

He looks toward the west, toward Gaza. "I hope for better days. Not just for us, but for all of humanity. For Palestinians, too." The sound of an artillery shell exploding is heard in the distance.

Someone asks him about the anti-Israel, pro-Hamas protests in the West. They ask about antisemitic propaganda that is seemingly everywhere. Someone else asks if he'll ever come back to Kfar Aza.

Eilon Kutler thinks about all that for a few moments, then says only this about the protests, the propaganda, the hate. "Those people? They misunderstand the situation.

"We are Jews. We have nowhere else to go. This place is home."

He looks back toward the west again. "And I am a Jew."

There are, were, two wars. There was the multifront military war that Israel—and, occasionally, its allies—are waging against terrorist groups and the supporters of terrorism. That war went on longer than many expected it to. But Israel was always most likely to win it.

The other war—the information war, the propaganda war—is different. In that war, even Israelis agree, those who wish for the destruction of Israel are winning, or have won. Online metrics, public opinion surveys, media content analysis studies: all show the same trend. Enemies of Israel and the West are dominating everywhere.

Unsurprisingly, the global propaganda campaign of Hamas and its axis—online and in the real world—hasn't stopped. In truth, the campaign against Jews, the Jewish state, and Western democracy has gotten bolder and more aggressive. Because it has faced little to no pushback—and because they've enjoyed more success than even they expected—agitators in the West have ramped up their activity everywhere. It would be a mistake to believe they will one day fade away.

It won't. And ignoring it won't work. The Democratic Party thinker and author David Shenk once told me in an interview about the name he had for this phenomenon: data smog. Every day, via the internet, regular people get overwhelmed by hundreds of thousands of words and images. They get buffeted with disinformation and propaganda. It's relentless—and in wartime it gets worse. So, Shenk postulates, people just tune it out. There's too much information. It's data smog. They turn it off.

Too often, this leaves the information battlefield to the liars and the haters. Information voids don't stay empty for long. It's much better, experts agree, for citizens to always be aware and skeptical. Always harness the power of doubt. If particular words or images cause a strong emotional reaction, it's worth keeping in mind that that's the reaction propagandists value more than any other: an emotional response before a rational one.

So, individual citizens can take steps to keep propaganda out. Rely only on news sources that are established and sourced—and that welcome more than one point of view. Be very wary of social media influencers and "citizen reporters." Avoid "like" and "share" buttons online, since those are the main way that algorithms— the propagandist's best friend—track people and offer more and more extreme content. And, of course, avoid extreme content in the first place.

Those are just some of the things individuals can do to avoid being held hostage by haters and extremists in the information war. But what can governments and non-governmental organizations do? At a societal level, Hamas and Hezbollah, and Iran, and China, and Russia, and the rest are having a greater impact than ever before. What can be done to fight that?

Ten ways. There are of course many more, but these are the ones I recommend first and foremost. In many cases, citizens already possess the means to do these things, and some of these ideas are already in place. What we lack, too often, is the will to enforce them.

1. **Defeat anonymity.** In the streets, the bad guys wear masks. Online, they use false names and fake accounts. Without anonymity, the haters would have nowhere near the strength they presently do. The main reason they hide their identities—masks over their faces, fake names online where their real names should be—is to avoid consequences, legal and otherwise. The law therefore needs to be changed to create meaningful penalties for those who wear masks while intimidating others—and to create bubble zones around places of worship, as is done for abortion clinics and health centres. Social media platform owners need to be told (using the force of the law, if necessary) that online anonymity should only be permitted in the rarest of circumstances. Openness and transparency must be the rule.

2. **Penalize haters and apply the law.** Most countries already deport newly arrived non-citizens for serious crimes, and have done so for decades. So, if a non-resident individual is found to have violated laws prohibiting the wilful promotion of hatred against an identifiable group—and, since October 7, that group is over-whelmingly Jews—they can reasonably be expected to be sent back to their country of origin. Throughout Western democracy, the necessary laws are already in place. They just need to be applied with more rigour.

3. **Pass effective, constitutional anti-hate laws.** Where anti-hate laws don't already exist, governments must create laws prohibiting the wilful promotion of hatred. Where those laws do exist, they need to be used more effectively than they presently are. Equally, just as there are laws that prohibit promoting hatred, there needs to be a commitment to creating laws against promoting listed terrorist organizations such as Hamas or Hezbollah and their known symbols. Promoting listed terrorist entities is as bad as promoting hate. Laws need to reflect that.

4. **Target online antisemitism and hate.** Hamas and its allies have flooded the internet with bots and fake accounts to give the impression of strength and to spread disinformation and conspiracy theories. Governments must take this threat more seriously and use their regulatory powers to penalize online platforms—up to and including imprisonment, as France recently did with one of the owners of Telegram—that do not take action against the proliferation of cyberhatred. The billionaire owners of online platforms can and must do better at stamping out the haters they platform.

5. **Force better moderation of social media platforms.** YouTube, X, Facebook, Instagram, and TikTok et al. possess the means to provide much better moderation of hateful, terroristic content. They are not doing so, they claim, because of cost—even though many of them possess larger budgets than many countries.

Governments and regulators need to compel the platforms to adopt basic moderation standards to reduce (and ideally eliminate) hatred on social media. They need to simply enforce their own end-user agreements. If they don't comply, they need to face serious sanctions that will force them to act.

6. **Penalize universities, colleges, and schools for hate.** If a place of education is receiving any public monies, they're already subject to prohibitions and laws against promoting and permitting hate. If they are private educational institutions, human rights and civil rights laws still apply to them. So, if a school allows any wilful expressions of antisemitism and hate—whether at an encampment or in the classroom—they should be penalized for doing so. Hate is not free speech, particularly in places of learning; hate is always a lie, and the absence of knowledge. So countries need to commit to funding and teaching about genocide. Students clearly need to receive better education about the Holocaust and related genocides. Nothing breeds hate more than ignorance. In places that can't quickly afford to do so on their own, bring in one of the many accredited private groups to fill the gaps in the curriculum.

7. **Fund public awareness campaigns.** Governments are fond of advertising advocacy campaigns about everything from the environment to public health. But, as noted, nothing breeds hatred better than ignorance.

Governments need to do what the private sector often doesn't—communicate some basic truths on mass media. Namely, what hate is and why it's unwelcome.

8. **Reform non-profit and charity laws.** Across the West, antisemitic, pro-Hamas protestors and organizers are frequently getting paid to disrupt and shut down society. Funding, too, is also being sent overseas to Hamas and its axis. Their efforts are often being funded by non-profits and charities. Any non-profit or charity that has links to a designated terrorist entity—by extending them material or rhetorical support—should swiftly lose their non-profit or charity status and, in the most serious cases, be prosecuted.

9. **Educate police, prosecutors, and politicians—and reform the system.** Police and prosecutors say they're feeling overwhelmed by the amount of antisemitic criminal activity they're seeing. Politicians are uncertain about the line between free speech and hateful incitement. In both cases, better resources and better education are required. Once that's done, governments need to mandate specialized prosecutors and courts for hate prosecutions. Some jurisdictions have done this, and it works. Among other things, it develops and centres expertise in the justice system, and it speeds up prosecutions of hate crimes. Many countries already do it for drug crimes; we clearly need to do it for hate crimes as well.

10. **Fund bias crime policing.** Where bias crime units don't exist, governments need to create and fund them. Most of the time, police agencies are a patchwork when it comes to hate; some places don't even have police officers trained to deal with the problem. So, governments need to fill in the gaps before the problem gets worse. In those few places where such specialized units already exist, resources are often minimal to nonexistent. If politicians are as serious about fighting hate as they claim to be, they need to ensure that the dollars are there for recruitment and training of knowledgeable police officers and prosecutors.

These are just a few ideas about how to fight the problem that this book has attempted to describe. There are others. And there are many people of goodwill who agree that we in the West need to do a much better job opposing the antisemitism and hatred that is seemingly everywhere since October 7, 2023.

As George Orwell said, "All the war propaganda, all the screaming and lies and hatred, comes invariably from people who are not fighting." That, across the West, is what the hidden hand has started—another war, one that is far from the frontlines in the Middle East.

And that war is all around us now.

W.K.

November 2025

ACKNOWLEDGMENTS

I want to sincerely thank my amazing colleagues at the Daisy Group and Facts Matter, who tirelessly provided advice as well as research and logistical assistance. Thanks, also, to my courageous editors and colleagues at Postmedia, who have supported me despite many threats and challenges. And thanks to the gifted producers and crew of our documentary, *The Campaign*, which arose out of this book.

I am immensely grateful to my partner, E.—and my kids, E., B., S., and J.—who always gave me love and the truth. And my friends, as well—and particularly H.M., T.R., and J.G.

INTRODUCTION

This chapter includes interviews with Rami Davidian and others at the site of the Nova Music Festival.

CHAPTER ONE

This chapter includes or relies upon interviews with Mosab Hassan Yousef, Yossi Klein Halevi, Eylon Levy, Rafi Mendelsohn, Bari Weiss, Trevor Asserson, Tal-Or Cohen Montemayor, Hillel Neuer, Lesley Klaff, Gary Wexler, and many others who wished to remain anonymous. The interviews were conducted in Israel, Europe, and North America.

Helpful documents and articles included: "A strong majority of voters say the recent attack on Israel was a terrorist act," Harvard CAPS/Harris Poll, December 14, 2023, p. 45; Center for Antisemitism Research, "Antisemitic Attitudes in America 2024," Anti-Defamation League website, February 29, 2024, adl.org; Becka A. Alper, Laura Silver, and Besheer Mohammed, "Rising numbers of Americans say Jews and Muslims face a lot of discrimination," Pew Research Center website, April 2, 2024, pewresearch.org; Becka A. Alper, "How U.S. Jews are experiencing the Israel-Hamas war," Pew Research Center website, April 2, 2024, pewresearch.org; Timothy Jones, "Antisemitism rising dramatically across the world—report," Deutsche Welle (DW) online, May 5, 2024, dw.com; "A survey of the American general population (ages 18+)," Ipsos, May 14, 2024; Robert Brym, "Jews and Israel 2024 Survey: Ten further insights," *Canadian Jewish Studies* 39, May 30, 2024, pp. 108–117, cjs.journals.yorku.ca; Shibley Telhami, "Study of change in U.S. public attitudes towards Jews and Muslims, 2022-2024," Critical Issues Poll, University of Maryland website, July 2, 2024, criticalissues.umd.edu; Jeffrey M. Jones, "Americans show heightened concern about antisemitism," Gallup website, July 1, 2024, gallup.com; "Jewish people's experiences and perceptions of antisemitism," European Union Agency for Fundamental Rights website, July 11, 2024, fra.europa.eu/en; *Zorchinsky c. SPHR Concordia*, 2024 QCCS 3646 (CANLII), Superior Court of Québec, October 3, 2024; "Antisemitism in Canada Report," National Center for Combating Antisemitism Association and the Ministry for Diaspora Affairs and Combating Antisemitism, October 14, 2024.

CHAPTER TWO

This chapter includes or relies upon interviews with Lauren Post, Lesley Klaff, Abraham J. Wyner, Terry Long, Yossi Klein Halevi, Jay Ulfelder, Tal-Or Cohen Montemayor, John E. Joseph, Tony Schwartz, David Duke, and others who did not wish to be quoted by name. The interviews, as with the others, were conducted in North America, Europe, and Israel.

On the use of antisemitic words to minimize and delegitimize the State of Israel, there is Lesley Klaff's invaluable "Word crimes against the State of Israel and the Jews: Holocaust inversion and the British context," Sheffield Hallam University Research Archive, 2019, https://shura.shu.ac.uk/22901. On the policy of Hamas, helpful documents and articles included: "The Avalon Project: Hamas Covenant 1988,"

Yale Law School Lillian Goldman Law Library website, August 18, 1988, avalon.law.yale.edu; "The covenant of the Islamic resistance movement" in Yale Law School Lillia Goodman Law Library by August 18, 1988; MEE staff, "Hamas in 2017: The document in full," *Middle East Eye* online, May 2, 2017, middleeasteye.net; Center on Extremism, "One year later: Antisemitic trends post-10/7," Anti-Defamation League website, October 2, 2024, adl.org.

CHAPTER THREE

This chapter relied upon interviews with Tal-Or Cohen Montemayor, Oded Vanunu, Avi Melamed, Ernst Zundel, Lane Kendall, Marc Ginsburg, Khaled Hassan, Rafi Mendelsohn, brave Israeli diplomatic officers, and several others who would participate in interviews only on condition of anonymity.

Invaluable data about the spread of false and antisemitic content on social media came from Cyabra reports and investigations into X/Twitter accounts spreading false information. Other helpful articles include: Dan Milmo, "X criticized for enabling spread of Israel-Hamas disinformation," *The Guardian* online, October 9, 2023, theguardian.com; Brian Fung and Clare Duffy, "The Israel-Hamas war reveals how social media sells you the illusion of reality," CNN online, October 14, 2023, cnn.com; Marianna Spring, "Who's behind Israel-Gaza disinformation and hate online?" BBC online, October 15, 2023, bbc.com; "Denial of the October 7 massacre on social media platforms," CyberWell website, January 22, 2024, cyberwell.org; Clint Watts, "Iran targeting 2024 US election," *Microsoft On the Issues* website, August 8, 2024, blogs.microsoft.com/on-the-issues.

On the rise of antisemitism online, helpful stories included: Center for Technology and Society, "Sliding through: Spreading antisemitism on TikTok by exploiting moderation gaps," Anti-Defamation League website, November 20, 2023, adl.org; Jeff Jacoby, "A generation of antisemites," *Aish* website, December 21, 2023, aish.com; Eliana Jordan, "Why is Holocaust denial rampant on Gen Z's favourite news source," *The Jewish Chronicle* online, February 28, 2024, thejc.com; Jonathan A. Greenblatt, "The growing antisemitism among young Americans," *Time* online, March 21, 2024, time.com; Zina Rakhamilova, "TikTok's dangerous antisemitism problem—opinion," *The Jerusalem Post* online, March 28, 2024, jpost.com; "Yom HaShoah 2004: Online Holocaust hate speech narratives and trends," CyberWell website, April 2024, cyberwell.org; Jack Jedwab, "Perceptions of hate and prejudice and its victims in Canada and the United States," Metropolis Institute and the Association for Canadian Studies website, June 2024, acs-metropolis.ca; Jacob Ware, "The third generation of online radicalization," GW Program on Extremism website, George Washington University, June 16, 2023, extremism.gwu.edu; "The evolution of online antisemitism, pre- and post-October 7," CyberWell website, October 10, 2024, cyberwell.org; Wills Robinson, "Adolf Hitler had 'some good ideas', a fifth of Gen Z Americans believe," *Daily Mail* online, October 12, 2024, dailymail.co.uk.

On the overarching strategy and messaging of Hamas's social media campaign, helpful articles included: Rita Katz, "How terrorists slip beheading videos past YouTube's censors," *Vice* online, May 26, 2017, vice.com; Rita Katz, "To curb terrorist propaganda online, look to YouTube. No, really," *Wired* online, October 18, 2018, wired.com; Toby Luckhurst, "TikTok: How Israeli-Palestinian conflict plays out on social media," BBC online, May 14, 2021, bbc.com; Omer Kabir, "Israel is losing on the online advocacy front: 15 times more posts with pro-Palestinian tags," *Ctech* website, September 11, 2023, calcalistech.com; Sheera Frenkel and Talya Minsberg, "Hamas hijacked victims' social media accounts to spread terror," *The New York Times* online,

October 17, 2023, nytimes.com; Drew Harwell and Elizabeth Dwoskin, "Hamas turns to social media to get its message out—and to spread fear," *The Washington Post* online, October 18, 2023, washingtonpost.com; Samuel Rubinstein, "Gen Z has an Israel problem," *UnHerd* website, November 6, 2023, unherd.com; Perry Bacon Jr., "Social media has played a huge role in the coverage of the Gaza conflict," *The Washington Post* online, May 10, 2024, washingtonpost.com; Cole S. Aronson, "Israel's TikTok problem," *Jewish Review of Books* online, March 13, 2024, jewishreviewofbooks.com; Carolina Hohagen and Juan Diego Solis de Ovando Bitar, "Gen Z: The polarization generation," Global Americans website, July 19, 2024, globalamericans.org; Paul Mozur, Adam Satariano, Aaron Krolik, and Steven Lee Myers, "How Telegram became a playground for criminals, extremists and terrorists," *The New York Times* online, September 10, 2024, nytimes.com; Mathilda Heller, "Qatar behind antisemitic influencers like Dan Bilzerian, Chikli tells 'Post'—interview," *The Jerusalem Post* online, November 7, 2024, jpost.com; Mason Goad, "Instagram the Intifada," National Association of Scholars website, November 9, 2024, nas.org.

On the use and rise of extremism and radicalization in social media, helpful documents and articles included: "ISIS online: Countering terrorist radicalization and recruitment on the Internet and social media," U.S. Government Publishing Office, July 6, 2016, govinfo.gov; Michael Jensen, Patrick James, Gary LaFree, Aaron Safer-Lichtenstein, and Elizabeth Yates, "The use of social media by United States extremists," Study of Terrorism and Responses to Terrorism (START) website, July 2018, start.umd.edu; Zeynep Tufekci, "YouTube, the great radicalizer," *The New York Times* online, March 10, 2018, nytimes.com; Sara Zeiger and Joseph Gyte, "Prevention of radicalization on social media and the internet," in *Handbook of Terrorism Prevention and Preparedness,* ed. Alex. P. Schmid (The Hague: International Centre for Counter-Terrorism,

2020), c. 12m pp. 358–395; Aaron Shaw, "Social media, extremism, and radicalization," *Science Advances* online, August 30, 2023, science. org; Joe Whittaker, "Online radicalisation: What we know," European Commission/Radicalisation Awareness Network, November 27, 2023, home-affairs.ec.europa.eu; Michael Starr, "Terrorist guide taught in Toronto by PFLP-tied group," *The Jerusalem Post* online, July 22, 2024, jpost.com.

CHAPTER FOUR

Many journalists were interviewed for this chapter; the majority could not be named, fearing discipline, dismissal, or threats. Those who spoke on the record included Brian Lilley, Matti Friedman, Noam Sheizaf, Khaled Hassan, Trevor Asserson, Rafi Mendelsohn, Mosab Hassan Yousef, and others. The interviews were conducted in North America, Europe, and Israel.

On media bias and coverage of the Israel–Hamas war, helpful articles included: Chris McGreal, "Can we trust casualty figures from the Hamas-run Gaza health ministry," *The Guardian* online, October 26, 2023, theguardian.com; Dan Kennedy, "With Israel and Hamas at war, here are some free reliable sources of quality news," *Media Nation* website, October 9, 2023, dankennedy.net; Ian Youngs and Paul Glynn, "BBC defends policy not to call Hamas 'terrorists' after criticism," BBC online, October 11, 2023, bbc.com; Paul Ricard, "Media reporting on Israel-Hamas war face singular challenges," *The Japan Times* online, October 31, 2023, japantimes.co.jp; Kelly McBride, "The audience has a lot to say about coverage of the Israel-Hamas war. We're listening," NPR online, November 2, 2023, npr.org; Robert Philpot, "The BBC is under fire for its coverage of the Israel-Hamas war—rightly so," *The Times of Israel* online, November 3, 2023, timesofisrael.com; Becket Adams, "The US media's moral blindness over Hamas is showing, and it isn't pretty," *The Hill* online, November 6, 2023, thehill.com; "Broken borders: AP & Reuters pictures of Hamas atrocities raise ethical questions," *HonestReporting* website, November 8, 2023, honestreporting.com; Benjamin Lindsay, "CNN fires Gaza-based photojournalist discovered to be embedded with Hamas," *The Wrap* website, November 9, 2023, thewrap.com; HR staff, "The eight categories of media bias," HonestReporting website, December 10, 2023, honestreporting.com; David Akin, "PCO poll finds many do not trust the media and do not believe news outlets are closing," Global News online, December 27, 2023, globalnews.ca; Adam Johnson and Othman Ali, "Coverage of Gaza war in the *New York Times* and other major newspapers heavily favored Israel, analysis shows," *The Intercept* website, January 9, 2024, theintercept.com; Charlotte Tobitt, "Trust in media: UK drops to last place in Edelman survey of 28 nations," *PressGazette* online, January 18, 2024, pressgazette.co.uk; David Folkenflik, "Newsroom at 'New York Times' fractures over story on Hamas attacks," NPR online, March 6, 2024, npr.org; "Hamas-run Gaza health ministry admits to flaws in casualty data," Foundation for Defense of Democracies website, April 9, 2024, fdd.org; Dr. Yvette Alt Miller, "Media bias against Israel," *Aish* website, April 10, 2024, aish.com; Laura Silver and Maria Smerkovich, "Israel views of the Israel-Hamas war," Pew Research Center website, May 30, 2024, pewresearch.org; Trevor Asserson, "The Asserson Report: The Israel-Hamas war and the BBC," Asserson Law Offices, September 1, 2024, asserson.co.uk; "What to know about media bias in coverage of Hamas' attack on Israel," American Jewish Committee website, October 17, 2023, ajc.org.

On the related social media information war, helpful articles included: Steven Lee Myers, "Fact or fiction? In this war, it is hard to tell," *The New York Times* online, October 13, 2023, nytimes.com; Liv Martin, Clothilde Goujard, and Hailey Fuchs, "Israel floods social media to shape opinion around the war," *Politico* online, October 17, 2023, politico.eu; Stephanie Burnett, Stephen Farrell, and Hardik Vyas, "Disinformation surge threatens to fuel Israel-Hamas conflict," Reuters online, October 18, 2023, reuters.com; Simon Montlake, "Israel-Hamas information war challenges media, public," *The Christian Science Monitor* online, October 24, 2023, csmonitor.com; Will Bedingfield, "Generative AI is playing a surprising role in Israel-Hamas disinformation," *Wired* online, October 30, 2023, wired.com; Jason Abbruzzese, David Ingram, and Yasmine Salam, "On Instagram, Palestinian journalists and digital creators documenting Gaza strikes see surge in followers," NBC News online, November 3, 2023, nbcnews.com; Laura Wagner and Will Sommer, "Hundreds of journalists sign letter protesting coverage of Israel," *The Washington Post* online, November 9, 2023, washingtonpost.com; Ines Eisele and Uta Steinwehr, "Fact check: AI fakes in Israel's war against Hamas," Deutsche Welle (DW) online, November 10, 2023, dw.com; "Israel-Hamas war misinformation is everywhere. Here are the facts," Associated Press online, November 14, 2023, apnews.com; Eric Cortellessa and Vera Bergengruen, "Inside the Israel-Hamas information war," *Time* online, December 22, 2023, time.com; Michael Schwartz, Tim Lister, Kareem Khadder, Abeer Salman, and Lauren Said-Moorhouse, "Israel orders shutdown of Al Jazeera in the country, seizes equipment, in 'dark day for democracy,'" CNN online, May 5, 2024, cnn.com; Josh Levs, "The mainstream media is biased against Israel. I know, I was part of it," *Newsweek* online, May 7, 2024, newsweek.com.

CHAPTER FIVE

This chapter commences with interviews conducted with "Garon Amuk," one of many who could not be identified because of the positions they currently hold, or because they were not authorized (like

Garon Amuk) to speak on behalf of their government on sensitive matters. Those who were prepared to speak on the record included Professor Gerald M. Steinberg, Neil Schwartzman, Beryl Wasjsman, Adam Swart, Shai Davidai, Palestine Action, Alex Gandler and some of his colleagues in Israel's Ministry of Foreign Affairs, FBI Special Agent Donald Bartnik, and several others.

On the international funding and promotion of antisemitism discussed in this chapter, helpful documents and articles included: "Matching Fund—Gaza Humanitarian Emergency," Global Affairs Canada, July 2024; "Humanitarian Response to Hostilities in Gaza, West Bank, and Neighboring Areas," Global Affairs Canada, March 2024; Seth Mandel, "China is building an anti-Semitic leviathan," *Commentary* online, October 15, 2024, commentary.org; "United States and Canada target key international fundraiser for foreign terrorist organization PFLP," U.S. Department of Treasury website, October 15, 2024, home.treasury.gov; Steven Lee Myers and Sheera Frenkel, "In a worldwide war of words, Russia, China and Iran back Hamas," *The New York Times* online, November 3, 2023, nytimes.com.

On the funding and influence of pro-Palestinian encampments and rallies across North America, helpful articles included: "Iran, Libya, Syria: Prospects for Radical Cooperation," U.S. Central Intelligence Agency, written on March 26, 1985, approved for release on March 18, 2011, cia.gov; Stuart Gibson, "Wake up and smell the coffee—who is pulling the strings of the pro-Hamas protesters," *The Daily Northwestern* online, May 9, 2024, dailynorthwestern.com; "Contagious disruption: How CCP influence and radical ideologies threaten critical infrastructure and campuses across the United States," Network Contagion Research Institute website, May 13, 2024, networkcontagion.us; Frannie Block and Eli Lake, "Rashida Tlaib speaks at Detroit conference tied to terrorist group," The Free Press website, May 28, 2024, thefp.com; Marc

Rod, "U.S. director of national intelligence says Iran is influencing and funding Gaza war protests," *Jewish Insider* website, July 9, 2024, jewishinsider.com; Avril Haines, "Statement from Director of National Intelligence Avril Haines on recent Iranian influence efforts," Office of the Director of National Intelligence website, July 9, 2024, dni.gov; "Iran supporting and funding pro-Hamas protests in the U.S.," Foundation for Defense of Democracies website, July 10, 2024, fdd.org; Jason M. Brodsky, "The truth about Iran's efforts to promote Gaza protestors," *Time* online, July 30, 2024, time.com; Isabel Vincent, "Iranian regime funneling money into anti-Israel groups and campus protests through 'grassroots activist' groups," *New York Post*, August 30, 2024; Negar Mojtahedi, "Iran masterminded anti-Israel protest in Canadian university," Iran International online, August 2, 2024, iranintl.com.

On charities with terrorism links, information regarding Canadian, American, and European charities was sourced using public government charity returns along with the respective charities' social media posts.

CHAPTER SIX

Caryma Sa'd, Ryan Mauro, Arsen Ostrovsky, Hillel Neuer, Guy Goldstein, Gerard Filitti, Eilon Kutler, and others were interviewed for this chapter. Representatives of the U.S. Campaign for Palestinian Rights, several pro-Palestinian charities, and the Canadian branch of the Muslim Brotherhood were also interviewed for parts of this chapter.

On the Hamas leadership and funding in North America, helpful legal documents and articles included: *Parizer et al v. AJP Educational Foundation Inc.* (1:24-cv-00724), Virginia Eastern District Court, May 1, 2025; Park MacDougald, "The people setting America on fire," *Tablet Magazine* online, May 6, 2024, tabletmag.com; "Jewish family among major backers of anti-Israel campus protests," i24 News online, May 29, 2024, i24news.tv; "Submission to the Standing Committee on

Public Safety and National Security for its study on Bill C-70, *An Act Respecting Countering Foreign Interference*," B'nai Brith Canada website, June 6, 2024, bnaibrith.ca; Danielle Berjikian, "Watch: Campus jihad and the dark money behind the Hamas protests," *Louder with Crowder* website, June 3, 2024, louderwithcrowder.com; *United States of America v. Yahya Sinwar et al* (24 MAG 438), U.S. Attorney's Office Southern District of New York, September 3, 2024.

On those involved in pro-Palestinian encampments, helpful stories included: Derek Lief, Mora Deitch, Alon Berkman, and Jesse R. Weinberg, "New figures reveal: The number of demonstrations against Israel has soared," Institute for National Security Studies website, November 9, 2023, inss.org.il; Jay Ulfelder, "Crowd counting consortium: Update on Israel/Palestine Protests," Ash Center for Democratic Governance and Innovation website, Harvard Kennedy School, November 28, 2023, ash.harvard.edu; Park MacDougald, "The people setting America on fire," *Tablet Magazine* online, May 6, 2024, tabletmag.com; Adam Kredo, "Inside the campus playbook to build a nationwide 'Unity Intifada' in support of Hamas," *The Washington Free Beacon* online, May 9, 2024, freebeacon.com; Ari David Blaff, "Meet the student group—with alleged links to Hamas—driving the anti-Israel encampments," *National Post* online, June 15, 2024, nationalpost.com; Matthew Levitt, "Introducing the Iranian external operations map and timeline," Washington Institute for Near East Policy website, August 2, 2024, washingtoninstitute.org; Ryan Mauro, "Marching toward violence: The domestic anti-Israeli protest movement," Capital Research Center website, October 9, 2024, capitalresearch.org.

Few books have been written on the global propaganda campaign against Israel and the West in recent years. Books I relied upon included my own: *Unholy Alliances: Terrorists, Extremists, Front Companies, and the Libyan Connection in Canada* (Lester, 1992); *Web of Hate: Inside Canada's Far Right Network* (HarperCollins, 1994, 2001); *Recipe for Hate* (Dundurn, 2017); *New Dark Ages* (Dundurn, 2018); and *Age of Unreason* (Dundurn, 2019).

Other invaluable texts included:

Abella, Irving, and Harold Troper. *None Is Too Many: Canada and the Jews of Europe, 1933–1948*. Toronto: Lester & Orpen Dennys, 1983.

Achcar, Gilbert. *The Clash of Barbarisms: The Making of the New World Disorder*. London: Paradigm Publishers, 2006.

Anti-Defamation League of B'nai Brith. *Extremism on the Right: A Handbook*. New York: B'nai Brith, 1988.

Anti-Defamation League of B'nai Brith. *Hate Groups in America: A Record of Bigotry and Violence*. New York: B'nai Brith, 1988.

Ariely, Dan. *Misbelief: What Makes Rational People Believe Irrational Things*. New York: HarperCollins, 2023.

Barrett, Stanley R. *Is God a Racist? The Right Wing in Canada*. Toronto: University of Toronto Press, 1987.

Beam, Louis R., Jr. *Essays of a Klansman: Being a Compendium of Ku Klux Klan Ideology, Organizational Methods, History, Tactics, and Opinions, with Interpolations by the Author.* Hayden Lake, ID: A.K.I.A. Publications, 1983.

Beller, Steven. *Antisemitism: A Very Short Introduction.* Oxford: Oxford University Press, 2017.

Bennett, David H. *The Party of Fear: From Nativist Movements to the New Right in American History.* New York: Vintage Books, 1990.

Bercuson, David, and Douglas Wertheimer. *A Trust Betrayed: The Keegstra Affair.* Toronto: Seal Books, 1987.

Beverley, James A. *Web of Error: An Analysis of the Views of Malcolm Ross.* Sackville, NB: Mount Allison University, 1990.

Bill, Steven. *The Death of Truth: How Social Media and the Internet Gave Snake Oil Salesmen and Demagogues the Weapons They Needed to Destroy Trust and Polarize the World—And What We Can Do.* New York: Alfred A. Knopf, 2024.

Bostom, Andrew G. *The Mufti's Islamic Jew-Hatred: What the Nazis Learned from the 'Muslim Pope.'* Washington: Bravura Books, 2013.

Brake, Mike. *The Sociology of Youth Culture and Youth Subcultures: Sex and Drugs and Rock 'n' Roll?* London: Routledge, 1980.

Bremmer, Ian. *The Power of Crisis: How Three Threats—and Our Response—Will Change the World.* New York: Simon & Schuster, 2022.

Carlson, Caitlin Ring. *Hate Speech* (The MIT Press Essential Knowledge series). Cambridge: MIT Press, 2021.

Coates, James. *Armed and Dangerous: The Rise of the Survivalist Right.* New York: Noonday Press, 1987.

Darshan-Leitner, Nitsana, and Samuel M. Katz. *Harpoon: Inside the Covert War Against Terrorism's Money Masters.* New York: Hachette Books, 2017.

Davies, Alan, editor. *Antisemitism in Canada: History and Interpretation*. Waterloo, ON: Wilfrid Laurier University Press, 1992.

Delisle, Esther. *The Traitor and the Jew: Anti-Semitism and Extreme Right-Wing Nationalism in Québec from 1929 to 1939*. Montreal: Robert Davies Publishing, 1993.

Dolan, Edward F. *Anti-Semitism*. New York: Franklin Watts, 1985.

English, Richard. *Does Terrorism Work?: A History*. Oxford: Oxford University Press, 2016.

Findley, Paul. *They Dare to Speak Out: People and Institutions Confront Israel's Lobby*. Westport, CT: Lawrence Hill, 1985.

Fisher, Max. *The Chaos Machine: The Inside Story of How Social Media Rewired Our Minds and Our World*. New York: Little, Brown & Company, 2022.

Flynn, Kevin, and Gary Gerhardt. *The Silent Brotherhood: Inside America's Racist Underground*. New York: Signet Books, 1989.

Frantzman, Seth J. *The October 7 War: Israel's Battle for Security in Gaza*. New York: Post Hill Press, 2024.

Galloway, Scott. *The Four: The Hidden DNA of Amazon, Apple, Facebook and Google*. New York: Portfolio/Penguin, 2017.

German, Mike. *Thinking Like a Terrorist: Insights of a Former FBI Undercover Agent*. Washington: Potomac Books, 2007.

Giridharadas, Anand. *The Persuaders: At the Front Lines of the Fight for Hearts, Minds, and Democracy*. New York: Knopf, 2022.

Goldhagen, Daniel Jonah. *Hitler's Willing Executioners: Ordinary Germans and the Holocaust*. New York: Vintage Books, 1996.

Goldhagen, Daniel Jonah. *The Devil That Never Dies: The Rise and Threat of Global Antisemitism*. New York: Little, Brown and Company, 2013.

Government of Canada, Senate Special Committee on Terrorism and Public Safety Report. Ottawa: Supply and Services Canada, 1987.

Hebdige, Dick. *Subculture: The Meaning of Style*. London: Routledge, 1979.

Hill, Marc Lamont. *Except for Palestine: The Limits of Progressive Politics*. New York: The New Press, 2021.

Hill, Ray. *The Other Face of Terror: Inside Europe's Neo-Nazi Network*. London: Grafton Books, 1988.

Hoffman, Michael A. *The Great Holocaust Trial*. Torrance, CA: Institute for Historical Review, 1985.

Horn, Dara. *People Love Dead Jews: Reports from a Haunted Present*. New York: W.W. Norton and Co., 2021.

Jacoby, Susan. *The Age of American Unreason*. New York: Vintage Books, 2008.

Katz, Rita. *Saints and Soldiers: Inside Internet-Age Terrorism*. New York: Columbia University Press, 2022.

The Klanwatch Project. *Hate, Violence and White Supremacy*. Montgomery, AL: Southern Poverty Law Center, 1989.

The Klanwatch Project. *The Ku Klux Klan: A History of Racism and Violence*. Montgomery, AL: Southern Poverty Law Center, 1991.

Klassen, Ben. *The White Man's Bible*. Otto, NC: Church of the Creator Press, 1981.

Knight, Nick. *Skinhead*. London: Omnibus Press, 1982.

Lacquer, Walter. *Fascism: Past, Present, Future*. Oxford: Oxford University Press, 1997.

Lee, Martin A. *The Beast Reawakens: Fascism's Resurgence from Hitler's Spymasters to Today's Neo-Nazi Groups and Right-Wing Extremists*. New York: Routledge, 2000.

Lethbridge, David. *This Is Racism*. Salmon Arm Coalition Against Racism, 1992.

Levitt, Cyril H., and William Shaffir. *The Riot at Christie Pits*. Toronto: Lester & Orpen Dennys, 1987.

Lévy, Bernard-Henri. *Israel Alone*. New York: Post Hill Press, 2024.

Lipstadt, Deborah E. *Antisemitism: Here and Now*. New York: Schocken Books, 2019.

Litvinoff, Barnet. *The Burning Bush: Anti-Semitism and World History*. London: Collins, 1988.

Lutz, Chris. *They Don't All Wear Sheets: A Chronology of Racist and Far Right Violence*. Atlanta, GA: Center for Democratic Renewal, 1987.

Martinez, Thomas. *Brotherhood of Murder: How One Man's Journey Through Fear Brought the Order—The Most Dangerous Racest Gang in America—To Justice*. New York: McGraw-Hill, 1988.

McIntyre, Lee. *On Disinformation: How to Fight for Truth and Protect Democracy*. Cambridge, MA: The MIT Press, 2023.

McIntyre, Lee. *Post-Truth* (The MIT Press Essential Knowledge series). Cambridge, MA: The MIT Press, 2018.

Mertl, Steve, and John Ward. *Keegstra: The Trial, the Issues, the Consequences*. Saskatoon: Western Producer Prairie Books, 1985.

Montell, Amanda. *Cultish: The Language of Fanaticism*. New York: Harper Wave, 2021.

O'Neill, Brendan. *After the Pogrom: October 7, Israel and the Crisis of Civilization*. London: Spiked Ltd., 2024.

Payne, Keith. *Good Reasonable People: The Psychology Behind America's Dangerous Divide*. New York: Viking, 2024.

Picciolini, Christian. *White American Youth: My Descent into America's Most Violent Hate Movement—and How I Got Out*. New York: Hachette Books, 2017.

Protzer, Eric, and Paul Summerville. *Reclaiming Populism: How Economic Fairness Can Win Back Disenchanted Voters*. Cambridge: Polity Press, 2022.

Putnam, Carleton. *Race and Reason: A Yankee View*. Washington, D.C.: Public Affairs Press, 1961.

Quinley, Harold E., and Charles Y. Glock. *Anti-Semitism in America.* New Brunswick, NJ: Transaction Books, 1979.

Razzaque, Russell. *Human Being to Human Bomb: Inside the Mind of a Terrorist.* Cambridge: Icon Books, 2008.

Renton, David. *Never Again: Rock Against Racism and the Anti-Nazi League 1976–1982.* London: Routledge, 2019.

Richardson, Louise. *What Terrorists Want: Understanding the Enemy, Containing the Threat.* New York: Random House, 2007.

Ridgeway, James. *Blood in the Face: The Ku Klux Klan, Aryan Nations, Nazi Skinheads, and the Rise of a New White Culture.* New York: Thunder's Mouth Press, 1990.

Robin, Martin. *Shades of Right: Nativist and Fascist Politics in Canada, 1920 to 1940.* Toronto: University of Toronto Press, 1992.

Rothschild, Mike. *Jewish Space Lasers: The Rothschilds and 200 Years of Conspiracy Theories.* Brooklyn: Melville House, 2023.

Schmidt, Michael. *The New Reich: Violent Extremism in Unified Germany and Beyond.* New York: Pantheon Books, 1993.

Sher, Julian. *White Hoods: Canada's Ku Klux Klan.* Vancouver: New Star Books, 1983.

Shermer, Michael, and Alex Grobman. *Denying History: Who Says the Holocaust Never Happened and Why Do They Say It?* Berkeley: University of California Press, 2000.

Simmons, Shraga. *David and Goliath: The Explosive Inside Story of Media Bias in the Mideast Conflict.* Jerusalem: Emesphere Productions, 2012.

Simons, Jake Wallis. *Israelophobia: The Newest Version of the Oldest Hatred and What to Do About It.* London: Constable, 2023.

Singer, P.W., and Emerson T. Brooking. *Likewar: The Weaponization of Social Media.* New York: Mariner Books, 2018.

Slayton, Philip. *Antisemitism: An Ancient Hatred in the Age of Identity Politics.* Toronto: Sutherland House, 2023.

Sokatch, Daniel. *Can We Talk About Israel?: A Guide for the Curious, Confused, and Conflicted.* New York: Bloomsbury Publishing, 2022.

Tibon, Amir. *The Gates of Gaza: A Story of Betrayal, Survival, and Hope in Israel's Borderlands.* New York: Little, Brown and Company, 2024.

Troper, Harold, and Morton Weinfeld. *Old Wounds: Jews, Ukrainians and the Hunt for Nazi War Criminals in Canada.* Toronto: Penguin Books Canada, 1988.

Van Der Breggen, Hendrik. *Untangling Popular Anti-Israel Arguments: Critical Thinking about the Israel-Hamas War.* Amazon KDP, 2024.

Van Der Linden, Sander. *Foolproof: Why Misinformation Infects Our Minds and How to Build Immunity.* New York: W.W. Norton and Co., 2023.

Weiss, Bari. *How to Fight Antisemitism.* New York: Crown, 2021.

Yaron, Lee. *10/7: 100 Human Stories.* New York: St. Martin's Press, 2024.